THE LAYMAN'S BIBLE COMMENTARY

THE LAYMAN'S BIBLE COMMENTARY
IN TWENTY-FIVE VOLUMES

THE LAYMAN'S BIBLE COMMENTARY

Balmer H. Kelly, *Editor*

Donald G. Miller   *Associate Editors*   Arnold B. Rhodes

Dwight M. Chalmers, *Editor, John Knox Press*

VOLUME 5

THE BOOK OF
DEUTERONOMY

THE BOOK OF
JOSHUA

Edward P. Blair

JOHN KNOX PRESS

ATLANTA, GEORGIA

© M. E. Bratcher 1964

10 9 8 7 6 5 4 3 2

Complete set: ISBN: 0-8042-3086-2
This volume: 0-8042-3065-X
Library of Congress Card Number: 59-10454
First paperback edition 1982
Printed in the United States of America
John Knox Press
Atlanta, Georgia 30365

PREFACE

The LAYMAN'S BIBLE COMMENTARY is based on the conviction that the Bible has the Word of good news for the whole world. The Bible is not the property of a special group. It is not even the property and concern of the Church alone. It is given to the Church for its own life but also to bring God's offer of life to all mankind —wherever there are ears to hear and hearts to respond.

It is this point of view which binds the separate parts of the LAYMAN'S BIBLE COMMENTARY into a unity. There are many volumes and many writers, coming from varied backgrounds, as is the case with the Bible itself. But also as with the Bible there is a unity of purpose and of faith. The purpose is to clarify the situations and language of the Bible that it may be more and more fully understood. The faith is that in the Bible there is essentially one Word, one message of salvation, one gospel.

The LAYMAN'S BIBLE COMMENTARY is designed to be a concise non-technical guide for the layman in personal study of his own Bible. Therefore, no biblical text is printed along with the comment upon it. This commentary will have done its work precisely to the degree in which it moves its readers to take up the Bible for themselves.

The writers have used the Revised Standard Version of the Bible as their basic text. Occasionally they have differed from this translation. Where this is the case they have given their reasons. In the main, no attempt has been made either to justify the wording of the Revised Standard Version or to compare it with other translations.

The objective in this commentary is to provide the most helpful explanation of fundamental matters in simple, up-to-date terms. Exhaustive treatment of subjects has not been undertaken.

In our age knowledge of the Bible is perilously low. At the same time there are signs that many people are longing for help in getting such knowledge. Knowledge of and about the Bible is, of course, not enough. The grace of God and the work of the Holy Spirit are essential to the renewal of life through the Scriptures. It is in the happy confidence that the great hunger for the Word is a sign of God's grace already operating within men, and that the Spirit works most wonderfully where the Word is familiarly known, that this commentary has been written and published.

THE EDITORS AND
THE PUBLISHERS

THE BOOK OF

DEUTERONOMY

INTRODUCTION

The Importance of Deuteronomy

Deuteronomy is not one of the biblical books most read by contemporary Christians. The first Christians, however, like their Lord before them and the Jews around them, pondered deeply and repeatedly the teachings of this book.

Deuteronomy is one of the four Old Testament books most frequently quoted in the New Testament (the others being Isaiah, Psalms, and Genesis). That Jesus' mind was well stocked with Deuteronomy's warmhearted exhortations is evidenced by the stories in Matthew and Luke of his temptation in the wilderness. In response to the voice of the Tempter he is said to have used three passages from Deuteronomy: "Man shall not live by bread alone, but by every word that proceeds from the mouth of God"; "You shall not tempt the Lord your God"; and "You shall worship the Lord your God and him only shall you serve" (Matt. 4:4, 7, 10).

The popularity of Deuteronomy in the Judaism of Jesus' time is apparent in part from the many fragments of the book found in the caves of Qumran by the Dead Sea. Sharing prominence with Deuteronomy among the sectarians who lived at Qumran were the books of Isaiah and the Psalms.

A high regard for Deuteronomy in both Judaism and Christianity is unmistakably attested in their agreement concerning the primary demand of God: "You shall love the LORD your God with all your heart, and with all your soul, and with all your might" (Deut. 6:5; compare Matt. 22:37; Mark 12:30; Luke 10:27; and the twice-daily recital of this Deuteronomic passage by Jews).

Deuteronomy is believed by most scholars to have been the first book of the Bible to be regarded as canonical; that is, as containing an authoritative standard for the life of the Covenant people.

It appears that King Josiah, in the year 622 B.C., regarded this book (or a part of it) as setting forth the divine will for the nation and that he sought to bring the attitudes and actions of his people into conformity with its requirements. From this time on, Israel became more and more a people of "the Book," as ever more literary material was recognized as containing the word of God for national and personal life.

The Basic Nature of the Book

The name "Deuteronomy," meaning "second [repeated] law," arose through a misunderstanding of a Hebrew phrase in Deuteronomy 17:18 by the ancient translators of the Old Testament into Greek. The phrase means not "second [repeated] law" but "a copy of this law." The title has persisted because the book has been regarded as containing a second utterance of the Mosaic Law for the benefit of the new generation about to enter the Promised Land.

Actually, most of the contents of the book are not so much law as preaching about the Law, in order to enhance its authority in national and personal life. Although chapters 12-26 contain a large body of legal material, a close scrutiny shows that this matter is interspersed with homiletical comment and is represented as belonging to sermons preached by Moses. The book would be better titled, "Preaching of the Covenant."

In the sermons Moses is pictured as recounting the gracious deeds of God for the benefit of a generation of Israelites once removed from the events of the Exodus and the Covenant at Horeb (Sinai) and about to enter the Promised Land. On the basis of what God has done, Moses prescribes what Israel must do if it is to participate in the glorious future God has planned for his people.

It is said that the God of the fathers brought the nation into being; redeemed it from bondage; revealed his holy will to it; guided, protected, and disciplined it; and planned for it peace and prosperity in a good land allotted to it. God chose Israel to be his own and showered his love upon it. In view of his gracious attitudes and acts, the worship of any other god or gods would be ingratitude of the basest sort. God's love should be reciprocated with love, and this love should flow out into obedience to his righteous will in all areas of personal and national life. The meaning of his will is spelled out in detail by a repetition of the terms of the Covenant which God is said to have given Moses at the holy mountain.

The central notes of Deuteronomy are "remember," "obey," "behold": *remember* God's gracious attitudes and deeds; *obey* his words in unswerving loyalty and fidelity; *behold* what he has in store for you as a people! If you remain faithful to him, "he will set you high above all nations that he has made, in praise and in fame and in honor" (26:19), but if you turn from him in disobedience and ingratitude "you shall be a horror to all the kingdoms of the earth" (28:25) and shall be utterly destroyed by famine, pestilence, and the sword. "See, I have set before you this day life and good, death and evil. . . . choose life . . ." (30:15-20).

This is preaching of the purest sort. Deuteronomy must be seen more as a book of sermons than as a code of laws. But the book contains more than a collection of sermons enjoining obedience to the Law, as chapters 27 and 31-34 clearly indicate. Portions of these chapters present historical and poetic materials quite different in type and purpose from the sermonic. The acceptance by Israel of the Covenant at Shechem is anticipated in chapter 27. The appointment of Joshua, the writing down of the Law, and the closing events associated with the passing of the old leader are noted (chs. 31-34). These materials suggest that we have here not only a book of sermons but also a book of worship and a kind of historical writing.

It is now believed that the sermons of Deuteronomy must be seen as traditional proclamations delivered in connection with periodic recitations of the Law and renewals of the Covenant relationship with God by the nation. Exhortation, recitation of the terms of the Covenant, commitment to the Covenant, and the announcements of blessings and curses for obedience and nonobedience—these are elements of a great service of worship into which the people of Israel entered. The Book of Deuteronomy thus enshrines a portion of the liturgy of ancient Israel.

Some interpreters believe that Deuteronomy is to be seen as the first member of a long historical work comprising now in our Bible the books of Deuteronomy through Second Kings—a Deuteronomic history of Israel in the land of Palestine, reaching from the period before the conquest of the land to the fall of the nation at the hands of the Babylonians. It was the author's purpose to evaluate Israel's national life from the standpoint of certain convictions: principally, its adherence or non-adherence to the worship of one God in one sanctuary by one people. If this view of the Book of Deuteronomy is correct, traditional materials of many kinds (worship, legal, historical, and the like) have been woven into a lengthy historical work, to which Deuteronomy is the introduction.

The Circumstances of Writing

The identity of the Deuteronomic writer or writers and the readers originally intended is not certainly known. Supporters of the traditional position—that Moses himself was both preacher and author of the book (at least in essentially its present form)—are still to be found. Samuel has been suggested as the author. The writing of the central portion of the book (chs. 12-26) has been placed by others in the time immediately before Amos (eighth century B.C.). Since the closing years of the nineteenth century, most interpreters have identified Deuteronomy with the book of the Law found in the Temple in the time of Josiah (II Kings 22) and have held that it was written in the early days of Josiah's reign or in the black years of his predecessor Manasseh. Still others have argued that the book could not have been written until after the fall of the Southern Kingdom and the Babylonian Exile.

While no one view has won the field, many are now inclined to look with favor on the position that the bulk of Deuteronomy was written shortly after 701 B.C. by a country Levite who, by the use of traditions reaching back to the great Covenant Festival of the Lord participated in by the federation of tribes at Shechem in the period of the Judges, attempted to turn his contemporaries away from polytheism to the exclusive worship of the Lord.

According to this view three characteristics of the book point to such an origin: a strong interest in old ceremonial materials; a fierce martial spirit expressed in the repeated sanctioning of the institution of "holy war"; and the sermonic cast of the whole writing. This view maintains that only Levites would have access to the old ceremonial traditions preserved in Deuteronomy and would have the ability and inclination to reinterpret them homiletically for the needs of a later situation. Their martial spirit is explained as due in part to the impact of the militaristic spirit of the old tribal traditions, of which the Levites were the custodians, and in part to the special conditions of the period after Sennacherib's invasion of Israel. Their sermonic and interpretative skill belonged to the essential nature of their calling: they were interpreters and inculcators of the laws of God.

It is evident that this hypothesis will account satisfactorily for the major part of the text of the present Deuteronomy. But it seems equally clear that some parts of the present text are later than others and that additions to the book were made from time to time. It may be, as some have argued, that the central core—and thus the oldest part—of Deuteronomy is contained in 4:44—26:19 and chapter 28 and that this has been expanded by the addition of the materials now contained in 1:1—4:43, chapter 27, and chapters 29-34. As the book now lies, the laws which are to be obeyed (chs. 12-26) are preceded by two lengthy introductions (1:1—4:43 and 4:44—11:32). It may be that the first introduction (1:1—4:43) was intended to introduce the Deuteronomic history of Israel (Deuteronomy through Second Kings) and that it was added to the older core when this core was woven into the history, probably shortly before or after the fall of Jerusalem in 587 B.C. Chapters 29-34 probably constitute additions to the core also, but when they were made we do not know. The central fact to be kept in mind is that the material which became the present Book of Deuteronomy has a long history. The experiences of a living community lie behind it, and the materials were adapted to the needs of a changing community.

But why have interpreters so largely abandoned the traditional position that Moses himself was the author of Deuteronomy, especially in view of the explicit statements in 31:9, 22, 24 that Moses "wrote this law" and "wrote this song"? Only a partial answer can be attempted here.

1. Mosaic authorship for the book as a whole is not claimed in 31:9, 22, 24. For obvious reasons, even the most conservative students do not hold that Moses wrote the account of his death (ch. 34). Furthermore, "this law" (31:9, 24) may refer only to a portion of the preceding material (possibly to the "statutes and ordinances" of chapters 12-26). In 27:3 "all the words of this law," which were to be written on plastered stones, can hardly refer to the lengthy contents of Deuteronomy but only to some portion thereof. Mosaic authorship of the book as we now have it is clearly not claimed in the text.

2. The impressive, flowing, oratorical style of Deuteronomy is quite unlike the earliest known pieces of Israelite literary material but is strikingly similar to the prose sermons of Jeremiah and even to certain aspects of the style of some nonbiblical correspondence of the same period—the Lachish letters of about 588 B.C.

3. The theology of Deuteronomy reflects the convictions of the great ethical prophets of Israel, long after the time of Moses. The teaching concerning God's love for Israel and Israel's love for God is reminiscent of the insights of Hosea. The emphasis in Deuteronomy on justice and mercy toward fellow men (the so-called "humanitarianism" of this book) seems to presuppose the teachings of Amos, Micah, and other prophets.

4. The situation in the life of Israel in which Deuteronomy best fits is the late monarchic, rather than the Mosaic, period. Nostalgia for the past was a widespread phenomenon in the lands of the Near East (including Palestine) in the seventh century B.C. Old orders were crumbling; old securities were being shaken. In Egypt, Mesopotamia, and Phoenicia, men were seeking inspiration and direction from the ancient days. "Remember the days of old" (Deut. 32:7) was a common injunction in this tired and fearful age.

Deuteronomy exhibits a marked nostalgia for the past—for the glorious days when God chose Israel for his own and by mighty deeds gave evidence of his presence with his people. It is the fervent wish of the author that the glory of those days should return to Israel, that the nation should organize its life after the pattern revealed in the days of old. The call to remembrance, therefore, reverberates throughout the book.

Deuteronomy fits the general spirit of the world of the seventh century; it would also speak cogently to the situation of that time in Palestine. During the long reign of Manasseh (about 687-642 B.C.) the country lay under the heel of Assyria, paying tribute as the price of vassalage and recognizing the gods of Assyria (see II Kings 21:1-16). Altars to Assyrian astral deities were erected in the Temple of the Lord. Pagan fertility rites (including sacred prostitution) were practiced in the Temple and at local sanctuaries. Divination and magic, highly popular in Assyria, flourished in Jerusalem. The ancient practice of the sacrifice of first-born children was revived. Injustice, oppression, and violence abounded. Reforming prophets of the time of Hezekiah (about 715-687 B.C.) and their sympathizers were executed or driven underground.

It is probable that Manasseh and his associates argued that God's claim on the life of his people had not been infringed. Had it not always been affirmed that the God of Israel was surrounded by a heavenly host? Were not the Assyrian astral deities members of his heavenly court and thus entitled to veneration alongside the worship of the supreme God? But for all Manasseh's possible rationalizations, sincere or otherwise, the hard fact was that the nation had fallen into polytheism of the crassest sort, with dire consequences in personal and national life.

Deuteronomy contains a powerful antidote for the poison at work in Israel. This antidote was administered by King Josiah in 622 B.C. The break-up of Assyria that followed on the death of Asshurbanipal (about 633 B.C.) gave Josiah an opportunity to strike for freedom and to re-establish the authority of the Davidic line of kings over the entire country. Religious sanction for his sweeping reforms seems to have come from the Book of Deuteronomy, for it apparently was this book, perhaps in a somewhat shorter form, that was found in the Temple by the priest Hilkiah (II Kings 22). So powerful an impression did it make on Josiah when it was read to him, that he immediately set into operation its prescriptions for the life of the nation.

Specific contacts between admonitions of the Book of Deuteronomy and the reforms of Josiah are not far to seek. The most important are Josiah's attempts to root out polytheism and to re-establish the exclusive worship of the God of Israel in the life of the nation (II Kings 23)—also the central concern of Deuteronomy. As a means to this end, Josiah destroyed the local sanctuaries and caused worship to be centralized in one sanctuary at Jerusalem (II Kings 23)—a requirement apparently laid down in Deuteronomy 12 (see comment). Pagan practices opposed both in Deuteronomy and by Josiah are: child sacrifice (Deut. 18:10; II Kings 23:10); sacred prostitution (Deut. 23:17-18; II Kings 23:7); and the practice of divination and magic (Deut. 18:11; II Kings 23:24). The provision of Deuteronomy 18:1-8, by which the Levites were to be allowed full priestly rights at the central sanctuary, was apparently guaranteed to them by Josiah but not made use of (II Kings 23:9). Josiah's vigorous advocacy of reform seems to have been stimulated by the blessings and the curses of Deuteronomy 28, to judge by the reaction attributed to him when the book of the Law found by Hilkiah was read in his presence (II Kings 22:11-13).

Josiah's break from Assyria and the destruction of the paraphernalia of foreign religions were certainly under way before the discovery of the core of our present Deuteronomy in 622 B.C. Clear evidence of this is the fact that the Temple of the Lord was being repaired when the book was found. The book added tremendous impetus to the reform movement and gave it direction. It was now seen that the whole Mosaic tradition—the ancestral law of Israel—demanded reform of the most radical character. The Deuteronomic core of preached law, as assembled by a northern Levite and brought to Jerusalem at some time before 622 B.C., was admirably designed to stimulate and direct the reform.

This view of the origin of the Book of Deuteronomy recognizes the antiquity of much of its material. It holds that the book enshrines the Levitical preaching of the Covenant in the days since its formal ratification at Shechem. This preaching may indeed contain reminiscences of actual words of Moses. We may say that Deuteronomy is to the historical teaching of Moses what the Gospel of John is to the historical teaching of Jesus. Authentic notes of each teacher are undoubtedly preserved in each writing, but both bodies of teaching have been transposed into a different key and made applicable to new situations. Moses stands behind Deuteronomy, even as Jesus stands behind the Fourth Gospel.

OUTLINE

First Address of Moses: What God Has Done. Deuteronomy 1:1—4:43

Introduction (1:1-5)
The "Mighty Acts" Between Horeb and Beth-peor (1:6—3:29)
The Call to Exclusive Loyalty to God (4:1-40)
Appendix: The Cities of Refuge (4:41-43)

Second Address of Moses: What God Requires. Deuteronomy 4:44—28:68

Introduction (4:44-49)
The Meaning and Obligation of the Covenant Relationship (5:1—11:32)
The Specific Terms of the Covenant Relationship (12:1—26:19)
The Publication and Enforcement of the Terms of the Covenant (27:1—28:68)

Third Address of Moses: What God Proposes. Deuteronomy 29:1—30:20

A Covenant in Perpetuity with Israel (29:1-15)
A Covenant Involving Total Obedience (29:16-29)
A Covenant Including the Possibility of a Second Chance (30:1-10)
A Covenant Requiring Radical Decision (30:11-20)

Connecting Narrative: The Change in Leadership. Deuteronomy 31:1—34:12

The Promise of Victorious Conquest (31:1-6)
The New Leader (31:7-8)
The Use of the Law Book (31:9-15)
The Song Concerning the Lawsuit of God (31:16—32:44)
The Passing of the Old Leader (32:45—34:12)

COMMENTARY

FIRST ADDRESS OF MOSES:
WHAT GOD HAS DONE

Deuteronomy 1:1—4:43

Introduction (1:1-5)

The Book of Deuteronomy begins with a general introduction which is meant to orient the reader with respect to its contents. They are characterized as "words that Moses spoke to all Israel" (1:1). These words are not represented as utterances of God through the lips of Moses but as Moses' attempt "to explain this law" (1:5), that is, the law embodied in the Book of Deuteronomy.

Only rarely in Deuteronomy is God represented as speaking in the first person to Israel (7:4; 11:13-15; 17:3; 28:20; 29:6). The book is thus not represented as a code of laws delivered directly by God to his people but as an exposition by Moses of previously given law.

Where the exposition is regarded as having occurred is not altogether clear from this introduction. The opening verse seems to place it in the great wilderness somewhere south of the Dead Sea. By "the Arabah" apparently is meant here the deep rift lying between the Dead Sea and the Gulf of Aqabah. Paran and Hazeroth lie in the southern portion of the Sinai peninsula, and Tophel probably was located in Edom. In 1:5 the locale is said to be "the land of Moab," considerably farther north. It appears that two traditions concerning the place of the Deuteronomic exposition of the Law have been combined in this introduction.

The "Mighty Acts" Between Horeb
and Beth-peor (1:6—3:29)

The deeds of God are presented in Deuteronomy as the ground of his requirements. Everywhere the mighty hand of God is in view or in the background. It is the writer's intention that the readers shall exclaim with Moses: "What god is there in heaven or on earth who can do such works and mighty acts as thine?" (3:24).

At Horeb (1:6-18)

The Deuteronomist begins his story at the holy mountain, called by him "Horeb" ("drought," or "desert"), but more frequently in the Old Testament "Sinai." Here God had revealed his glory and his will to Israel and made the new nation peculiarly his own in the solemn ceremony of a blood covenant (Exod. 24). Israel had accepted the responsibilities of the Covenant with the words, "All that the LORD has spoken we will do, and we will be obedient" (Exod. 24:7).

At length the time of revelation and vision came to an end, and the hard task of realizing the promises inherent in the Covenant lay before the young nation. But the promises were God's, and the strength to bring them to pass would be supplied by him.

Specifically, the promise centered in the land which God had promised to Abraham, Isaac, and Jacob and to their descendants (vs. 8). This land lay between the Euphrates River on the northeast and the territory of Egypt on the southwest. Among its inhabitants are said here to be the Amorites and the Canaanites, the former being the Deuteronomist's name for the pre-Israelite occupants of the hill country on both sides of the Jordan River and the latter being his term for the dwellers on the seacoast of northern Palestine. The Negeb is the southland, the Beer-sheba and Kadesh-barnea area.

What is a nation without a habitable land? The inhospitable desert in which Israel had been wandering for a generation might sustain wandering bands of relatively few people and animals but hardly a nation as numberless as the stars (Gen. 15:5). The realization of the promise depended absolutely on the availability of suitable territory.

Israel was not the only people to cast envious eyes on the "Fertile Crescent" which stretched from the Euphrates to Egypt. Especially in times of drought and famine, nomads from the deserts to the east and south attempted to overrun this good land. To guard against this, the cities were highly fortified and their defenders skilled in the art of war. But Israel's determination was nurtured on its faith that God had destined this land for his people. Though there were reverses and many heartaches, the land ultimately fell before their intrepid feet. On them then devolved the task of defending it against other claimants, which task they discharged with all the fanatical zeal they had exhibited in conquering it. Few nations have loved their land as intensely as Israel.

In addition to the challenge concerning the land set before Israel at Horeb, the Deuteronomist notes the organization of the people there under tribal leaders or judges (1:9-18). According to the Book of Exodus (Exod. 18:13-27), Moses' father-in-law, Jethro, initially suggested the appointing of tribal leaders to assist Moses in the heavy judicial work. Here this detail is passed over and the credit given to Moses himself, who, of course, was ultimately responsible for the action.

It is not altogether clear why this incident from the Horeb experience is introduced at this point, unless it is to highlight Moses' authority as the divinely appointed leader and head over all subordinate authorities and to illustrate the alternation between obedience and disobedience in the life of Israel. The focal verses here seem to be: "And I commanded you at that time all the things that you should do" (1:18); and "The thing that you have spoken is good for us to do" (1:14). Deuteronomy, like the other books of the Old Testament, is the story of the coming of the word of God to his people and the people's alternation between obedience and disobedience.

From Horeb to Kadesh-barnea (1:19-46)

This section provides a shortened form of the narrative in Numbers 13-14 concerning the spies. There the appointing of the spies arises from a command of the Lord (Num. 13:1-2) but here from the wishes of the people (1:22-23). The Deuteronomic writer seems to want to put the people's unbelief in as strong a light as possible: even the sending of spies was an act of mistrust of the God who promises and lavishly fulfills what he promises, provided only that his people trust him implicitly. Spies are sent to determine whether *men* are able, not whether *God* is able!

The sentiments of the people, as here presented, run through five stages: trusting hope, hesitation, unbelief, presumption, and despair. They set out from Horeb with some enthusiasm, traversing "that great and terrible wilderness" in obedience to the commands of God (1:19) and arriving at length at the oasis of Kadesh-barnea, the southern doorway of the Promised Land. Here Moses bids them enter and take possession of the land promised by the God of their fathers.

But fear sets in. Is God really adequate for what lies ahead? Ought not one to know what the opposition is like, what the odds are? Why not spy out the land to see whether it actually can be taken? Moses acquiesces, and spies are appointed. But the report of the spies simply deepens the people's fears. They hear that the land is a goodly one but that its defenses and defenders are formidable. The "sons of the Anakim" (in Hebrew folklore, a race of giants; vs. 28; see 2:10, 21; Num. 13:22, 28, 33) live there, and who can possibly prevail against such monsters?

Hesitation then turns to unbelief. The people sit disconsolately in their tents and murmur against God. They accuse him of hating them and bringing them out of Egypt to die in the wilderness at the hands of their enemies. Moses' efforts to move them to remembrance of God's gracious acts in their behalf in Egypt and in the wilderness prove unavailing. They refuse to believe that God has been bearing them in his arms as a father bears his young son (vs. 31). As they read the facts of the moment, it seems evident that God has abandoned them to the fury of their enemies.

Moses' stinging rebuke and the revelation of God's bitter judgment on their stubborn rebellion finally shock the people awake: their heritage is now to be the inhospitable wilderness; Caleb, Joshua, and the next generation are to inherit the Promised Land. Such a prospect becomes unbearable. Have they not borne the heat of the days and the terrors of the way? They are determined not to die in the wilderness while others enter the land and gorge themselves on the fruit of Eshcol (1:24-25). Now, too late, in self-willed desperation, and in defiance of God's warning, they throw themselves against the securely entrenched inhabitants of the goodly land. But, alas, God is not with them! Their enemies chase them, as bees do, into the wilderness, in a disastrous rout. There they weep bitterly and sit alone in their despair.

The story is true to human nature and experience. Unwavering trust in God and unswerving loyalty to his will are both man's privilege and his obligation. God's call to the life of trust and obedience is backed by the record of his gracious dealings with men—collectively and individually. But in the presence of mountainous difficulties we quail, in spite of God's blessed assurances. At times we fall into downright unbelief—not that God is, but that he is actively concerned about us and will see us through. Then we seek to force our will on the future, rather than to find and do his. And the consequences are the same: we find ourselves shattered, lost, and licking our wounds in the desert of our infidelity and unbelief. The promises belong to those who wholly follow the Lord (1:36).

Through Southern Transjordan (2:1-25)

Israel's long stay at Kadesh-barnea is to be explained by the copious supply of water there. It appears that these wanderers in the wilderness were not camel-nomads but ass-nomads, who therefore could never stray far from oases. Unable to storm Canaan from the south, they temporized for a generation until courage and fighting power moved them to an assault on the land from the east.

Their wanderings, according to this passage (see also Num. 20:22-23; 21:4-9), took them southward along the great depression below the Dead Sea, known as the Arabah (2:8), to the vicinity of Ezion-geber (Elath), where Solomon later constructed copper smelters. Then they turned northward. They were expressly forbidden to molest three peoples, each bound to them by family ties: the sons of Esau in Mount Seir (Edom); the Moabites, descendants of Lot; and the Ammonites, also Lot's progeny. Prudence, if not ties of family, would have dictated a "go slow" policy. We now know from archaeological exploration that the borders of Edom and Moab were secured by numerous strong fortresses in this period. The unbrotherliness of Edom's king (Num. 20:14-21) must have galled the hungry and thirsty travelers.

Though the exact line of march northward cannot be determined, it is likely that the Israelites made their way eastward along the Brook Zered, the boundary line between Edom and Moab, and that they then detoured Moab on the east.

The antiquarian notes in verses 10-12 and 20-23 inform us about Israel's beliefs concerning the aborigines of the area. These were given various names (here listed) by the various peoples. The large stone structures, called dolmens, of the New Stone Age, found in many areas of the world, are in part responsible for the origin of traditions concerning aboriginal giants.

Several notes of importance are sounded in this section: (1) God can work out his gracious purposes only with people who are ready to work with him. When the new generation heard the command "turn northward" and set its feet resolutely in that direction until the battle for the Promised Land was won, the nation became a hinge on which the divine purpose in history turned. (2) God is gracious even to those who spurn his call: "these forty years the LORD your God has been with you; you have lacked nothing" (2:7). The Father of all "makes his sun rise on the evil and on the good, and sends rain on the just and on the unjust" (Matt. 5:45). The evil share God's goods but not his Good. They are not forgotten in the present, but they cannot share in the blessed future he has planned for his people. (3) God's purpose embraces other peoples besides the Israelites. He not only gives Israel its homeland but gives other peoples (Edom, Moab, Ammon) theirs as well. (4) He is a covenant-keeping God; his promises to Abraham's family and descendants were to be honored perpetually. He is forever loyal to his people and to his word.

Conquest of Heshbon and Bashan (2:26—3:11)

Israel's first victories converted the territories east of the Jordan (except for Moab and Ammon, which, as we have seen, were spared) into a base for military operations west of the Jordan.

The two kingdoms which first fell to Israel were the Amorite kingdoms of Sihon of Heshbon (immediately east of the north end of the Dead Sea) and of Og of Bashan (east and southeast of the Sea of Galilee).

The Amorites (from *Amurru,* meaning "Westerners") originally came from northwestern Mesopotamia and northern Syria. They overran Mesopotamia and Palestine early in the second millennium B.C. and therefore were established in the latter area before the coming of Abraham (see Gen. 14:7, 13; 15:21; Exod. 3:8). According to Numbers 21:26-30 the kingdom of Sihon consisted of territory wrested from the king of Moab. It appears from archaeological evidence that between about 2000 and 1300 B.C. there was a gap of varying proportions in the sedentary occupation of Transjordan, southern Transjordan remaining especially open until the thirteenth century B.C. It is likely that both these Amorite kingdoms were of fairly recent origin when the Israelites invaded them.

It is significant that Moses offered Sihon terms of peace. Moses' objective is declared to be the territory west of the Jordan; he wished only to pass through Sihon's land. But Sihon's refusal made it necessary for Israel to besiege his fortified towns and capture the entire kingdom. The Deuteronomic writer in retrospect regards Sihon's refusal as providential. He even writes that God "hardened his spirit and made his heart obstinate" (2:30). In the Old Testament, before the rise of the idea of Satan, evil attitudes and acts are sometimes attributed to divine instigation. What is struggling for expression here is that, in the providence of God, good often comes out of evil: God makes the wrath of men to praise him. Men may choose what course of action they will; but they cannot determine the consequences of their choices. These are determined by him who is the Lord of history.

The second kingdom to fall to the invaders in Transjordan was that of Og, king of Bashan. He is described in 3:11 as a giant, the last of the Rephaim (one of several names in the Old Testament for the alleged aboriginal giants; see 2:10-11; Num. 13:33). It is probable that the "bedstead of iron" was a sarcophagus of black basalt, some thirteen and a half feet by six feet, which in later times was pointed out as the coffin of Og.

The destruction of the two kingdoms was thoroughgoing. The cities and their inhabitants were "utterly destroyed" (2:34; 3:6). Only the cattle and certain booty from the cities were appropriated by the victors. We have here the first mention in Deuteronomy of what is known as "holy war." For Israel, as for other ancient peoples, war was from first to last a religious act. The victory was accomplished by the tribal deity. Since the enemies and their property belonged to a foreign deity now opposing himself to Israel's God, both must be obliterated before the face of the conquering deity.

In actuality, there was some variation in the extent of the destruction wrought by Israel. The instructions for the obliteration of Jericho (Joshua 6:17-19) exempted Rahab and all in her house, as well as the silver and gold and the vessels of bronze and iron. The valuable objects mentioned were to be turned over to the treasury of the Lord. Saul spared Agag, the king of the Amalekites, and the best of the livestock, to the wrath of Samuel, who believed that everything should have been destroyed (I Sam. 15). It is probable that humanitarian and material considerations, in addition to special agreements and covenants, affected the application of the principle of complete destruction, although in the main it was rigorously carried out. Laws governing the destruction of conquered peoples are set forth in some passages of Deuteronomy (7:1-5; 20:10-18). (For the theological issue involved in the oft-recorded command of God concerning the extermination of conquered peoples, see the comment on 7:1-26 and 20:1-20.)

Assignment of Conquered Lands (3:12-22)

The defeat of Og was an event of magnitude in the life of Israel. This monster was the last obstacle to the entrance of the Promised Land. Many centuries later the slaying of both Sihon and Og was celebrated in the hymnody of Israel (Pss. 135:11; 136:19-20). All credit was given to God, "who smote many nations and slew mighty kings" (Ps. 135:10).

The conquered territory was assigned to the tribes of Reuben and Gad and half of the tribe of Manasseh. Reuben received the southern half of Sihon's kingdom, Gad the northern half, and half-Manasseh the kingdom of Og. But the warriors of these three tribal groups were not yet free to settle down on their lands. They had yet to fight side by side with their brethren beyond the Jordan until all had received their inheritance. "One for all and all for one" was the principle by which Israel lived. No man was free to enjoy the fruits of his conquests until all were free. The spirit of brotherhood here displayed rebukes our contemporary indifference to individuals and nations who have yet to enter into their God-appointed inheritance.

The passage also elucidates the relationship between God and man in the historical process. Though the Hebrews gave all credit to God, they knew full well that God does not work in history alone. Men are his instruments, and it is by their wholehearted co-operative effort that God's ends are accomplished. The Israelite warrior, as he pressed forward in battle, feared not his enemies, for he believed that the Lord his God was fighting for him (3:22). Paul expressed the same truth on a deeper level when he wrote, "Work out your own salvation with fear and trembling; for God is at work in you, both to will and to work for his good pleasure" (Phil. 2:12-13).

Rejection of Moses' Prayer (3:23-29)

Moses died on the east side of the Jordan without setting foot in the Promised Land proper. This was the fate of almost all the adult people he led out of Egypt, the only exceptions apparently being Caleb and Joshua, the two affirmative spies (1:34-40; Num. 13-14). The great leader himself was denied the privilege of

seeing the consummation of his lifework—a bitter disappointment which was hardly mitigated by a distant view of the land
from the top of the Moabite plateau overlooking the north end
of the Dead Sea.

Pisgah was a projecting point of the Abarim Mountains, a
short distance from Mount Nebo and connected by a saddle to
the latter. It is about 2,600 feet above sea level and nearly 4,000
feet above the Dead Sea. Projecting westward from Mount Nebo,
which is behind and slightly higher, Pisgah offers a magnificent
panorama in clear weather: Mount Hermon to the far north;
Mount Tabor to the northwest; the peaks of Ebal and Gerizim in
Samaria, between which ancient Shechem lay; the rugged mountains of Benjamin and Judah, with the Mount of Olives clearly
identifiable; the tumbling hills to the south of Jerusalem, in which
Bethlehem and Hebron lie; the Jordan rift, with a green gash of
life winding crazily through its barren bottom; the Dead Sea,
shimmering eerily under the haze of its massive evaporation; and,
directly north, the lush forests of Gilead. To one standing here,
especially if he had come out of the merciless deserts behind him,
it would seem life's ultimate catastrophe to be denied the right
to step across the Jordan into the goodly land.

Moses' spirit here exhibits the qualities which so clearly marked
his career. Although he was old, he was still full of adventure
and dauntless courage: "O LORD God, thou hast only begun to
show thy servant thy greatness and thy mighty hand . . ." (3:24).
He knows full well that the toughest battles lie ahead, but he is
eager to get on with the struggle and personally to participate in
it. But when it becomes clear to him that his work is done and he
will have to pass the leadership over to Joshua, he accepts his
disappointment with equanimity and seeks to prepare his successor for the role that he himself so much wanted to play. Humble
submission to the will of God and the role marked out for him by
God, with no claim to special prerogatives, is the essence of that
meekness which was so prominent a characteristic of Moses
(Num. 12:3).

The reason for Moses' failure to get into the Promised Land is
not clearly indicated in the Old Testament. It is suggested in
Numbers 20:2-29 that Moses and Aaron in smiting the rock at
Kadesh, instead of speaking to it, were guilty of unbelief and rebellion against God. Deuteronomy 32:48-52 also lays the blame
on Moses' and Aaron's own sin. But other passages place the
blame upon the people and suggest that Moses, though personally

innocent, somehow shared in the punishment meted out by God
to the people (Deut. 1:37; 3:26; 4:21). Perhaps the explanations
are not mutually exclusive (see Ps. 106:32-33). Aaron defected
seriously in the incident of the golden calf (Exod. 32), and we
are not led to believe that Moses' faith and obedience were perfect. But that Moses suffered bitterly because of the sins of his
people, far beyond any consequences of his own doing, is altogether clear. The good often suffer with the evil while they seek
to rescue them from their evil. In this respect Moses was like
the Second Moses—Jesus Christ—and the prototype of the
Servant of the Lord of Isaiah 53.

It must be borne in mind, of course, that the explanations of
Moses' death outside the Promised Land are only "explanations."
The theology of the early Hebrews tended to view every misfor-
tune as punishment for sin, and this is particularly true of Deuteronomy. Natural factors in the death of Moses—he is said to
have been 120 years old at the time of his death (34:7)—must
not be overlooked.

The Call to Exclusive Loyalty to God (4:1-40)

The contents of Deuteronomy are strongly sermonic (see Introduction). The homiletical nature of these materials is particularly clear in 4:1-40, although it has been evident throughout the
narration up to this point that a preacher has been interpreting
history, showing that obedience to the word of God brought life
to some faithful men but that disobedience brought death to
almost an entire generation.

The words "And now" (4:1) introduce the final appeal of this
first address of the book. Since God is what he is, since he has
done what he has done and said what he has said, Israel must
bring its attitudes and life into harmony with the will of God
if the people are to live and prosper in the world.

The Wisdom of Obedience to the Covenant (4:1-14)

The thrust of the appeal is first of all the wisdom of obedience
to the terms of the Covenant entered into at Horeb. The Covenant is here defined somewhat narrowly as the Ten Commandments (4:13), although it is immediately suggested that "statutes
and ordinances," taught by Moses, are also included in the Covenant (4:14).

It now appears that the Covenant between God and Israel

made at Sinai is closely similar to the suzerainty covenants known from Hittite documents of about 1450-1200 B.C. By these covenants the Hittite kings bound their vassal states to unswerving loyalty to the throne and brought about amicable relationships among the covenanted vassals.

These covenants followed a clear form: a preamble, in which the author of the covenant is named, with his titles, attributes, and genealogy; a historical prologue, describing in "I—thou" language the benevolent acts performed by the Hittite king for the benefit of the vassal; a statement of the detailed obligations imposed upon and accepted by the vassal (such as exclusive loyalty to the king, respect for equality of co-vassals, military support of the king when requested, unlimited trust in the king, and loyalty in word as well as in deed); a provision for the deposit of the covenant document in the temple and its periodic public reading; a list of deities who stand as witnesses to the covenant; and blessings and curses as sanctions of the covenant.

The Covenant at Horeb (Sinai), as reflected in Israel's historical traditions, contains most of these elements: a preamble—"I am the LORD your God" (Deut. 5:6; Exod. 20:2a); a historical prologue—"who brought you out of the land of Egypt, out of the house of bondage" (Deut. 5:6b; Exod. 20:2b); the obligations—commandments relating to duties toward God (Deut. 5:7-15; Exod. 20:3-11) and commandments relating to duties toward fellow men (Deut. 5:16-21; Exod. 20:12-17). The deposit of the Covenant document in the Ark is noted (Deut. 10:5; 31:26) and periodic reading of the Law of Moses is enjoined (Deut. 31:9-13). Blessings and curses as sanctions of the Covenant are said to have been uttered (Deut. 27-28).

The Covenant was conceived as arising out of God's gracious election of Israel, as an expression of his desire to enter into communion with his Chosen People and to bless them with his presence and gifts. Men could establish no claim on God. But God willed to be gracious to his people and would be so under certain conditions. These conditions were not arbitrary but were set by his character and his purposes. If men accepted these conditions and faithfully observed them, God would fulfill the promises made to them.

The emphasis in the closing section of the first great Deuteronomic sermon is on Israel's obligation with respect to the requirements of the Covenant made at Horeb. These must be meticulously obeyed, in the form shortly to be set forth in the book. Nothing is to be added to or removed from them (4:2). The memory of that awesome moment when these requirements were delivered to Israel from the burning mountain must be kept alive in the hearts of each successive generation.

Reasons for complete obedience are introduced again and again: "that you may live," and not die as did the men who became involved in the idolatrous worship of the Baal of Peor (Num. 25:1-9); that you may "go in and take possession of the land"; that you may enjoy the approbation of other nations when they see your close relationship to God and the essential rightness of your laws.

It may be noted here in passing that Israel's greatness in the world has in fact resulted from the very presence of God with his people (supremely in the Incarnation) and in the revelation of his will for the life of mankind. It is significant that these, and not wealth or military power or artistic achievement, are pointed out as the measure of Israel's greatness.

The Spirituality and Uniqueness of God (4:15-40)

The preacher has now emphasized Israel's responsibility for obedience to the terms of the Covenant. For him these terms are summed up in the Ten Commandments. He comments on two of these in order to show specifically how they should be observed.

He takes the second commandment first: "You shall not make for yourself a graven image . . . for I the LORD your God am a jealous God . . ." (5:8-10). This is elaborated and applied in 4:15-31.

The preacher finds evidence of the spirituality of God in the fact that at Horeb the Israelites heard the voice of God but saw no form (4:12, 15, 33, 36). He infers that since they saw no form of God, they are to worship nothing which man can see.

It is a significant fact that in all of the archaeological excavations conducted in Palestine no representations of Israel's God have ever been found. Images of the human male figure are likewise missing. It is true that the Israelites used Astarte figurines (nude representations of the Canaanite goddess of fertility), perhaps to promote human and animal fertility, but these are obviously intrusions from Canaanite religion and culture and foreign to Israel's normative faith and life. The evidence is strong that the Covenant with God entered into by Israel at Horeb prohibited the making of images.

Images, of course, seriously limit the worshiper's concept of the deity being worshiped. Even when the image is conceived only as the abode of the deity, the place of his manifestation to man, the effect is still to limit the conception of the god to the way he has been represented. Ancient peoples around Israel thought of their gods as personifications of the forces of nature, as supermen, who related to one another as men do. By magical practices they could be moved to activities beneficial to their worshipers. When God is conceived as a man writ large, little damage to the God idea will result from the making of images. But when God is conceived as in some respects like man but in other respects wholly other; when he is identified with no force of nature but held to be the Creator of all and the Lord of nature; when it is believed that he cannot be localized; and when his activities are conceived to be the governing of both nature and human history —then images of him appear altogether stultifying and repugnant to his essential nature.

It is true that Israel did not and could not altogether escape anthropomorphisms (the representing of God in human terms). God is said to see, speak, hear, smell, laugh; he is represented as having eyes, ears, hands, feet, arms, and the like. He feels joy, jealousy, disgust. He even repents of this or that course of action. If God is to be thought of as in any way personal, it is inevitable that certain qualities which men possess will be predicated of him. It is the glory of Israel's faith that neither his likeness to men nor his difference from them was sacrificed. Both were held in creative tension. Israel made selective and discriminating use of anthropomorphisms, decisively rejecting some and employing others.

Thus in this passage the voice of God out of the midst of the fire at Horeb is an anthropomorphism acceptable to the writer. Voice suggests presence, command, will. Israel is to be concerned not about God's form but about his acts and his purposes for its life. He is the "living" God, the creative, vitalizing, and purposive Power behind and in all. The essential for man's life and salvation is not a picture of God but understanding of his activity and his will.

The second part of the appeal (4:32-40) stresses the importance of the first commandment: "You shall have no other gods before me" (5:7). It is clear that the phrase "before me" really means "besides me," or "apart from me" (5:7; see margin). Allied to this are the statements found in 4:35 and 39: "the LORD is God; there is no other besides him"; and "the LORD is God in heaven above and on the earth beneath; there is no other."

Israel is to have no other god because there is actually no other God than he! Is this the meaning here? The surprising statement in 4:19-20 to the effect that God has ordained the worship of sun, moon, stars, and all the host of heaven for other nations but that he has redeemed Israel "to be a people of his own possession" seems to fall much nearer to henotheism or monolatry (both terms meaning essentially the worship of one god by one people, without denying that other gods exist) than to monotheism (which holds that there is only one God; others are alleged to exist but the claim is false).

The nature of Israel's "monotheism" and the time of its emergence in the life of Israel have been much discussed. Though reputable interpreters are not in complete agreement, the conviction is growing that Israel's faith from the time of the Horeb experience may in a broad sense be termed monotheistic. Though the existence of other gods than Israel's was not flatly denied (see, for example, Judges 11:24; I Sam. 26:19; II Chron. 2:5; Pss. 95:3; 97:9), the power of these gods was. Israel's God alone was Creator and Ruler of the world and history; at best other gods were subordinate to him, members of his heavenly court and council (Job 1:6-12; 2:1-6; Ps. 82:1) and of the heavenly hosts around his throne (Deut. 33:2; Neh. 9:6; Ps. 29:1). Israel was forbidden to worship these lesser beings, although the nations, because of their lack of knowledge, might be allowed to do so (thus perhaps we may understand Deuteronomy 4:19). The realm of God's authority was universal, but his unique revelation was given to the people of Israel. Here only, among his Chosen People, were his true nature and purposes known. The gods of the nations were no gods in any proper sense of that term, and the idols of these nations were creations of the hands of men. This is at least "practical," if not "theoretical," monotheism. Even in Christianity, angels and demons are granted existence under the sovereignty of God.

The meaning here is not so much that Israel is to have no other God because there is no other God than he, but that Israel is to have no other God because this God, who is the God of all the earth, came to Israel and in the Covenant made Israel "his own possession"; because he revealed himself to his people in his mighty and compassionate works; and because he seeks in love

to discipline his people (4:36) and to show mercy to them forever. The God of Israel is no passive God, who theoretically
exists behind and in all things, but the active God of redemption,
whose claim on Israel's loyalty is absolute and inescapable.

Appendix: The Cities of Refuge (4:41-43)

This brief reference to the cities of refuge comes in abruptly.
It serves to separate the first and the second addresses of Moses,
the latter of which begins in 5:1, after the brief introduction of
4:44-49. It perhaps was put here to make explicit the connection
of the appointment of cities of refuge with Moses, in view of
another tradition which assigned the cities of refuge to Joshua
(Joshua 20:1-9, especially verse 8; on the purpose of the cities
of refuge see the comment on Deuteronomy 19:1-13).

SECOND ADDRESS OF MOSES: WHAT GOD REQUIRES

Deuteronomy 4:44—28:68

It is likely that the original Book of Deuteronomy began at
4:44 and that the material preceding this point was written at a
somewhat later date as an introduction to a history of Israel in
Palestine from the Deuteronomic point of view covered in Deuteronomy through Second Kings (see Introduction). Thus when
1:1—4:43 was added to the original Book of Deuteronomy, two
introductions to the laws of Moses were included: 1:1—4:43 and
4:44—11:32. There is a good deal of overlapping between these
two introductions. Each is complete without the other. There are,
however, differences in emphasis.

Chapters 5-11 are nearer in contents and general point of
view to 4:1-40 than to chapters 1-3. In the latter, the deeds of
God in the wilderness experience of Israel are elaborated; in
4:1-40 the people are urgently exhorted, in view of what God
has done, to accept wholeheartedly his will for their life as disclosed in the revelation given them at Horeb. Chapters 5-11 stress
this theme, particularly obedience to the first commandment,
and point out the importance of such obedience for the future
of the nation in the land into which it is soon to come.

Introduction (4:44-49)

Four terms are used here to characterize the content of the legislation delivered to the people by Moses just prior to their entrance into the land: "law," "testimonies," "statutes," and "ordinances." Although there is in the Old Testament some distinction in the usage and meaning of the Hebrew words thus translated, in Deuteronomy the terms appear to be synonymous, as the occurrence of three of them in 4:8 seems to show. All refer to the divinely revealed will for the life of man on its many sides, as detailed in the Book of Deuteronomy. They include man's relationship to God in its inner, spiritual aspects as well as its outward forms, and his relation to his fellow men in all areas of his life.

The Meaning and Obligation of the Covenant Relationship (5:1—11:32)

This section is difficult to analyze logically. In general it seeks to prepare the reader for the detailed exposition of the laws contained in chapters 12-26 by explaining to him precisely why he should regard them seriously and endeavor to obey them faithfully. In spite of the lack of logical development, the section contains the most appealing and religiously significant chapters of the entire book.

The thought centers around God's graciousness in entering into a Covenant with Israel. His love for Israel, quite unmerited and in fact inexplicable, should evoke love and reverence in the beloved. The glorious destiny marked out for God's people in the goodly land should arouse in them genuine humility and dedication to his purposes. One feels here the pulsebeat of true religion.

God's Direct Commands (5:1-21)

The Decalogue is prefaced here by a summons to hear, learn, and obey the terms of the Covenant made at Horeb. It is affirmed that this Covenant was made "with us . . . all of us here alive this day," not with "our fathers" (vs. 3).

It might seem that the writer does not know of, or has overlooked, the generation lost in the wilderness, which generation—and not the present one—actually stood at the holy mountain. But it is more likely that he means to stress the perpetual contemporaneity of the Covenant's obligations. From the Hebrew perspective the children are seminally in the loins of the fathers; they are in him and he is in them. The patriarch represents the tribe he heads, puts his distinctive stamp on it, and determines its destiny. Obligations he assumes remain obligations of his progeny. God's Covenant was with the people of Israel. The people before Moses at the Jordan are now this people. They cannot therefore shrug off their responsibilities.

It is possible also that the words in 5:2-3 stem from the liturgy of the renewal of the Covenant used in successive generations of Israel's history. By this liturgy each generation shared at first-hand in the formative events of Israel's past.

The commandments as here given closely resemble those re-corded in Exodus 20. Both obviously derive from a common source. Whether the Decalogue actually comes from the time of Moses has been much debated. A growing number of present-day scholars affirm that it is essentially Mosaic, for it fits into the pat-tern of suzerainty covenants known to be in vogue in the time of Moses (see comment on 4:1-14). And the fundamental con-ception of religion it enshrines seems to agree with the spirit and work of Moses, so far as we are able to make it out. It is possible that in their earliest form some of the commandments were con-siderably shorter, consisting only of a succinct injunction without qualifying phrases (for example, simply, "You shall not make for yourself a graven image"—Deut. 5:8).

The Decalogue falls naturally into two parts: commandments defining man's proper relationship to God and commandments regulating man's relations with his fellows.

The first two commandments, the first stressing the unity and the second the spirituality of God, have already been treated (see comment on 4:15-40). It needs also to be noted that idolatry is by no means simply an ancient problem. The temptation to worship something less than the true and only God is ever with us. While images of false gods do not now smile or frown upon us from mantles and street-corner pedestals, the gods of money, sex, the state, and the like, subtly shackle our minds and lead to-ward individual and corporate destruction.

The one true God is said here to be "a jealous God" (vs. 9). In Hebrew the word for "jealous" does not mean "envious," as in some religions where the gods are envious of one another and even of men who are succeeding too well. It means rather that

God maintains his exclusive rights over the created order and the worship of man. God stands alone. He shares his glory with no other. Men who attempt to become like God are cut down. And he will allow no other to infringe on his domain. The jealousy of God is inherent in and necessary to monotheism.

The statement that God visits the iniquity of the fathers upon the children to the third and fourth generation (vs. 9) has given offense to many. But it is true, first, that the children to many generations are affected for good or ill by the choices and deeds of their forebears. If the fathers sow the seeds of idolatry, the children will hardly reap a harvest of ethical monotheism. Second, God's judgment on idolatrous practices is to be seen in part in the individual and social consequences of these practices. The degradation of mankind is itself the wrath of God at work (Rom. 1:18-32). Third, this statement must be balanced by the complementary affirmation that every man is responsible for his own sins (Jer. 31:29-30; Ezek. 18:2-4).

The third commandment prohibits the misuse of the divine name. The name of God, representing as it does his character and power, was to be regarded as holy (compare the petition, "Hallowed be thy name," in Matthew 6:9). It was not to be treated lightly and used for unworthy purposes, such as in magical formulas, in false oaths, in curses irresponsibly uttered, and the like.

The fourth commandment enjoins observance of the Sabbath. The Deuteronomic form is considerably longer than that in Exodus, chiefly because of the different reason given for observing it. In Exodus the Sabbath rest is grounded in God's rest after the six days of creative activity; in Deuteronomy it is to be separated from other days both as a day of rest and as a reminder of the deliverance from Egypt. Rest for servants is especially stressed in Deuteronomy (vs. 14), in line with the persistently humanitarian outlook of the book (15:12-18; 16:9-12; 24:17-18).

Some basic truths underlie the institution of the Sabbath, as represented in Exodus and Deuteronomy. (1) The rhythm of work and rest has divine sanction. "Six days you shall labor, and do all your work" underscores the importance of work in the life of man and the danger of idleness. But man and beast can work too much. Rest is required for the good of both. God cares for all of his creatures, and the rights of all must be respected. (2) The Sabbath stands as a reminder of what God has done. He is

both Creator and Redeemer, and men need perpetually to be reminded of this. Though worship of God on the Sabbath is not
here specifically enjoined, it is certainly implied. (3) The Sabbath symbolizes God's claim on all of man's time. In Hebrew
thought and practice a part frequently represents the whole (as
in the giving to God the first fruits of the harvest, the first-born
son, and the like). God owns all but allows us to keep the larger
share. Thus the Sabbath represents his claim on us altogether.
Christians have seen God's deed and his claim supremely in Jesus
Christ; hence, their weekly day of rest and worship is no longer
reminiscent of the Passover and the deliverance from Egypt but of
the greater deliverance accomplished on the day of Christ's resur-
rection.

The fifth commandment ("Honor your father and your
mother") heads the list of obligations to our fellow men. Reverence for parents is deeply embedded in Hebrew life, both ancient
and modern, and forms the basis for family solidarity in the Jewish and the Christian traditions. Respect for parental authority
(see Exod. 21:15, 17; Deut. 21:18-21) and care for the aged
(see Mark 7:9-13) constitute what is meant by "honor."

The sixth commandment ("You shall not kill") gives evidence
of the high value placed on human life in the community of
Israel. It was meant to safeguard the members of the Covenant
community against unauthorized acts of killing. Apparently not
included in the prohibition are the slaying of animals for food
(Gen. 9:3), the killing of Israel's enemies (Deut. 20:1-4), and
capital punishment (Exod. 21:12-17). It is significant that for
crimes against property the death penalty was not exacted in
Israel as was the case among other peoples of the ancient Near
East—further evidence of the high value placed on human life.
Cities of refuge were provided for persons taking life accidentally
(Deut. 4:41-43; 19:1-13). Suicide—extremely rare in Israel
(for cases see I Sam. 31:4-5; II Sam. 17:23; I Kings 16:18)—
is condemned not by specific prohibitions but by the whole attitude of Israel toward the sanctity of life.

The seventh commandment ("Neither shall you commit adultery") emphasizes the sanctity of marriage, a state instituted by
God, according to the Book of Genesis (2:18-24). While the
prohibition here relates only to the conduct of married persons,
and not to sexual activities of the unmarried (fornication), Hebrew law as a whole has a stringent attitude toward sexual re-

lationships. Sodomy, bestiality, and incest were punished by death (Lev. 20:11-16). Polygamy was not forbidden, but it is never represented in a light way—as an opportunity for increased sexual gratification—but as a means of responsible procreation. In the fertility religions around Israel sexual license was widely tolerated and strongly encouraged by the rituals of the cult, but in Israel such conduct was abhorred (Deut. 23:17; Lev. 19:29). Jesus brought Israel's teaching on the sanctity of sexual relationships to its highest expression in the forbidding of the lustful attitude as well as the act (Matt. 5:27-28).

The eighth commandment ("Neither shall you steal") adds to the sanctity of life and marriage the sacredness of property. Behind the commandment lies the belief that a person is entitled to enjoy the fruits of his labors and not be deprived of them by those who have done nothing to merit them. The commandment is meant to encourage industry and thrift and to protect the industrious and thrifty from the irresponsible and the indolent. Without such a law, organized society could scarcely exist.

The ninth commandment ("Neither shall you bear false witness against your neighbor") is intended to ensure justice in the courts. The Hebrew here is literally, "And you shall not answer against your neighbor, as a vain witness," while in the Exodus form of this commandment the word is "false." A "vain witness" apparently means an insincere, untruthful witness. Then as now, the administration of justice depended upon the availability and reliability of witnesses. If integrity is lacking in the courts, grave injury can be done the innocent.

The tenth commandment ("Neither shall you covet . . .") strikes at the root of the evil actions prohibited in the preceding commandments. It is in the heart of man that adultery, stealing, and insincere witnessing are spawned. As Jesus pointedly put it, "The good man out of the good treasure of his heart produces good, and the evil man out of his evil treasure produces evil; for out of the abundance of the heart his mouth speaks" (Luke 6:45). Here Jesus developed an insight deeply embedded in Deuteronomy.

Jesus and New Testament writers took the commandments of the Decalogue seriously. They did not argue their validity—they assumed it (see Mark 10:17-22; Rom. 13:9). They were careful to point out, however, that no formal obedience to these laws is adequate. God wants men who are good inwardly as well as outwardly (Matt. 5:21-48). He desires that a man should love him with all his heart and love his neighbor as himself (Mark 12: 28-31; Rom. 13:8-10). "Love is the fulfilling of the law" (Rom. 13:10). In according to love the central place in ethics, Jesus and the Church were but following the lead of the Old Testament (Deut. 6:4-5; Lev. 19:18).

The People's Response (5:22-33)

It is clearly stated here and in the Book of Exodus (Exod. 19: 16-20; ch. 20) that the Ten Commandments were given by God directly to the people but the rest of the Law came to them through the mediation of Moses. This distinction serves to highlight the importance of the Decalogue. The phrase here, "and he added no more" (5:22), also indicates the writer's sense of the finality and authority of the Ten Commandments.

The people's reaction to God's direct revelation of his will in the Decalogue oscillated between gratitude and fear. What a sublime privilege it was to hear the very voice of God, to see "his glory and greatness"! (vs. 24). They marveled that they had not been consumed by his awful Presence. But they want no more face-to-face relationships with him. Let Moses draw near to him and bring them word concerning his demands in detail!

How shallow Israel's pledge of obedience on this occasion was is shown in the incident concerning the molten image and subsequent acts of rebellion in the period of wilderness wandering (Deut. 9:12-24). There is pathos in God's words, "Oh that they had such a mind as this always, to fear me and to keep all my commandments, that it might go well with them and with their children for ever!" (5:29).

The Great Commandment and Israel's Obligation (6:1-25)

God's revelation to Moses, the mediator nominated by the people and accepted by God (5:27-31), now begins to be delineated. Its importance is stressed repeatedly in chapter 6 and following. It is on hearing and obeying it that the nation's future in the land soon to be possessed will depend.

Moses rightly sees that God's central requirement is recognition of his unity and uniqueness, and love of and loyalty to him on the part of man's whole being (6:4-5).

That verse 4 stresses the unity and uniqueness of God, and thus puts positively what the first commandment of the Decalogue states negatively, seems clear in spite of the ambiguity of the

Hebrew phrase which, literally translated, is simply: "The LORD
our God the LORD one." The several possibilities of translation
are listed in the margin of the Revised Standard Version. The
problem centers in the meaning of the word "one." Does it
affirm that Deity is not to be thought of as comprising many
beings, each with differing characteristics, functions, and places
and forms of worship, but rather as a unity? Does the passage
affirm monotheism as against polytheism, "one" in contradis-
tinction to "many"? Probably so; and if the Deity is truly one,
then he is the only One. His unity and his uniqueness go together.

Having affirmed what God is, the passage next defines what
man's attitude toward him should be. It is not to consist in a fearful and servile recognition of his sovereignty, and therefore a
dutiful obedience to his will, but in a glad and wholehearted response to him—a response of the total self, which only the word
"love" can express.

The command to "love" the Lord can be understood only in
the light of later statements about God's lavish and uncondi-
tioned love for Israel (7:7-8; 10:15; see comment). It is necessary
to see here that the command to love God has meaning and com-
pulsive power only in relation to God's prior love.

The Hebrew verb, like our English word "love," has a wide
range of usage in the Old Testament: such as loving food (Gen.
27:4), sleep (Prov. 20:13), the soil (II Chron. 26:10), wisdom
(Prov. 4:6), the good (Amos 5:15), evil (Micah 3:2), oneself
(I Sam. 20:17), one's neighbor (Lev. 19:34), one's offspring
(Gen. 22:2), and the opposite sex (licitly or illicitly—I Sam.
18:20; II Sam. 13:4). Hosea apparently was the first to use the
word in a religious sense, for God's love for Israel (Hosea 3:1;
9:15; 11:1, 4; 14:4). The earliest use of the word to characterize
man's proper attitude toward God seems to be in Deuteronomy.
Here it is said again and again (5:10; 7:9; 10:12; 11:1, 13, 22;
13:3; 19:9; 30:6, 16, 20) that what God basically wants of the
people of Israel is their wholehearted love and loyalty and the
obedience to the terms of the Covenant relationship which love
and loyalty will inspire.

The importance of the Lord's commands is emphasized by practical instructions: commit them to memory; impress them upon
your children; talk about them incessantly; hold them before
your eyes always.

The injunction to bind the commands on the hand, to wear

them on the forehead, and to write them on the doorposts may originally have been meant figuratively (see Exod. 13:16), but Jews of the time of Jesus and later followed the command literally. They inscribed Exodus 13:1-10, 11-16, and Deuteronomy 6:4-9 and 11:13-21 on tiny scrolls of parchment, inserted them in cases of skin or metal, and bound them on the left arm and on the forehead at the time of reciting the Shema (see below). In addition, they affixed a *mezuzah* (a small cylinder enclosing a parchment inscribed with Deuteronomy 6:4-9 and 11:13-21) to the upper part of the right-hand doorpost. The "phylacteries" of Matthew 23:5 are the cases worn on the arm and the forehead.

Deuteronomy 6:4-9 is one of the great passages of the Bible, judged both by its contents and by its influence on Judaism and on Jesus and the Church. It is one of three passages comprising Israel's basic affirmation of faith (the other two being Deuteronomy 11:13-21 and Numbers 15:37-41). It is called the "Shema" (meaning "Hear"), from the first Hebrew word of Deuteronomy 6:4. Loyal Jews for more than two millennia have been reciting this confession twice daily. Jesus joined Deuteronomy 6:4-5 and Leviticus 19:18 into a summary of the heart of the Law (see Mark 12:28-34).

The material surrounding and including the great commandment, like much of the contents of the Book of Deuteronomy, falls into a simple pattern: what Israel should do, what it should not do, and why in both cases. Israel has just been commanded to love the only true God. It is now instructed concerning the dangers ahead with respect to the fulfillment of this command, the tragic consequences of failure (6:10-15), and the rewards of obedience (6:2-3, 18-19, 23-25).

These dangers are, first, that unearned material abundance, lavished on the conquering nation, will dull its awareness of God and the memory of his gracious deliverance from Egypt (6:10-12). Jeremiah found that prosperity freely bestowed by God led not to gratitude and loyalty to God's will but only to selfish indulgence and gross immorality (Jer. 5:7-9). Jesus warned his disciples repeatedly concerning the seductive and soporific power of riches (Matt. 6:19-21; Luke 12:13-21).

The second danger is that Israel will fall to worshiping the gods of the peoples around. It would be natural to attribute the prosperity of the Canaanites to the fertilizing power of the god

Baal. In the Ras Shamra tablets of the fourteenth century B.C., Baal is said to make the heavens rain fat and the wadis (gorges) to flow with honey. Hosea had to remind the people of his time that Israel's God, not Baal, was the giver of agricultural abundance (Hosea 2:5-23). It is emphasized once again in 6:15 that the Lord is a "jealous" God. He demands exclusive loyalty. To love him means to fear (reverence) him, to serve him alone, and to invoke only his name in oaths (6:13).

Thirdly, there is the danger of unbelief, of questioning God's presence and providence in the life of Israel (6:16-19). At Massah (meaning "testing," "proving"), Israel openly doubted by asking, "Is the LORD among us or not?" (Exod. 17:7; compare Deut. 9:22; 33:8). Of what significance is it to believe that God is one if he is unconcerned about his worshipers? To deny that he is graciously active in the life of his Chosen People is as great a sin as to deny his unity and uniqueness. The God of Israel is the God who acts dependably and persistently in fulfillment of his Covenant promises and responsibilities. To deny his presence is to accuse him of infidelity and inconstancy. His fidelity to the Covenant in spite of Israel's infidelity was one of the chief emphases of the great prophets; and likewise of Paul, who wrote: "What if some were unfaithful? Does their faithlessness nullify the faithfulness of God? By no means! Let God be true though every man be false . . ." (Rom. 3:3-4).

The last paragraph of this chapter (Deut. 6:20-25) is concerned not with the obedience of the generation about to enter the Promised Land but with the fidelity of its descendants, a subject briefly mentioned in verse 7. There it is suggested that the responsibility lies with the parents, but here the initiative comes from the children. These curious little creatures are always asking "Why?" and intelligent answers are due them. If the faith of the fathers is to become a living faith in the children, something more than parental commands must become operative. The answer to be given them, the passage suggests, is in chief part a story: We obey God's laws because of what he has done for us.

It is widely held today that the story of the deliverance from Egypt, as here formulated (see also Deuteronomy 26:5-9 and Joshua 24:2-13), comprises one of the earliest confessional statements of Israel, long antedating the Book of Deuteronomy. For centuries children had been told the story of God's love for Israel as manifested in his deeds, culminating in the giving of the

Law and the gift of their homeland. But besides gratitude as a motive for obedience, the consequences of obedience are pointed out. Obedience is "for our good always" (vs. 24). Later chapters show again and again that through obedience to God's righteous will the nation will find life, peace, and prosperity in the good land appointed for it, but catastrophe through disobedience. The assertion that "it will be righteousness for us, if we are careful to do all this commandment" (vs. 25) probably does not mean merit before God or uprightness of life but salvation, deliverance, vindication.

Safeguarding the Covenant Relationship (7:1-26)

After having set forth God's basic requirements in chapters 5 and 6, the author now considers the practical dangers to the observance of these requirements which the conquest of the land will pose. In this section two fundamental counsels are offered: be separate or holy (7:1-16, 25-26) and be unafraid (7:17-24).

The first will involve utter extermination of the nations inhabiting the land. They are to be given no quarter: no political intercourse (vs. 2; "no covenant with them"); no marital intercourse (vs. 3); no religious intercourse (vss. 4-5, 25-26). The reason for the policy of extermination and nonintercourse is clearly stated: "they would turn away your sons from following me, to serve other gods" (vs. 4).

The precise number and exact identity of the ethnic groups in Canaan at the time of the Conquest is unknown. Seven are listed here (vs. 1). In other passages the numbers are: two (Gen. 13:7; 34:30), three (Exod. 23:28), five (Exod. 13:5; I Kings 9:20), six (Exod. 3:8, 17; Deut. 20:17; Judges 3:5), seven (Joshua 3:10; 24:11), and ten (Gen. 15:19-21). The basic groups appear to have been the Canaanites (chiefly along the seacoast) and the Amorites (chiefly in the hill country), with other groups here and there.

All had been assimilated more or less into the culture of the Canaanites, including the latter's polytheistic fertility religion centering in the worship of the high god El, his dramatic storm-god son or grandson, Baal, and their fecund and bloodthirsty consorts (Asherah, Anath, Ashtoreth). As givers of fertility, these deities and others were worshiped in orgiastic rites of a most debased character. Worship was carried on at "high places" (see II Kings 23:5, 8; Jer. 2:20) and in elaborate temples.

Archaeologists have uncovered Canaanite places of worship. At Megiddo an elaborate altar for burnt offering, dating about 1900 B.C., was found. It consisted of a circular platform of large stones, some six feet high and twenty-nine feet in diameter at the base. Stone steps led up the side. At their foot lay burned animal bones. Other objects at these places of worship included a sacred tree or post, apparently the symbol of the goddess Asherah (these posts are called "Asherim" in Deuteronomy 7:5), and a sacred stone pillar, perhaps the symbol of the male deity El or Baal. Images of El and Baal, cast from copper and over-laid with gold and silver leaf and others cut in relief on large blocks of stone, have been found. Clay plaques depicting a nude fertility goddess, holding lilies in her outstretched hands and with a serpent draped around her neck, were used in homes as fertility amulets. These may be referred to in 7:26.

The reason for the extermination of the Canaanites is said to be God's election of Israel to be his especially prized people, a people set apart ("holy") to God out of all the peoples on earth (7:6-11). The Hebrew root lying behind the word "holy" means basically a "cut" or a "separation," and in the Old Testament the word is used of places, things, and persons which are separated from the sphere of ordinary life and dedicated to the deity. By virtue of their relationship to the deity they are characterized by a mysterious supernatural potency. In the Old Testament the word often suggests not the opposite of unclean but the opposite of profane. The Hebrew words for the male and female cult prostitutes of Canaanite religion mean literally "holy men" and "holy women" (Deut. 23:18; I Kings 14:24; Hosea 4:14), for they are set apart from ordinary people for a special function in relation to the deity. In other passages a moral element is to be seen in the term "holy" (for example, Isa. 6:1-5; Pss. 15:1; 24:3), as is the case in the New Testament. The one who belongs to God belongs to a God of moral perfection, who has acted in the history of Israel and in Jesus Christ in such a way as to make possible man's ultimate moral perfection (Rom. 6:19, 22; Eph. 1:4-7; I Thess. 4:3). In Deuteronomy 7:6-11 the meaning of "holy" is basically "separated," though the moral emphasis is not wholly absent. Israel's holiness involves obedience to God's laws, and in Deuteronomy these laws often require relationships and conduct of a highly ethical character.

The second fundamental counsel here is: Be unfraid! (7:17-

24). Two reasons for fearlessness are offered: the remembrance of what God did at the time of the Exodus from Egypt; and the certainty that that "great and terrible God" is still in the midst of his people, giving victory to them in seemingly impossible circumstances.

This section states clearly the traditional concept of "holy war," as reformulated by the Deuteronomic writers. In the period of the Judges the tribes were banded together for the carrying on of cultic practices and defense against their enemies. After consultation of the Deity to ascertain his readiness to help and save, trumpets were blown, the victory cry was raised, the men of war were consecrated, a priestly blessing was uttered, and the warriors plunged into the battle with reckless abandon, confident that God would send a great panic ("confusion," vs. 23) on their enemies. This would lead to blind self-destruction. This may be what is meant by the Hebrew word translated by "hornets" (vs. 20). Thus the victory would be gained not by force of arms but by God's miraculous intervention. What was needed, therefore, was faith in God, not in the arm of flesh.

That this conception of God and the reckless abandon that accompanied it led to fantastic victories over militarily superior forces is abundantly attested in the books of Joshua and Judges. And that the destruction of the corrupt Canaanite civilization led to certain consequences favorable to the spread of ethical monotheism in the world can scarcely be denied.

But we must beware of eliminating from the decision to exterminate the inhabitants of the land the element of human choice. The Israelites *chose* to do what they did. The consequences which flowed from their choices, like the consequences of all human decisions, were made by the Lord of history to serve his redemptive purposes. As God brought good out of the choice of the Assyrian and Chaldean kings to overrun and subjugate Israel, it turned out that even Israel's bloody wars—which must be seen in themselves as the evil they really were—were made by God to serve his purposes. God makes the wrath of men to praise him. Men are free to choose, but they cannot determine the consequences, immediate or ultimate, of their choices.

In reading the stories about Israel's past it must therefore be remembered that the human element in decisions has been swallowed up in the realization *after* the events that God effected consequences beyond human deserving or expectation. Thus even the choice is assigned to him. Exterminating wars can hardly be attributed without qualification to the instigation of the God of Jesus Christ!

Learning Dependence Upon God (8:1-20)

The wilderness period was variously interpreted by the writers of Israel. To Hosea and Jeremiah it was an idyllic age when Israel lived in intimate fellowship with God, before the abominable practices of Canaanite Baalism were learned and passionately espoused. In the time of Jesus the inhabitants of Qumran by the Dead Sea glorified the wilderness by fleeing to it and making of it a habitation of God and his devout worshipers, a place of preparation for entrance into the Promised Land of the Messianic Kingdom. They patterned their institutions after the forms set up by Moses in the wilderness.

But some of the psalmists thought of this time as one of ceaseless rebellion against God (see, for example, Ps. 106), and Paul and the author of Hebrews were chiefly impressed by the failure of so many of God's people to get into the Promised Land—a warning to the complacent and the sensual in the Christian Church (I Cor. 10:1-13; Heb. 3-4).

The Deuteronomic writer here thinks of the wilderness period as a time of schooling for God's children. There they learned humble dependence on God—to wait for his will and his word, and to be grateful for his providential care. The writer is particularly impressed by the gift of manna to the hungry people (vss. 3, 16). This substance is now believed to be the excretion of insects which suck the sap of the tamarisk tree and leave a sweet deposit on the trees and bushes of the Sinai area in early summer. Starving people would find this sweet deposit a strength-giving delicacy.

A basic sin of life, as the Deuteronomic writer sees here, is man's spirit of self-sufficiency. He feels adequate for every problem and in need of no help from God. When prosperity comes to him, he gloats inwardly; and he secretly boasts, "My power and the might of my hand have gotten me this wealth" (vs. 17). He forgets the good hand from which all good things come, and settles down to self-gratification.

The view set forth here is that God is a merciful and benevolent Father who ever wills his children's good (vs. 16). Their well-being depends on complete trust in him and obedience to his will. He will satisfy not only their physical but also their spiritual needs, if they trust him implicitly. Bread for the stomach he will provide, but more—bread also for the spirit: "Man does not live by bread alone, but . . . man lives by everything that proceeds out of the mouth of the LORD" (vs. 3). The Jesus who rejected the temptation to turn stones into bread for himself and others by the use of this verse from Deuteronomy (Matt. 4:4; Luke 4:4) is reported to have said also, "My food is to do the will of him who sent me, and to accomplish his work" (John 4:34). It is this spirit that marks a true son of the Father.

The Ground of Israel's Acceptance by God (9:1—10:11)

The sins of the spirit are subtle but devastating. In the preceding section Israel was warned against proud self-sufficiency and here against self-righteousness. These walk hand in hand, and either will destroy the person or nation.

Success is pleasant but perilous. It leads often to the "see-what-I-have-done" attitude or to the smug feeling that the Deity loves me because of my lovableness. When Israel comes into possession of the good land, she is to remember that this land is God's unmerited gift.

In the assertion that salvation is the unmerited gift of God, the Deuteronomic theologians stand on common ground with New Testament writers. Acceptance before God cannot be earned, for all are sinners and cannot make themselves acceptable. Acceptance is God's act alone and rests purely on his gracious forgiveness. The bulk of chapter 9 aims to prove that Israel's acceptance and favored position have nothing to do with inherent righteousness. It was said before that God's love is to be explained by no characteristics or qualities of the object (7:7).

Proof of Israel's stubborn rebelliousness is offered aplenty. The greatest attention is given to the incident of the golden calf (vss. 8-21), with minor attention to other incidents (vss. 22-23). Moses summarizes his experience with Israel by saying flatly, "You have been rebellious against the LORD from the day that I knew you" (vs. 24).

Moses' role as an intercessor stands out sharply here, as it does in other strata of the tradition about him (Exod. 32:11-14, 31-32; 33:12-16; 34:9; Num. 14:13-19). His work in the life of Israel was many-sided. He was a political and military leader, a prophet of God, a priestly mediator, and a vicarious sufferer. In him God found the kind of obedience he desired from Israel as a whole. The Bible offers many illustrations of the truth that "the prayer of a righteous man has great power in its effects" (James 5:16; compare Gen. 18:23-32; I Kings 18:36-39; Acts 4:23-31). Had it not been for Moses' selfless intercession and God's merciful forbearance, the nation would have been destroyed.

In 10:1-5 the completeness of God's forgiveness is emphasized. The sinful nation is restored without qualification to God's favor. The Ten Commandments are rewritten and deposited in the Ark of the Covenant as Israel's permanent possession. The forgiveness the Bible talks about is radical and absolute. Since God removes our transgressions from us "as far as the east is from the west" (Ps. 103:12), we ought to forgive absolutely those who transgress against us (Matt. 18:21-22; Luke 17:3-4).

Summary of Israel's Obligations (10:12—11:32)

The warmhearted Deuteronomic preacher now attempts to summarize his appeal to the national conscience and move his readers to action. In view of God's gracious deeds in the national history, what should be Israel's response?

The summation of God's requirements in 10:12-13 is worthy to stand alongside that in Micah 6:8. Both contain high expressions of Israel's majestic faith. To "fear" God is to reverence him, to have high regard for what he is, what he has done for men, and what he requires of them. It suggests the kind of veneration and respect that issues in obedience to his will. To "love" God involves more than sentimental response to him. It means to serve him with all one's heart and soul (vs. 12), to offer one's total self to him in exclusive loyalty. The proper issue of fear and love is obedient service, a service which itself issues in well-being (vs. 13).

To circumcise the foreskin of the heart (vs. 16) means to open the self to God's word and direction, as the expression, "be no longer stubborn," immediately following implies. Uncircumcised ears are closed ears (Jer. 6:10; see margin); uncircumcised lips open and speak only with difficulty (Exod. 6:12, 30). God's openhearted love to Israel should evoke openhearted love to him. This will mean loving what he loves: justice for the fatherless and the widow and mercy toward the sojourner (vss. 18-19). God's concern for the weak and the oppressed is a strong note in Deuteronomy.

Chapter 11 summarizes emphases of the preceding ten chapters: the mighty deeds of the Lord in Egypt and in the wilderness; the promise of the land and God's guaranteed assistance in its conquest and cultivation; warning against idolatry and its fearful consequences; the injunction to meditate on God's laws and to teach them to the children. The summary concludes with a final appeal to consequences. Obedience will lead to "a blessing"; disobedience will bring "a curse" (vs. 26), a subject given full treatment later (chs. 27-28).

The Specific Terms
of the Covenant Relationship (12:1—26:19)

With the beginning of chapter 12 the reader of Deuteronomy encounters the beginning of a long section of laws which express in detail God's will for the life of Israel on its many sides. They are called "statutes and ordinances." They are not general principles, expressive of the basic character of Israel's religious faith, as in the Ten Commandments, but detailed prescriptions—ceremonial, civil, criminal—for the regulation of daily life. Some seventy laws are here set forth.

The context in which they are presented is still that of preaching. Moses is represented as recounting these laws in his sermons to the second generation just prior to the entry into Canaan. Interspersed among the laws are to be found exhortations to obedience and motivating explanations. The atmosphere is not greatly different from that encountered in chapters 1-11.

The present-day reader of Deuteronomy may be tempted to skip over chapters 12-26 as of little importance for the life of our times. It is true that the laws here contained reflect and seek to regulate life in an ancient, Near Eastern, agrarian civilization, radically different from our own. But before crossing them off as irrelevant two considerations, at least, should be faced.

First, the entire Bible presents the word of God in relation to and in the idiom of a culture other than ours. The word of God spoken by Jeremiah to Zedekiah, the king, at the time of the foul betrayal of the liberated slaves, after the lifting of the siege of the Babylonian army (Jer. 34:8-22), can be exactly relevant to no other situation. It was formulated for that one time. But the Spirit of God can make that historical word unmask our shallow insincerities when we, like those ancient slaveholders, in a time of crisis make promises to God which we only half mean and which we deny when the crisis is past.

Second, a thoughtful consideration of these ancient laws which are based on the principles enunciated in the Ten Commandments—in other words, on the basic convictions underlying ethical monotheism—will lead us to ask to what extent our own laws express the spirit and outlook of ethical monotheism. How can the kind of God revealed in the events of Israel's history be served in the everyday activities and relationships of contemporary life? Who can say that such reflection is irrelevant and unimportant?

Laws Concerning Religious Institutions and Worship (12:1—16:17)

This section deals with the following subjects: the proper locale of public worship (12:2-28), the handling of idolatry and idolaters (12:29—14:2), permitted and forbidden foods (14:3-21), and sacred dues and seasons (14:22—16:17). It is appropriate that Israel's relationship to God should be regularized before human relations are considered.

The first law orders the destruction of Canaanite places of worship and the establishment of public worship of God at a place to be selected by himself alone. The name of this place is not given, but Jerusalem is probably intended, at least by the man or men who put together the old Levitical traditions collected in Deuteronomy (see Introduction).

It is a well-known fact that in earlier days of Israel's life in Canaan the God of Israel was worshiped at many sanctuaries: at Shiloh, Gibeon, and Shechem, for example. Exodus 20:24 seems to allow for the construction of many altars of sacrifice. It is furthermore demonstrable that the Israelites converted many Canaanite high places into places of worship of their own God. After the death of Solomon the northern tribes under Jeroboam split off from the southern and founded a separate kingdom. Sanctuaries for the continued worship of the God of the fathers were established at Bethel and Dan. The golden calves (probably golden bulls) set up by Jeroboam seem to have been wooden statues covered with gold plate. It appears that these were regarded as God's seat or footstool, for in the ancient world, deities were frequently represented as riding on the back of an animal. It is clear, then, that the worship of the Lord was carried on at many different places in the earlier centuries of Israel's existence in Palestine.

Two kings of Judah, Hezekiah and Josiah, undertook to centralize worship in Jerusalem. Hezekiah removed the high places and altars and said to Judah and Jerusalem, "You shall worship before this altar in Jerusalem" (II Kings 18:22; Isa. 36:7). The Northern Kingdom had fallen, and Hezekiah wanted to unite his nation around a central sanctuary. Under Manasseh, Hezekiah's successor, the centralizing program was reversed and the many local sanctuaries restored. Josiah in 622 B.C., after the discovery of the Book of Deuteronomy in the Temple, renewed vigorously Hezekiah's policy of religious centralization. Deuteronomy 12, plus the many explicit commands elsewhere in the book to root out Canaanite places of worship, provided the stimulus and driving power.

In Deuteronomy 12:5 (and in some twenty other places in the book) the nation's great place of worship is called the place where the Lord God has caused his name to dwell (literally, to "tabernacle"). In contrast with many passages of the Old Testament in which God's actual presence in the Temple at Jerusalem is referred to, the Deuteronomic writers prefer to say that his name tabernacles there. How could an earthly temple contain the God whose true dwelling is in heaven? (See I Kings 8:27.) But his name, which represented his character and his will to shepherd and save his people, could "tabernacle" there. Israel could hold fast to this name as the sufficient assurance of God's revelation and presence.

It is made clear in 12:15-28 that the command to offer the prescribed sacrifices at the central sanctuary and to consume portions of them in the sacred festivals there is not meant to prohibit the eating of meat at home. In ancient Israel the slaughter of animals was regarded as a sacrificial act, and before the flesh could be eaten the fat and the blood had first to be presented at an altar (Lev. 17:1-7). Now a distinction is to be made between slaughtering animals for food and slaughtering them for sacrifice. With only one sanctuary in existence it is no longer feasible to present at one altar portions of all animals slain; hence, only sacrificial victims must be presented there. Although in nonsacrificial slaughtering the blood need not be presented at an altar, it is absolutely not to be eaten, "for the blood is the life, and you shall not eat the life with the flesh" (vs. 23). As the seat of life, the blood was regarded as too sacred for human consumption; it belonged solely to God. Hence, it was to be poured out on the earth that it might return to its Giver.

Deuteronomy as a whole says relatively little about sacrifices;

they are dealt with here only in connection with the law concerning the one sanctuary and in chapter 18 in connection with the rights of Levitical priests. For a detailed picture of Israel's sacrificial system the Book of Leviticus must be consulted. But Deuteronomy presupposes the legitimacy of the sacrificial system. What meaning did Israel see in the sacrifices of the Temple? The question is one of great difficulty. But it is likely that at least three conceptions underlay the sacrificial system.

First, the sacrifices were regarded as a gift to the Deity from whom all good things come. It is right that man should give back to God part of that which has been given him. By a gift of that which is precious to him man acknowledges his debt to God, expresses his gratitude, and to an extent binds the Deity to gracious attitudes and actions in the future.

Second, certain kinds of sacrifices were thought to establish and maintain communion between God and man. Some sacrificial victims were divided three ways: the fat and the blood for God, certain parts for the priests, and the rest for the worshipers. The holy meat was consumed in solemn ritual in the Temple and thereby God, the priests, and the worshipers were united, even as men who seal a contract by eating together strengthen the bonds between them (see Gen. 26:28-31; 31:44-54).

Third, sacrifices, when accompanied by sincere repentance, were thought to bring about forgiveness of sin. The blood was considered to be peculiarly efficacious: "it is the blood that makes atonement, by reason of the life [that is in it]" (Lev. 17:11). The sacrifices were of various kinds for people of different rank and economic status. In some cases the blood was carried into the Holy of Holies and sprinkled against the veil, rubbed on the corners of the altar of incense or on the horns of the altar of burnt offering, and poured at the foot of the latter. On the Day of Atonement the high priest entered the Holy of Holies and sprinkled the mercy seat with the blood of a bull and of a goat. In the offering up to God of the very life of the victim, of a possession valuable to man, in a spirit of true repentance, it was felt that God's anger was turned away, the sin covered, and fellowship with God restored.

In some parts of the New Testament, Jesus is presented as the flawless sacrificial victim by whose death forgiveness of sins is effected (Heb. 9:11-14; see II Cor. 5:21). "Without the shedding of blood there is no forgiveness of sins" (Heb. 9:22).

The second group of laws here concerns the handling of

idolatry and idolaters (12:29—14:2). The earlier chapters of Deuteronomy drive home the importance of monotheism and the peril of idolatry; now practical procedures are suggested for ensuring the perpetuation of the former.

Several sources of enticement into idolatry are envisaged: a false prophet, who attempts to authenticate his vicious teachings with miraculous deeds (13:1-5); a family member or intimate friend (vss. 6-11); a particular community, led astray by "base fellows" (vss. 12-18). In 17:2-7 any Israelite, male or female, is considered a possible seducer.

The penalty in all these cases is to be death: when individuals are responsible, by stoning (13:10; 17:5); when a whole community is involved, by the sword and burning (13:15-16).

Such a penalty seems extreme to us, the method of establishing guilt—the testimony of at least two witnesses (17:6)—inadequate, and the way of execution repulsive and inhuman. It is inconceivable to us that a man should stone his own wife or child!

It must, however, be remembered that idolatry struck at the very foundations of Hebrew national life as founded on the Covenant at Horeb. The religion of the Canaanites and surrounding peoples was a debased form of nature worship, with revolting moral standards and practices (see the comment on 7:1-26; note the mention of child sacrifice in 12:31). We may not like the exact way in which the Hebrews sought to deal with their subversives, but we can recognize the legitimacy of their abhorrence of the offense and of their desire to guard against it. They were anxious, therefore, to keep out any marks of pagan customs, even mourning rites of bodily mutilation and shaving of the head (14:1-2). The barriers against pagan standards and practices must be high and thick, lest the nation eventually be engulfed by them.

The third group of laws concerned with religious institutions and worship has to do with permitted and forbidden foods (14: 3-21). Since God is holy ("cut off," "separated" from the common and profane), Israel must likewise be set off from the common and profane. This extends to the realm of foods. It is not simply a question of physical contamination, such as might result from improper slaughtering and handling, but of the impurity of the genus itself. Why some classes of animals were regarded as unclean is not known. Some unquestionably were sacred to heathen gods; the repulsive appearance or uncleanly habits of others may have offended early Hebrews; some may have been thought to be possessed of evil spirits; sickness, rightly or wrongly, may have been associated with the eating of certain animals. The prohibition against boiling a kid in its mother's milk (vs. 21) is a protest against the Canaanite practice of preparing a sacrifice by cooking it in milk.

Though Jesus unquestionably abided by most of the food laws of Judaism, he shifted the emphasis from defilement by external to defilement by internal causes: "Whatever goes into a man from outside cannot defile him . . . What comes out of a man is what defiles a man" (Mark 7:18-23). Mark, seeing the radical implication of this, adds, "Thus he declared all foods clean" (Mark 7:19). Against Gnostic ascetics of the second century, who forbade the use of "foods which God created to be received with thanksgiving," the author of First Timothy retorted that "everything created by God is good, and nothing is to be rejected if it is received with thanksgiving" (I Tim. 4:3-4). In the Gentile church, at least, sin was not a matter of eating the wrong food (as was partially the case in Judaism) but of harboring the wrong spirit (see Gal. 5:19-23).

The fourth group of laws in this section concerns sacred dues and seasons (14:22—16:17). A tenth of the agricultural products and of the firstlings of herds and flocks—or the equivalent in money—is to be taken to the central sanctuary two years out of three. There the tenth—or equivalents purchased on the spot —is to be consumed in sacred feasts before the Lord. These feasts are meant to remind God's people that the land is his and that all good things come from his hands. At the end of the third year the tithe is to be kept in the areas where it was produced and is to be distributed to the landless and the poor.

Nothing is said here about gifts for the support of the priests officiating at the central sanctuary. However, in 18:3-4 designated portions of sacrificial animals and first fruits of grain, wine, oil, and the first shearing of sheep are prescribed. But in Numbers 18:21-24 the tithes are all said to belong to the Levites, the priestly clan. The difference between Deuteronomy and Numbers on the use of the tithes probably is to be explained by assuming that the former book reflects the practice of northern Israel and the latter that of Jerusalem.

Deuteronomy's view—that the tithes are meant to keep Israel

mindful of its debt to the Lord, the Giver of all, and to provide relief for the poor and landless—gives genuine religious and social meaning to this practice. If the tithe is considered to be simply a tax to support the religious establishment or if prosperity for the giver is held up as the reward of tithing—as in some modern-day preaching on tithing—the religious quality of the practice soon evaporates.

The provisions concerning the seventh year (Sabbatical) release highlight Deuteronomy's constant concern for brotherly mercy (15:1-18). The appeal runs: since God has been merciful to us all in the events of our history and in his continuing providential care, we should be merciful to one another (vss. 14-15).

Jesus, who apparently nourished his life on Deuteronomy (see Introduction), emphasized strongly that we should imitate God's attitudes and activities in our dealings with others. The injunctions to "open wide your hand to your brother, to the needy and to the poor, in the land" (vs. 11) and to release debtors gladly during the Sabbatical year stand close to Jesus' admonition: "Give to every one who begs from you; and of him who takes away your goods do not ask them again" (Luke 6:30). Jesus, of course, was more inclusive in his definition of one's "brother." He did not limit the range of his ethical requirement to fellow Israelites, as does Deuteronomy (15:3; compare 14:21).

The sacred seasons of national life and the offerings appropriate to them are next set forth (15:19—16:17). According to 16:16, three times a year all Hebrew males with their sacrifices and offerings must appear before the Lord God at the central sanctuary: at the Feast of Unleavened Bread (Passover); at the Feast of Weeks (later called Pentecost); and at the Feast of Booths (Tabernacles). The hardship involved in this requirement of thrice-yearly attendance at Jerusalem led to relaxation in practice, so that in the time of Jesus attendance once a year was expected of those living in Palestine (see Luke 2:41). Jews living in the Dispersion were able at best to make the pilgrimage a few times in a lifetime.

The feasts of Unleavened Bread and Passover were originally separate feasts. The former was an agricultural feast, probably taken over from the Canaanites soon after Israel's settlement in the land. It marked the beginning of the barley harvest, the first crop to be harvested. During seven days, bread was made only with the new grain of the harvest. The feast marked a new beginning and gave expression to the people's joy over the coming of a new harvest. The Passover seems originally to have been a feast of nomads. It centered in the sacrifice of a young animal with a view to securing fertility and prosperity of the flocks. Blood was put on the tent poles to drive away evil spirits. The sacrifice was offered and the flesh eaten during the full moon. The participants were belted, shod, and equipped with a shepherd's stick. There is evidence that its origin lies far behind the time of the Exodus from Egypt.

Since the Feast of Unleavened Bread and the Feast of Passover both fell in the spring, at almost the identical time, after the settlement in the land it became natural to associate them. The Passover was observed on the night of the full moon of the month Abib and the Feast of Unleavened Bread followed on the next seven days. From the time of Josiah's centralization of worship in Jerusalem the two seem to have been observed together in the Temple at Jerusalem.

The meaning Israel put into these ancient feasts was new. Both became occasions on which the deliverance from the bondage of Egypt was commemorated, as Exodus 12 shows. This great event in which God delivered and sealed his people with Covenant bonds overshadowed all and reshaped many of Israel's institutions and rituals. National ceremonies inevitably reflect the ongoing experiences of the people observing them.

The Feast of Weeks (Greek "Pentecost," meaning "fiftieth") fell on the fiftieth day after the beginning of the Feast of Unleavened Bread (that is, fifty days after the first barley had been cut). This feast marked the end of the cereal harvests. Thus Unleavened Bread and Weeks celebrated the beginning and end of harvest. Both were times of great rejoicing.

The ceremonies of the latter centered in the offering to the Lord of two loaves made out of new flour, baked with leaven. It is a farmer's feast, by which gratitude for the crops is expressed to the Deity. Israel poured its own content into this Canaanite agricultural festival also. By the time of Jesus it had become an occasion for commemorating the giving of the Law at Sinai (Horeb). The Essenes at Qumran, who called themselves the "community of the new covenant," renewed their covenant with God at the Feast of Weeks. This for them was the most important feast of the year.

The Feast of Booths (Tabernacles) was the most popular and joyous feast of all. Josephus, the Jewish historian, called it "the holiest and the greatest of Hebrew feasts." In Exodus 23:16

and 34:22 it is called "the feast of ingathering." It was held after all the crops were in and was celebrated with seven days of worship, feasting, and dancing. Its purpose was to give thanks to God for the gift of the harvest. After the Exile an eighth day of rest and worship, before the return to normal life, was prescribed (Lev. 23:36, 39; see John 7:2, 37). During the seven days of the feast proper the people lived in huts, constructed from the branches of trees. This practice probably arose in ancient times when the reapers lived in such shelters in the orchards and vineyards at harvest time, both for the sake of convenience and for protection of the crops from thieves. By the time of Deuteronomy the festival had been centralized at Jerusalem. At some unknown time in its history, like the other feasts we have discussed, this feast was infused with new meaning: the huts were thought to commemorate the huts in which the fathers lived during the period of wandering in the wilderness (Lev. 23:42-43).

Through reinterpretation of ancient festivals, the deeds of God in the nation's past were kept before the minds of the people. In the time of Jesus and later, as a result of the growth of the Messianic hope, the confidence grew that the God who had delivered Israel from the Egyptian bondage would again deliver his people from the bondage of the heathen (Rome); and that under a prophet like Moses, who would prepare the way for a Messiah like Moses (see 18:15, 18), God's people would enter the blessedness of a new Promised Land. The three great festivals thus fanned the hope for the coming of a second miraculous exodus. Against this background one can understand why the author of the Gospel of John presents Jesus—the Messiah—as the fulfiller and actualizer of the inner meaning and intent of the great feasts of the Jews.

Laws Concerning National Leaders (16:18—18:22)

The code of laws in Deuteronomy 12-26, according to modern standards of logical organization, needs rearrangement. The dominant subject in 16:18—18:22 is clearly the appointment and responsibilities of leaders: of local judges (16:18-20), of a superior court (17:8-13), of a king (17:14-20), of Levitical priests (18:1-8), of prophets (18:9-22). Some sections fit only loosely into this category (16:21—17:7); they properly belong to the previous section on religious institutions and worship.

Local judges and officers ("officers" here probably means "clerks" serving under the judges) are to be appointed in every town. These judges may have been "elders," that is, heads of families in the various clans, and thus the leading citizens. Or they may have been professional judges appointed by the king (see II Chron. 19:4-7). Their function is to render impartial justice: "you shall not show partiality" (16:19; literally, "you shall not regard faces"); and "you shall not take a bribe." Bribery as a means of securing a favorable decision in courts was extremely common in the ancient Near East (see 10:17; 27:25; Ps. 15:5; Isa. 1:23; 5:23; Ezek. 22:12; Micah 3:11).

In Israel the concept of justice (that is, seeing to it that every man receives his proper due) was deeply rooted in the concept of the Covenant relationship: since God and his people are linked together in the bonds of Covenant love or Covenant fidelity, individual members of this covenanted community must treat each other as brothers. They must act responsibly and faithfully toward one another, even as God acts responsibly and faithfully toward them all. This meant that all members of the community were equal before the law, regardless of class or status. The prophets regarded violations of this principle with abhorrence. Brotherhood and justice are twin concepts.

In 17:8-13 provision is made for appeal to a higher court in difficult cases. This court, consisting of priests and an officiating judge (vs. 9) or a priest and a judge (vs. 12), sits in Jerusalem ("the place which the LORD your God will choose"). The judgment of this court is final. Its competence is assured for all kinds of cases, for the judges represent both the religious and the civil realms. Disobedience to the verdict of this court is punishable by death.

In 17:14-20 the office of a king is halfheartedly allowed. In effect the passage says, "You may have a king, like the nations around you, if you think you must. But severe restrictions must govern his selection and subsequent conduct. He is to be a limited, not an absolute, monarch." The point of view is close to that in I Samuel 8 and 12:6-25. Prior to the selection of Saul as Israel's first king, the nation was organized as a federation of clans, tightly bound together in loyalty to God and in fidelity to each other. They worshiped together at a common sanctuary and periodically renewed their loyalties to God and to each other.

In this passage, composed apparently long after unfortunate

experiences with kings like Solomon—who multiplied for himself horses and chariots (vs. 16; see I Kings 4:26; 10:26-29), wives (vs. 17; see I Kings 11:1-8), and silver and gold (vs. 17; see I Kings 10:14-25)—the marked democratic spirit that characterized Israel's life as a whole is to be seen. The king is to be completely subject to the law of God, as is every other Hebrew (vss. 18-19). He is to maintain a brotherly attitude and relationship with his subjects (vs. 20). He is to live simply, as a servant of the people, not to enrich himself and seek power and fortune in military conquests (vss. 15-17). In short, he is not to imitate contemporary despots. Since he rules by divine appointment and not by inherent right (vs. 15; see I Sam. 10:24), his tenure and that of his descendants will be contingent on obedience to God's laws (vs. 20). The gulf between Israel's conception of kingship (or at least that of certain groups in Israel) and the view that predominated in surrounding nations was wide.

The Levitical priests (literally, "the priests the Levites"), according to 18:1-8, are to receive their support from designated portions of the animal sacrifices brought to the central sanctuary and from the first fruits of the grain, wine, oil, and fleece presented there. Since they have no territorial inheritance, they are to be supported out of those revenues on which God has a claim. Levites who have been dispossessed of their source of livelihood at various altars throughout the country by the centralization of worship at Jerusalem may, if they wish, minister at the central sanctuary and receive there their share of the sacrifices and first fruits (vss. 6-8).

The origin, precise identity, history, and function of the Levites are much debated. Various suggestions concerning the meaning of the name "Levite" have been offered, the most probable perhaps being "a descendant of Levi," one of the sons of Jacob. It appears, however, that in the course of time the word became also a functional term (understood to mean perhaps "one pledged by vow"); it now included those of other parentage who nevertheless had been dedicated to and were performing priestly functions. Thus Samuel was reckoned as a Levite (I Chron. 6:28), though by lineage he was an Ephraimite (I Sam. 1:1). Moses and Aaron are said to have belonged to the tribe of Levi. Aaron and his descendants were set apart especially for priestly services (Exod. 29:9, 44; 40:12-15). Thus one family of Levites gained positions of special prominence in the cult and other Levites became assistants (Num. 3:5-10), priests at local sanctuaries, and local teachers of the Law of God. When worship was centralized at Jerusalem, the subordinate Levites were without sources of income. In Deuteronomy it is emphasized that these Levites have equal rights with the dominant group at the central sanctuary. Here one sees again the concern in this book for the needy and underprivileged.

In 18:9-22 the false and the true sources of religious knowledge are set forth. Israel is not to heed the word of diviners, soothsayers, sorcerers, wizards, necromancers, and the like—practitioners who abounded in the countries around Israel—but rather the word of divinely appointed prophets, a succession of men like Moses, whom God will raise up for Israel's guidance. These men will speak with the authority of the Lord himself. They are to be absolutely obeyed. Self-appointed prophets will be slain; and the word of all prophets is to be tested against the course of events.

The craving of men to unlock the secrets of the future and to know the purposes of God in critical situations was as strong in the ancient world as in our own. Equally strong was the desire to influence the deity or deities to a favorable course of action. The belief that certain men had unusual ability to determine the divine will and to influence the deities' actions was widespread in antiquity, as the many magical formulae and rituals known from the ancient Near East show.

One abominable practice carried on by such men is mentioned here: the sacrifice of children (vs. 10). The Phoenicians, both at home and abroad (particularly at Carthage), in time of national danger sacrificed their dearest children, as did the king of Moab when his capital city was under heavy siege (II Kings 3:27). In Judah, Ahaz and Manasseh made their sons "pass through the fire" (II Kings 16:3, margin; 21:6) in times of great danger, obviously to influence the deity in their behalf. This practice is unsparingly condemned in Deuteronomy and the Prophets, along with other heathen customs.

The true prophet will be an Israelite, not a foreigner (as many diviners were; see Num. 22:1-6; Isa. 2:6), and he will be like Moses (vss. 15, 18). The latter characteristic probably means that like Moses he will mediate and interpret the divine word to the people. But an allusion to the character and total prophetic role as exemplified in Moses is not to be excluded here. The

Deuteronomists—to whom Moses was a figure of colossal proportions, to say the least—certainly regarded him as the standard by which all messengers of God must be measured.

To test the verity of prophecy by its fulfillment in the course of events (vs. 22) is at best a partial test. Jeremiah appealed to this test in his dramatic exchange with Hananiah (Jer. 28:9). But a true prophet may predict events which do not come to pass because of a change in the moral character of those addressed (as Jer. 18:7-10 plainly allows). Furthermore, prophecy is much more than prediction of future events. It is a declaration of the will of God in relation to the practical conduct of men (consider the preaching of Amos, for example). Here the conscience is appealed to, and the test of true as against false prophecy will lie in the application of ethical standards as taught by great leaders of the past and accepted by the community at large. Thus Jeremiah holds up, as further tests, the lack of accord between the teaching of the false prophets and the prophetic tradition as a whole (Jer. 28:8-9) and the immoral character of their living (Jer. 23:9-15).

The promise of the coming of a prophet like Moses (18:15, 18)—while pointing, as the context shows, to a succession of prophets like Moses who will deliver the word of God to the people as need arises—was taken in the time of Jesus and later to refer to the coming of a single great prophet of the Last Days, a Second Moses, who would prepare the way for the Messiah's appearance. The Essenes who gave us the Dead Sea Scrolls expected the coming of this Prophet ahead of two anointed representatives (one priestly and the other a layman). Deuteronomy 18:18 was a favorite passage of theirs, as indicated by its presence in a list of Messianic passages found at Qumran by the Dead Sea. The authors of the Gospels of Matthew and John regarded Jesus, the Messiah, as like Moses in many respects.

Laws Concerning the Handling of Criminal Cases (19:1-21)

In this section three criminal matters are dealt with: homicide (unpremeditated and premeditated), stealing of land, and the method of establishing guilt.

Civilized societies regularly recognize the difference between premeditated and unpremeditated homicide and adjust the penalty accordingly. In ancient Israel, where the system of blood revenge prevailed as a deterrent to premeditated homicide (that is, where the next of kin was obliged to shed the blood of the person guilty of murder), some provision had to be made to protect a man-slayer until the nature of his motive could be determined. This provision was the establishment of cities of refuge. Deuteronomy authorizes three in Transjordan (4:41-43), three in the land west of the Jordan (19:1-3), and three more if Israel's territory is enlarged (19:8-9). If investigation by the elders of the city leads to the conclusion that the homicide was unpremeditated, blood vengeance will not be allowed; but in the contrary circumstance, the murderer will be taken from the city of refuge and turned over to the next of kin for "eye for eye," "tooth for tooth," and "hand for hand" treatment (19:21).

The moving of boundary markers, which consisted of a stone or a pile of stones, was relatively easy and apparently often done (Job 24:2; Prov. 22:28; 23:10; Hosea 5:10). The sanctity of inherited property was jealously guarded in Israel (see Lev. 25: 23-34; I Kings 21).

The administration of justice is to a large degree dependent on reliable testimony. Hebrew law attempted to guard against conviction on insufficient evidence by requiring two or three witnesses (19:15) and against perjured testimony by "eye for eye" punishment (19:16-19, 21). The supreme court at the central sanctuary (see 17:8-13) undertook to examine the credibility of witnesses on appeal. If perjury was established, the false witness was saddled with the penalty he sought to fix on the innocent. "Eye for eye" justice, while not in good repute among most Christians, was in actuality an attempt to limit vengeance to equitable proportions; otherwise a second injustice would be added to the first.

Laws Concerning Holy War (20:1-20)

The concept of "holy war," as held and practiced by the early Israelites, appears in Deuteronomy 7:17-24 (see comment). Here detailed prescriptions for it are laid down. Still other passages in Deuteronomy relevant to this theme are 21:10-14; 23:9-14; 24:5; and 25:17-19.

The large preoccupation with this subject in Deuteronomy is no evidence that the writers were violent men, who delighted in the massacre of whole populations. Rather does it grow out of their zeal for ethical monotheism. They and their predecessors had learned through sad experience that intermingling with and

tolerance of polytheistic peoples and practices led to tragic consequences in the life of Israel: the Covenant was broken and
Israel's vision of the one true God and his will for the life of men
was destroyed.

But neither should these men be praised overly much. They did
not rise to the insight that monotheism can best be preserved by
proclamation, demonstration of its beneficial results in life, and
subsequent conversion and assimilation of heathen groups. Such
an understanding of Israel's saving role in the world came with
the Prophet of the Exile, with Jesus, and with the Christian
Church. The Deuteronomists were heirs of a point of view that
was destined to pass away in God's fullness of time. Though they
mollified the brutalities and heartlessness involved in savage, exterminating wars, they did little to change the basic strategy of
international relationships.

Certain humane considerations appear in these directions concerning the conduct of "holy war": the exempting of men who are
on the verge of some high experience (the dedication of a new
house, the enjoyment of the fruit of a new vineyard, the consummation in marriage of a betrothal); the excusing of the fearful and
fainthearted; the avoiding of needless bloodshed in the offer of
terms of peace; the sparing of fruit trees (apparently to avoid
food shortage and famine) in the course of a siege. In 21:10-14,
unusual courtesy to a captive woman is enjoined: safe conduct to
the captor's house; a month's period of mourning for her relatives; an honorable position in the household; freedom rather
than sale into slavery if the captor no longer desires her. All such
humanitarian attitudes and actions are remarkable in time of war
in civilizations ancient or modern! It is evident that the Deuteronomists' call to right living and brotherly treatment of other persons had practical consequences in the tangled affairs of daily
life.

Miscellaneous Civil and Domestic Laws (21:1—25:19)

It is not necessary to comment on all of the laws in this mis-
cellaneous collection. They cover a wide range of relationships
and offer us a glimpse into many fascinating and strange dimen-
sions of ancient Hebrew life and thought. A few of them are
grouped here for discussion.

The Community's Relation to God. The view throughout is that
Israel is a holy community, dwelling in a holy land. God has

set apart both people and land from all that is evil and imperfect.

Evil is looked upon as something which defiles or contaminates the land and the community (21:9, 21; 22:21, 22, 24; 24:4, 7). All sin and guilt must be removed by some recognized means of expiation. When the evil has been dealt with—usually when the sinner has been punished—the stain is removed. But when the offender is unknown—as when a human corpse is found in open country—the offense still must not be overlooked. The guilt is to be transferred from the unknown offender to a heifer by the elders of the nearest town. The heifer then bears the punishment in the breaking of its neck, and a prayer for forgiveness of "thy people Israel" is to be offered (21:1-9).

It is suggested, furthermore, that the land is not only the dwelling place of a holy people but is also the place of God's visitation. In an army camp, pollution from human sources must be guarded against: "Because the LORD your God walks in the midst of your camp . . . therefore your camp must be holy, that he may not see anything indecent among you, and turn away from you" (23:14).

Eunuchs are to be excluded from the community (23:1). In surrounding countries this form of bodily mutilation in the service of a deity or a king was common. The Hebrews, as the sons of the Lord, are not to cut themselves (14:1), that is, to alter in any way the body given them by God. In Leviticus 21:16-23 it is stated that men with physical imperfections cannot serve as priests before God.

Bastards (23:2, probably meaning those born of any kind of illegal sexual relationship) and Ammonites and Moabites (23:3) are prohibited from membership in the community, the former apparently because the stain of their birth clings to them and their descendants, and the latter because of hostility expressed toward Israel at the time of the wandering in the wilderness.

The ideal underlying all the laws is that of a perfect community, with the members living in obedience to all of God's laws and no sin or imperfection tolerated.

Sex Relations. Adultery is forbidden in the Ten Commandments (5:18), as well as here (22:22). By adultery was meant any voluntary intercourse of a married (or betrothed) woman and a man other than her husband (or intended husband). In Hebrew custom, betrothal was tantamount to marriage. The bride price had been paid and the woman now belonged to her intended husband. The punishment for adultery was the death of both parties by stoning (apparently on the analogy of 22:24). In nations around Israel, adultery was also forbidden and severely punished.

In cases of rape, where a betrothed (or married) woman is involuntarily involved, only the man is held responsible and is punished by death (22:25-27). In seduction or rape of an unbetrothed virgin, the man is to pay the father of the woman the bride price (22:28-29). He is obliged to take her as his wife, and the possibility of divorce is denied him.

Relations with a stepmother are prohibited (22:30). In Leviticus 18:8-18 and 20:11-21 the prohibition is extended to a wide range of female relatives. Why only the stepmother relationship is mentioned here is not known. It may have been thought representative of the whole group of forbidden relationships, or it may have been a particularly frequent problem in a polygamous society in which wives were passed along with the rest of the property of an inheritance.

In 24:1-4 there appears a law against the remarriage of a divorced woman to her first husband after she has entered into a second marriage. The right of divorce by a husband is not provided for here or anywhere in the Old Testament. This right had been recognized so long in the ancient Near East that it was simply assumed everywhere. The ground of the husband's action is said to be "some indecency" (in Hebrew literally, "the nakedness of a thing"—apparently immodest or indecent behavior short of adultery, or the death penalty would be specified). The bill of divorce (a properly executed legal document, which probably required an appearance before a public official and called for formal delivery into the wife's hands) was meant to protect the wife from hasty and ill-considered expulsion. It is to be noted that no provision is made in the Old Testament for a wife's divorcing her husband.

While divorce of a wife was easy in Old Testament times, some Hebrew spirits were repelled by it. In Genesis 1-2 monogamous marriage is looked upon as God's will, and in Malachi 2:16 divorce is said to be hated by God. Jesus held that Moses permitted divorce because of the hardness of men's hearts, but that God's intention at the Creation was permanent and indissoluble marriage (Mark 10:4-9).

The prohibition of a return of a twice-married woman to her

first husband rests on the judgment that she is "defiled." In other words, she is an adulteress from the point of view of her first husband. This attitude provides the background for the statement in Matthew 5:32.

The sex laws here set forth reflect clearly the status of women as the property first of the father (22:29) and then of the husband or intended husband. But a woman is property of peculiar sanctity: she has rights as a person. If her husband unjustifiably slurs her moral reputation (22:13-21), or if she was seduced by him before betrothal and marriage (22:28-29), she is entitled to special protection: the husband loses the right to divorce her. Furthermore, the formalities involved in the preparation and delivery of the bill of divorce were meant to safeguard her position. The ideal for marriage here is considerably below Christian conceptions, but it probably was immeasurably above that of surrounding peoples at the time of the writing of Deuteronomy.

Family Relations. Closely related to the subject of sex relations is the matter of family relations. In one case here the two subjects overlap: in the law of levirate (from a Latin word meaning "husband's brother") marriage (25:5-10).

If a married man dies without a son, his brother, if living together with him on the same family estate, is to take the widow as his wife and beget a son for his brother. This son will bear the name and inherit the estate of the dead brother. If the surviving brother declines to do this, he must endure publicly a distasteful ceremony and bear, together with any children subsequently born, a disgraceful family name. This custom was designed to prevent the extinction of a family and to keep property from passing into the hands of a stranger who might marry the widow.

This law reveals some important things about ancient Hebrew belief: the strong sense of family solidarity, of brotherly responsibility; the importance of family survival; the subordination of the romantic and emotional aspects of love and marriage to the purpose of reproduction and the creation of new family units. It is to be remembered that the early Hebrews had no hope of a blessed immortality after death. They expected to live on in the life of their offspring, and they expected their children to perpetuate and give honor to the family name. Family pride was a strongly motivating factor in Hebrew life.

The rights and responsibilities of children in a household are spelled out here. In the matter of inheritance, justice must not be subverted by favoritism. The first-born son's right to a double portion of his father's goods is inviolable, even though his mother may not be the favorite wife and mother in a plural marriage (21:15-17). The most notable instance of violation of inheritance rights through the influence of a favorite wife was David's elevation of Solomon to the throne instead of Adonijah (I Kings 1-2).

But if children have rights, they have also responsibilities. First among these is to honor and obey their parents (21:18-21; see also the fifth commandment in 5:16). An oft-reproved but incorrigible son is to be turned over to the elders of the city for execution. The Hebrews insisted on stable family life as a prime factor in the stability of the community. Obedience to constituted authority, both divine and human, was a firm emphasis of Hebrew life.

Neighbor Relations. One of the most attractive features of the Book of Deuteronomy is the loving, faithful, and helpful spirit it fosters in neighbor relations. Members of the community stand in a Covenant relation with both God and men. God's love for Israel led to the inauguration of the Covenant relationship. Israel is to love God in return, to be loyal to him, and to show brotherly love and fidelity to fellow Israelites. Although the statement "You shall love your neighbor as yourself" is to be found only in Leviticus (19:18), the spirit of these words permeates the Book of Deuteronomy.

Lost property of known and unknown members of the community is to be restored as speedily as possible (22:1-4). No interest is to be charged on loans of money or goods to one's brother in the community (23:19-20); helpfulness, not the desire for profit, should characterize brotherly relationships. When security is to be given to assure repayment of a loan, the creditor may not seize what he wishes from the house of the borrower; he is to accept what the borrower brings out to him (24:10-11). If the cloak of a poor man is offered as security, it must be returned at sundown so that he may not suffer from the cold of the night (24:12-13). A widow's garment is not to be taken as security (24:17). Generosity toward the poor (the sojourner, the fatherless, the widow) will dictate leaving some of the harvest for gathering by them (24:19-21). Balustrades are to be erected on roofs for the protection of visiting neighbors (22:8). Fellow Israelites are not to be forced into slavery or sold (24:7). Oppression of hired servants (Israelite or foreign-born) and the withholding of wages from them are strictly forbidden (24:14-15). Refugee foreign slaves (who apparently have fled on account of ill treatment) are to be received considerately and not to be returned to their oppressive owners (23:15-16). Honest weights and measures must be used in all commercial transactions (25:13-15). Hunger may be satisfied from a neighbor's vineyard and field, but the privilege must not be abused by carting away the neighbor's produce (23:24-25).

We may pause to inquire briefly concerning the reasons offered for kindly, generous, brotherly attitudes. Again and again it is suggested in Deuteronomy that the motive for such attitudes and acts is the attitude and deeds of God. God loved and showed mercy on a weak, afflicted people: "You shall remember that you were a slave in Egypt and the LORD your God redeemed you from there; therefore I command you to do this" (24:17-22). The people are to treat the sojourner and the fatherless justly, to show especial consideration for the widow, and to provide generously for them all. In short, those who have been mercifully treated should show mercy in similar circumstances. Egyptians are not to be abhorred because (to a degree, at least) they showed hospitality to the needy Israelites (23:7-8), but the unmerciful, inhospitable Moabites and Ammonites stand condemned and excluded forever (23:3-4). The God of love and mercy requires love and mercy of those who live in fellowship with him.

Presentation of First Fruits and Tithes; Concluding Exhortation (26:1-19)

The collection of laws we have been surveying since the beginning of chapter 12 is rounded off by instructions concerning two ceremonies and a brief word of exhortation concerning obedience to all the laws commanded by God.

The first ceremony is meant to express gratitude to God for his gracious act of redemption from Egypt and for the gift of the Promised Land. First fruits of the soil are to be brought to the central sanctuary each year (presumably at the Feast of Weeks—16:9-12) and, through the priest officiating there, presented to God, from whose hand the gracious gifts have come. At that time a glad confession is to be uttered before the Lord, expressing gratitude for the miraculous deliverance from the Egyptian bondage and the gift of "a land flowing with milk and honey" (vs. 9).

The second ceremony commanded here is to fall in the year

(the third year) when tithes are retained in the home community and given for the relief of the Levite, the sojourner, the fatherless, and the widow (see 14:28-29). After the tithe is thus turned over to the needy, the Israelite is to appear at the central sanctuary (probably at the Feast of Booths) and declare before God that he has completely fulfilled the commandments concerning tithing. He is then to offer a prayer for God's continued blessing on the people of Israel and the land God has given them.

The two confessions or declarations contained here (vss. 5-10 and 13-15) are of great interest. In language and style they appear more ancient than the Book of Deuteronomy itself. It is believed that they formed part of the ancient confessional liturgy of Israel, perhaps that of the Tabernacle before the construction of Solomon's Temple.

Strikingly similar in content to the first of these confessions are Deuteronomy 6:20-24 and Joshua 24:2-13. These three passages recall God's great saving acts in the history of Israel—from the time of the Patriarchs to the gift of the land under Joshua—acts which brought the community of Israel into existence. We have in these confessions the basic outline later developed into the narrative contained in Genesis to Joshua; or, to put it the other way around, we have in these confessional statements the content of these books in miniature. From very early times Israel recalled in acts of worship the mercies of God in the choice and redemption of Israel and in gratitude pledged obedience to his gracious will. Likewise, the Christian Church has recalled in hymns, creedal declarations, and the Lord's Supper the deed of God in the gift of Jesus Christ and, as the New Israel created by him, has pledged loyalty to its risen Redeemer.

The concluding exhortation (vss. 16-19) may possibly come from the old ceremony of Covenant renewal (see the comment on 27:1—28:68). The words of these verses may have been spoken in the ritual after the laws had been read aloud and after the people had affirmed their willingness to obey them (see vs. 17). It is now pronounced that if the people are fully obedient, God will fulfill his Covenant promises: that Israel will be uniquely his own people; that the nation will be exalted among the nations; and that it will be a holy people.

Chapter 26 as a whole is an admirable conclusion to the section on "The Specific Terms of the Covenant Relationship" which began with chapter 12. The ceremonies here enjoined—including the words of remembrance to be spoken, the declaration of obedience, and the prayers to be offered—are meant to keep the laws of God fresh in the mind and to move the will to complete acceptance and obedience. We hear once more the appeal to Israel (and to ourselves) at the deepest levels of personal existence: "You shall therefore be careful to do them with all your heart and with all your soul" (repeated eight times in the book).

In concluding the discussion of chapters 12-26 three general observations may be helpful.

First, the material in chapters 12-26 is not civil law in the sense that we understand that term. It is the divine will for the life of man on its various sides. It is *"torah,"* that is, "teaching," "guidance," "instruction," "direction." It is a way of life, commanded by God, which should be followed out of gratitude and wholehearted acceptance. Furthermore, the will of God is not only set forth here; it is *preached*. Reasons why God's guidance should be followed are constantly suggested. This is not customary in civil codes. These laws belong to religion, not primarily to political and social science.

Second, the laws contained in these chapters fall into two basic types, known as apodictic law (categorical, policy law) and casuistic law (case or procedural law). The former type is found in the Ten Commandments and throughout chapters 12-26, where the divine demand is stated flatly and directly in the second person: "you shall not" or "you shall" (see, for example, ch. 14). This policy law sets forth the terms of the Covenant relationship. The God who entered into covenant with Israel defines the terms of that relationship. He speaks directly to his people and expects acceptance and obedience. The second type is concerned with specific cases and situations. It rests upon the fundamental principles enunciated in the apodictic law. Laws of this type begin with a conditional clause (introduced by "if" or "when"). (For illustrations see chapter 21.) This case-type law was the principal kind of law in the ancient Near East. Many of the cases presented in these chapters are obviously intended as representative of types of situations that arise. We have here no complete, detailed code of laws.

Third, it is important to note that the laws set forth in Deuteronomy are preponderantly person-centered rather than property-centered. Ancient law codes outside Israel were considerably more concerned with the protection of property rights and the regulation of economic affairs than were the Covenant laws of Israel. Here the dominant concern is with the God-man and the man-man relationships. It is assumed that if God and men live together in a fellowship of love and fidelity, economic relationships need not be governed by a highly detailed body of law. According to Deuteronomy, ethical behavior springs out of the dedicated and loving heart.

The Publication and Enforcement of the Terms of the Covenant (27:1—28:68)

Chapter 27 interrupts the second address of Moses, which, according to the book's general pattern, has been proceeding since the beginning of chapter 5. In chapter 27 the third, rather than the second, person form of address appears, and instructions are given by Moses and the elders concerning the publication and enforcement of the laws. In chapter 28 the second person reappears and the address continues. It is apparent that chapter 27 is logically out of place. The instructions of chapter 27 would more suitably come after chapter 28. How and why chapter 27 got in this position in the book is not known.

The material of chapter 27 centers in a great ceremony to be held after the entrance into the land. It was to consist first of all in the setting up on Mount Ebal of plastered stones on which the Deuteronomic law was to be written. It was a practice of antiquity to inscribe the laws of the land on slabs of stone and erect them in public places (the Code of Hammurabi, for example). The use of plastered stones as a writing surface was common in Egypt. Because of the dry climate there, such inscriptions were practicable, but in Palestine the dampness would soon cause the plaster and the writing to crumble away. It is not clear how much of the Deuteronomic law the writer regards as to be inscribed. "All the words of this law" (vss. 3, 8) elsewhere seems to mean the content of chapters 5-26. It is possible, however, that only chapters 12-26 are meant. The publication of the Law in this way would tend to fix its authority on the minds and hearts of the people.

The second element of the ceremony has to do with the erection of an altar of uncut stone, the offering of sacrifice upon it, and a festal celebration. The reason for the prohibition of cut stone (see also Exod. 20:24-26) may have been the belief that only things in their natural condition—things not interfered with by man—should be used for the service of God (see Num. 19:2; Deut. 21:3-4; I Sam. 6:7). The sacrifices and the customary feasting following would indicate the people's glad acceptance of the Law and the unity of the community with God and with one another. As covenants between men were sealed by their eating together (Gen. 26:28-31; 31:44-54), so the bond between worshipers and their God was sealed by his acceptance of a portion of the victim on the altar and by the worshipers' eating some of the meat in his presence. Thus Paul writes, "Are not those who eat the sacrifices partners in the altar?" (I Cor. 10:18).

The third element has to do with the ratification of the Covenant in a symbolical ceremony conducted between and on the slopes of the twin mountains Ebal and Gerizim near Shechem. The details of the ceremony cannot be fully reconstructed, even with the further data supplied by Joshua 8:30-35 and 24:1-28 (the latter apparently a record of the same ceremony). It is clear that the whole body of people was to be divided into two parts: six tribes (the sons of Jacob's wives) were to stand on the slope of Mount Gerizim to invoke blessing as the reward for obedience to the Covenant law; and six tribes (mostly the sons of Jacob's concubines) were to take a position on the slope of Mount Ebal to invoke curses as the punishment of disobedience. According to Joshua 8:33, Levitical priests and the Ark of the Covenant stood between the two sections. In the hearing of all, Joshua read the whole law and exhorted Israel to obey it (compare Joshua 24: 1-28). The people responded with ringing words of acceptance (Joshua 24:16-18, 21, 24). Some kind of formal act of entering into covenant with God (probably a formal oath, accompanied by the slaughter of an animal) was performed (Joshua 24:25-28). Blessings and curses were read aloud by Joshua and selected Levites (Joshua 8:34; Deut. 27:14-26) and probably were also chanted antiphonally by the two great six-tribe choirs. The people responded with "Amen" (meaning "assuredly," "verily"). Such seem to be the major elements of this great Covenant ceremony at Shechem, whatever the exact order in which they fell.

It is probable that the curses and the blessings contained in Deuteronomy 27:15-26 and 28:3-6, 16-19 belong to the liturgy of this ceremony. Ancient suzerainty covenants regularly ended with curses and blessings in which the gods were called on to mete out calamities and rewards to the vassal state in accord-

ance with its disobedience or obedience to the terms of the covenant (see comment on 4:1-14). In Hebrew curses and blessings
the agent of the curse or blessing is regularly undesignated and the
form is simply "Cursed [or blessed] be . . . !" The Hebrews and
ancient peoples in general regarded the spoken word as having
supernatural power to effect the results contemplated in the
utterance.

The twelve curses contained in 27:15-26 offer but a sample of
the many that must have been uttered at this great ceremony.
Most of the curses here fall upon those who sin secretly. The
implication is that God knows, even if men do not, that an evil
deed has been committed, and he will punish it. Secret sins will
pollute the land and destroy Israel's future. Three of the twelve
offenses listed here appear in the Ten Commandments (vss. 15,
16, 24). Most of the others are forbidden in some law code of
the Pentateuch (there is, however, no parallel to those in vss.
25-26). The offenses named here comprise sins against God, sins
against parents and neighbors, and flagrant types of sexual sins.
The list is to be regarded as typical; there seems to be no logic
behind the selection of these particular sins for condemnation.

The blessings and curses of chapter 28 revolve around the con-
trasting parallel lists of verses 3-6 and 16-19. As indicated above,
these lists are probably part of the liturgy of the Covenant renewal ceremony. The rest of the material of chapter 28 seems to
be a free composition by the Deuteronomic writer or writers on
the theme of the rewards and punishments contingent on obedience or disobedience. After the interruption of chapter 27, Moses
is represented as again speaking directly to Israel.

It is unnecessary to comment in detail on these rewards and
punishments. A thoughtful reading of them is a sobering experience. The effects of them on King Josiah were dramatic and
played a part in his sweeping reformation (II Kings 22-23; see
Introduction). The stark imagery of the chapter is calculated to
shock the will awake and to lead to vigorous action.

It should be noted that the blessings and curses are conceived of as primarily national, not individual, though the individual participates fully in the destiny of the nation. The basic
question is, What kind of future does the Covenant people have?
The nation stands between promise and fulfillment: God has
called it into being; he has revealed his will to it; he plans for it
a glorious future; he wants it to be the head and not the tail

among the nations of the world (vs. 13; see vs. 44); he longs to establish Israel "as a people holy to himself" (vs. 9). But the fulfillment of the promise is conditioned upon full obedience to God's will. The divine election does not automatically convey the divine blessing. With God's purpose must be linked human co-operation if the possibilities inherent in the Covenant relationship are to be realized. The point of view here is identical with that in Isaiah 1:19:

> "If you are willing and obedient,
>> you shall eat the good of the land;
> But if you refuse and rebel,
>> you shall be devoured by the sword;
>> for the mouth of the LORD has spoken."

The prophets of the Old Testament as a whole would second this utterance with a resounding "Amen!"

But does God reward nations for full obedience and punish them for disobedience? Does he bring pestilence, drought, famine, and the scorching, blinding sirocco? (The sirocco winds of the desert carried dust as fine as powder; see verse 24.) Does he send enemies against a disobedient nation to gobble up the produce of the land, to lay merciless siege to its cities, and to carry away its inhabitants into foreign lands where they will languish in bitter despair? Contrariwise, does he reward the obedient with full breadbaskets, abundant and healthy posterity, security from attacks of enemies, and pre-eminence among the nations? Throughout much of the Old Testament—in the Prophets, the Psalms, the Book of Proverbs—as well as in the Deuteronomic writings, the formula is to be found: obedience to the Law of God will bring individual and national prosperity, security, health, and religious and political leadership of the world.

That this emphasis is not the whole truth is evident in those questions and suggestions in the Old Testament that intimate that suffering may have causes other than man's sin. Job, knowing that he is innocent of wrongdoing, resigns himself to the wisdom of God and leaves the matter there. Others believe that God will finally vindicate the righteous and punish their evil oppressors (Pss. 37; 73; Hab. 1-2). Still others look on suffering as a divine education through which the sufferers will be led away from their sins to a new and higher relationship with God (Jeremiah; Second Isaiah). Jesus regarded suffering as his divinely given vocation (Mark 8:31; 10:35-45; Luke 12:49-50). New Testament writers find in the suffering of Jesus the means of man's reconciliation with God (Rom. 5:6-11; Heb. 9:11-14; I Peter 3:18). Christians are called upon to accept suffering as normative Christian experience (Acts 14:22; I Thess. 3:3; I Peter 4:12-19). They are to rejoice in their sufferings (Acts 5:41; Rom. 5:3; Col. 1:24), knowing that suffering brings cessation from sin (I Peter 4:1) and the ability to comfort others who are suffering (II Cor. 1:3-7). In the New Testament the suffering of the Christian is attributed to the hostility of evil men, inspired by the Devil (I Peter 5:8-9; Rev. 12:7-17; Eph. 6:12). It is rarely viewed as God's direct punishment of the sinner for his sin (but see I Cor. 11:29-30).

It is evident that Deuteronomy draws a straight line between sin and suffering. Its causes and its meaning, according to the Bible as a whole, are more complex than this. But it must be evident to all who stop to think that *some* suffering is the direct result of sin. The individual or the nation that flouts the laws of God governing personal, social, and international life will bring down on individual and corporate heads the "Furies" that seem so eager to rush in at the slightest infraction of moral and spiritual law. And who can know the wonders that might follow on the obedience of an entire nation to the Law of God? God is still looking for a nation that will test him out!

THIRD ADDRESS OF MOSES:
WHAT GOD PROPOSES

Deuteronomy 29:1—30:20

The third address of Moses (29:1—30-20) may have been added to the core of the Book of Deuteronomy (4:44—28:68, with the exception of chapter 27) after the experience of exile, probably that in Babylonia (sixth century B.C.). In 29:28 the phrase "as at this day" may point to the exilic or postexilic stance of the writer. He seems to know of the existence of the original Book of Deuteronomy (29:20, 21, 27), to whose laws he counsels unconditional obedience.

In chapters 29-30 the writer represents Israel as entering into a covenant with God in Moab, just prior to the entrance into Canaan. This covenant is a renewal of the Covenant sealed at

Horeb (29:1). It is likely that parts of these chapters, at least, contain elements of an old liturgy of Covenant renewal.

A Covenant in Perpetuity with Israel (29:1-15)

In verses 10-15 the nation is pictured as standing in the presence of God and Moses, ready to take upon itself the solemn obligations of the Covenant relationship. It is carefully indicated that *all* Israel was there, including children, women, sojourners, servants, and even unborn Israel (vss. 14-15). Not a single soul was to be exempt from the obligations of the Covenant relationship, and they were to be binding on the nation in perpetuity.

The ground of their obligation is again said to be God's gracious acts from the time of their deliverance from Egypt (vss. 2-9). Though Moses is talking to the new generation, it is said once again that those events took place before their eyes (vs. 3; compare 4:34; 6:22; 9:17). Israel past, present, and future is bound together in an indivisible whole. The Hebrews and other ancient peoples took seriously the concept of tribal solidarity: that individuals bear responsibility for and the consequences of the acts of all other members of the group; that no man "lives to himself, and none of us dies to himself" (Rom. 14:7). Our individualistic, pluralistic society rests upon concepts quite unknown to the ancient world. Many today feel that their sins will hurt no one but themselves, so why not indulge one's private appetites and lusts? But both sins and acts of righteousness have social consequences: in the family, in the world where we do our work, and on the generations that follow us. The history of families and social groups is determined by the decisions of individual members.

A Covenant Involving Total Obedience (29:16-29)

The responsibility of individual members of the community—the other side of the coin—is now emphasized. After the nation has entered into the Covenant, the individual must not be tempted to feel that God's protection and help will be assured by the obedience of others (vs. 19). Upon such a man the judgments of God, as recorded in the Book of Deuteronomy, will surely fall (vs. 21). And his secret sins will lead to tragic consequences for the entire nation—"to the sweeping away of moist and dry alike" (vs. 19). In other words, his evil deeds will lead not only to his own destruction (he is the dried-up plant) but to the annihilation of the innocent (the watered and green plants). It is a tragic fact of life that the innocent frequently suffer with the guilty.

A Covenant Including the Possibility of a Second Chance (30:1-10)

In this section Moses is represented as foreseeing the rebelliousness of the nation and its dispersal among foreign peoples, as predicted in the section concerning the curses (ch. 28). Here the point is that God takes no delight in the punishment of the wicked, but his will is that none "should perish, but that all should reach repentance" (II Peter 3:9). The message of the Old Testament, as well as the New, is that God loves his people with an everlasting love and seeks to bring them into a relationship of abiding fellowship and obedient service. If Israel will only turn to the Lord with all its heart and with all its soul (vss. 2, 10), then God will delight to be merciful and will open up to his repentant and obedient children the glorious future he promised to the fathers.

The Hebrew verb for the act of repenting is, literally, "to turn" and means not only a change of inner attitude but a complete redirection of life. If the sinner will "turn" to God, he will be empowered by God to live in obedience to the divine will; for God will circumcise the heart, "so that you will love the Lord your God with all your heart and with all your soul, that you may live" (vs. 6). The circumcised heart is the heart open to God's command and fully obedient to him (see Deut. 10:16; Jer. 4:1-4; Rom. 2:28-29). Openness and obedience are characteristic attitudes of those who are loved by God and who love him in return. In this passage the gospel of God's pursuing, redemptive, empowering love is eloquently set forth.

A Covenant Requiring Radical Decision (30:11-20)

But is not the loving obedience commanded by God impossible for man? Can he really know what God wants of him and, knowing it, can he obey it? That God's will is not inscrutable mystery which must be sought out by those who are able to ascend to heaven or traverse the seas—and therefore inaccessible to most men—the writer emphatically asserts: "The word is very near you; it is in your mouth and in your heart, so that you can do it" (vs. 14). The word is very near because God has brought it near: in the revelation he gave to Moses, in the terms of the Covenant which Israel is now taking upon its lips and into its heart. God has not revealed all his secrets to Israel (see 29:29), but he has told his people in unmistakable language what he wants them to know and to do. He asks nothing unreasonable of them.

A choice is thus presented to the will: to love God or not to love him; to obey or not to obey. The stakes are high: life or death, good or evil. Much is wrapped up in the term "life" here. It involves national stability and prosperity, abundant posterity, and the like, but it means more: to live in loving fellowship with God, obeying his voice, "cleaving" (that is, clinging in warm affection) to him (vs. 20). God's greatest gift is himself. To live apart from him is death.

The seriousness of the choice is indicated by the appeal to heaven and earth as witnesses (vs. 19). In Hittite suzerainty treaties, the gods of the contracting parties and phenomena of the natural world (mountains, rivers, springs, winds, clouds, the sea) were called on to serve as witnesses to the covenant agreement. It is likely that in those treaties the gods mentioned were also expected to punish infractions of the terms of the covenant. In Hebrew Covenant theology the gods of polytheism seem to have become the Lord's assembly or council of angels, his ministers and assistants in the administration of his universal dominions. The prophets called on this council, as original witnesses to the Covenant, to testify concerning the terms of that Covenant and thus to clear God of any charge of injustice in punishing his disobedient vassals (see the comment on 31:16—32:44). The Deuteronomic writer is saying here: If you break the terms of the Covenant, the angelic assembly will testify against you before God the Judge and your punishment will be speedy and severe.

The message is not simply an ancient one addressed to people of long ago. Life and death stand before us today as blessed and terrifying possibilities, and the condition remains the same: obedience or disobedience to the voice of God who calls us and all men into loving relationships with himself and with each other.

CONNECTING NARRATIVE:
THE CHANGE IN LEADERSHIP
Deuteronomy 31:1—34:12

With the end of chapter 30 the formal addresses of Moses have come to a conclusion. The remaining materials of the book form a historical connecting link with the Book of Joshua and the rest of the Deuteronomic history of Israel. We are told how Joshua, the new leader, was chosen, and how Moses, the old leader, passed from the scene. Moses' parting words, as contained in his Song and his Blessing, are offered for the warning and encouragement of his people.

The material is loosely put together and can best be treated by grouping similar sections. There is no clearly perceptible subject, but there is a dominant personality: God. The chapters may be viewed without undue forcing as setting forth what Israel may expect in the future under the leadership of God and Joshua.

The Promise of Victorious Conquest (31:1-6)

The aged Moses (the 120 years may be a round figure meaning that his life spanned three generations) now makes known to his people that he will be unable to lead them into the Promised Land. Joshua has been designated by God for this important work. But the real leader will be God himself. This is said repeatedly in verses 3-6. What God did to Sihon and Og (see comment on 2:26—3:11) is a symbol of what he will do to the inhabitants of the land. The land is to be his gift; Israel's part is to "be strong and of good courage" (vs. 6).

The similarity of this passage to Joshua 1:6-9 is striking. Both passages may come from the same hand.

The New Leader (31:7-8)

Moses is said to have summoned Joshua and informed him in the presence of all the people that he was to lead them, under the guidance and empowerment of God, into the Promised Land (vss. 7-8). The formal commissioning by God is placed in the Tent of Meeting (see vss. 14-15, 23). This term is explained in Exodus

25:22; 29:42; 30:36 as signifying the place where God met with Moses for the purpose of revealing to him his will. The "Tent of Revelation" would more accurately say what was meant. How the Lord commissioned Joshua in the Tent of Meeting is not indicated; only the commissioning words are given (vs. 23).

In Numbers 27:18-23 another account of Joshua's commissioning appears. There Joshua is said to have been commissioned by the laying on of Moses' hands in the presence of the priest Eleazar and of the whole congregation. Since the ceremony took place at the Tent of Meeting (the Tabernacle), the involvement of the officiating priest is inherently probable.

The Use of the Law Book (31:9-15)

Provisions for the deposit of the book of the Law alongside the Ark of the Covenant (see vs. 26)—only the tablets containing the Ten Commandments were deposited inside the Ark (Exod. 25:16; I Kings 8:9)—and for its periodic public reading at the central sanctuary (vss. 9-13) correspond to practices connected with Hittite suzerainty treaties (see the comment on 4:1-14). In Israelite conceptions the deposit of the book of the Law beside the Ark of the Covenant would give to the Law the highest possible sanctity and authority. Since it contained the definitive statement of the will of God for Israel and set forth the consequences contingent upon obedience and disobedience, it would serve as a norm for the measurement of Israel's conduct and offer testimony in God's defense if he was forced to punish his people (see vs. 26).

Here (vss. 9-13) the reading of the Law at the central sanctuary in the presence of all Israel every seventh year is prescribed for the Feast of Booths (Tabernacles). In the Hittite suzerainty treaties it was required that the reading of the terms of the treaty in the presence of the vassal king and his subjects be carried out much more frequently, varying from one to four times a year. Some interpreters have thought that there was an annual ceremony of Covenant renewal (including reading of the book of the Law) in Israel from early times, similar to one carried out by the sectarians who gave us the Dead Sea Scrolls. It now appears that, at least before the Exile, while the Covenant was *confirmed* at the time of a change in leadership of the nation, it was *renewed* only on those exceptional occasions when a national repentance was carried out. This usually resulted from a disaster which showed conclusively that the people's sins had cancelled their right to expect the protection and help of God. The purpose of the periodic reading of the Law is said here to be that all the people of Israel "may hear and learn to fear the LORD . . . and be careful to do all the words of this law" (vs. 12), and that their descendants might likewise know and obey it (vs. 13). This was precisely the purpose of the repeated reading of the Hittite suzerainty treaties.

The Song Concerning the Lawsuit of God (31:16—32:44)

Besides the book of the Law, which is to guide the life of God's vassal-subjects and to defend his character when he punishes his people, there is attributed to Moses here a second "witness" for God against the nation. It is in the form of a song which is to be learned and passed down to subsequent generations (31:19-21). When Israel callously breaks the Covenant by idolatry and experiences the awesome judgments of God, the song will remind the sufferers of the meaning of their misfortunes and of the justice of God in thus afflicting them. It will point out to them the baseness of their apostasy and show how they may once again experience God's mercy.

It is widely agreed today that the song contained in chapter 32 is old. It may have been composed as early as the eleventh century B.C. and is hardly later than about the seventh. Thus it had been in use for a considerable time before its incorporation in this section of Deuteronomy.

In form it seems to follow the pattern of the covenant lawsuit, which provided the thought framework for the activity of the great ethical prophets. The covenant lawsuit rests back on the covenant form proper, as seen in the Hittite suzerainty treaties and in the Israelite adaptation of this form. The prophets, seeing that the terms of the Covenant had been broken by Israel's idolatry, represented God as assembling his heavenly court and arraigning the guilty Israel before the bar of justice (see I Kings 22:19; Ps. 82:1). Heaven and earth—apparently meaning the heavenly beings who preside over heaven and earth (Deut. 32:8)—are called upon to bear testimony (or to hear the case) against Israel as violators of the terms of the Covenant (Ps. 50:4; Isa. 1:2-3; Jer. 2:12-13; Micah 6:1-2). Israel, being justly condemned in the court of heaven, is promptly sentenced. It is the role of the prophet, to whom this knowledge is revealed, to go to his people and make known Israel's guilt before the bar of God and the coming penalty, if immediate repentance is not forthcoming (Isa. 1:2-20; ch. 6).

The song in Deuteronomy 32 reflects many of the elements of the covenant lawsuit, although it develops them with some freedom. It begins with a summons to the witnesses, heaven and earth (vs. 1). It reviews the gracious attitudes and deeds of God, centering in his choice and loving care of Israel as his special people (vss. 4, 7-14). It proceeds to a formal indictment of the nation for its base ingratitude as manifested in its forsaking God and worshiping idols (vss. 15-18). It records God's condemnation and sentence, which consists of humiliation at the hands of enemies and affliction by natural calamities (vss. 19-29). It yet sets forth grounds for hope: God will not give his people up to utter destruction; his agents of judgment will themselves be judged when Israel turns away from impotent idols (vss. 30-38). The God who alone is sovereign will manifest his mighty power in the destruction of Israel's enemies (vss. 39-42). The song concludes with a summons to the nations to praise the God who vindicates his people and who cleanses away the defilement of their land (vs. 43).

There are many beautiful and theologically meaningful passages in the song, especially those which set forth the righteous character and provident care of God. He is the Creator-Father (vs. 6), who cares for his children as the parent eagle watches over the young eaglets. If, in their efforts to fly, their strength fails, the mighty parent bird swoops underneath and bears the fledglings up, until they can take to wing again (vs. 11). The Father is also "the Rock" (vss. 4, 15, 18, 30, 31), the firm support and refuge of his people. His sovereign power is directed by love. His aim is the purgation and establishment of his people (vss. 36-43). He will tolerate no infidelity; he alone is God (vs. 39).

The Passing of the Old Leader (32:45—34:12)

The Final Exhortation (32:45-47)

The song ended, Moses now offers his final exhortation to absolute obedience to the Law. The expression "all these words" of verse 45 refers to the Deuteronomic discourses as a whole, not to the words of the song, as the closing phrase of verse 46 plainly shows.

The listeners are told to "lay to heart [literally, "set your heart to"; that is, "take to heart"] all the words which I enjoin upon you [literally, "which I am testifying against you"]" and to teach them to their posterity. Here God's revelation of his will in the Law is considered as a testimony against man's sin. Obedience is a life-and-death matter, not a triviality with inconsequential results (vs. 47).

The Preparation for Death (32:48-52)

Moses is now instructed to ascend Mount Nebo in the Abarim Mountains opposite Jericho (about 12 miles east of the mouth of the Jordan) for a view of the land prior to his death. (For a discussion of the relation of Pisgah to Mount Nebo and the reasons for Moses' exclusion from the Promised Land see the comment on 3:23-29.)

The Parting Blessing (33:1-29)

In the ancient Near East the parting blessings of tribal and family heads were irrevocable last wills and testaments, as is evident from the story of Isaac's blessing of Jacob and Esau (Gen. 27) as well as from extrabiblical accounts from the fifteenth and fourteenth centuries B.C. Leadership in the tribe and family was conferred by these oral blessings. The dying patriarch's words were considered to be power-laden; when uttered, the future, whose secrets they ensnared, was unconditionally determined.

We have here Moses' alleged last will and testament. It is similar in form and content to that attributed to Jacob (Gen. 49). It now seems probable that this poetic blessing was composed in the eleventh century B.C. and written down during the period of literary activity of the days of David and Solomon in the tenth century. That it was not composed by Moses is clear from the reference to Moses in verse 4, from the allusions to the conquest of Palestine as already past (vss. 27-28) and the part taken in it by certain of the tribes (see vs. 21), and the non-mention of the tribe of Simeon (which after the period of the Judges was absorbed in Judah). Why the poem came to be attributed to Moses is unknown.

In structure the blessing falls into three parts: the introduction (vss. 2-5); the blessings (vss. 6-25); and the conclusion (vss. 26-29). It is possible that the introduction (with certain deletions) and the conclusion formed a separate poem of approximately the same date and that the blessings were inserted into it.

The introduction presents the Lord's glorious self-revelation to Israel in the wilderness, his giving of the Law through Moses, and his becoming king over the tribes of Israel.

The Hebrew text in this introduction has not been accurately preserved and cannot be translated precisely at many points (see the numerous footnotes in the margin of the Revised Standard Version). "Seir" is the territory of Edom, south of Canaan, and "Mount Paran" is also called "the wilderness of Paran" (Num. 10:12). Kadesh-barnea was located in or near it. The association of Israel's God with mountains and the description of his manifestations in the imagery of natural phenomena (the coming of the dawn, thunderstorms, fire, and the like) are frequent characteristics of Israel's poetry (Judges 5:4-5; Pss. 18:7-15; 68:7-9; Hab. 3:3-15). The myriads of "holy ones" (angels) attending him seem here to be instruments of his purposes. This passage gave rise to the belief in Judaism that the Law was given through angels (Acts 7:53; Gal. 3:19; Heb. 2:2). The word "Jeshurun" (vs. 5) is a poetical designation for Israel and means "the upright one."

The blessing of Reuben is short and modest, according well with this tribe's undistinguished history. The introduction to it apparently has dropped out (see, for example, vss. 7, 8, 12, 13). A blessing of Simeon should now follow (as in Gen. 49:5-7), but since this tribe had been absorbed in Judah by the time of the composition of the poem, it is passed by. Judah is in trouble with an enemy (perhaps the Philistines), and the Lord's help is besought. Levi, the bearer of the priestly office with its teaching, sacrificial, and divining functions (the "Thummim" and "Urim" were a kind of dice, carried by the chief priest in his breastpiece, and used for determining the divine will), is praised for its fidelity to the Covenant while in the wilderness. *How* Levi was faithful at Massah and Meribah is not said either here or in Exodus 17:1-7 and Numbers 20:2-13. Benjamin, beloved of God, is especially protected by him. The last line of verse 12 means either that God dwells in a sanctuary in the territory of Benjamin (at Nob during the reign of Saul?) or, more probably, that Benjamin tents between God's shoulders, and thus is especially secure. Joseph (the tribes of Ephraim and Manasseh), in a long and lavish blessing, is called "prince among his brothers" (vs. 16). Economic prosperity and military strength are to characterize these tribes. They obviously were flourishing at the time when the poem was composed. Zebulun and Issachar are to lead others in pure worship and are to profit from the treasures of sea and sand (maritime trade, fishing, and clam-digging operations?). Gad's broad lands east of the Jordan, seized by a lionlike people, are described as "the best of the land" (vs. 21). Gad is commended for assisting the other tribes in the conquest of the territory west of the Jordan. Dan, Naphtali, and Asher—all settled in the area later known as Galilee—are represented as aggressive and prosperous. The references to the "foot in oil" (vs. 24) alludes to the productivity of the olive tree in this part of the country. Asher will need defensive fortifications because of its location on the northern border and will need continuing strength against the pressure of enemies.

The conclusion (vss. 26-29) emphasizes the mighty God's speedy and persistent care of his people. This care has been manifested in the initial defeat of the inhabitants of the land, in the productivity of the soil, and in the undergirding support and protection of his people. Few verses have affected the life of man more powerfully than verse 27:

> "The eternal God is your dwelling place,
>   and underneath are the everlasting arms."

Almost equally beloved is the latter part of verse 25: "as your days, so shall your strength be."

The Death Itself (34:1-12)

The story of Moses' death is constructed out of pieces contributed by several writers. These are now woven together into an effective narrative concerning the great leader's last moments and an estimate of his importance in the purpose of God and the life of Israel.

First is recorded his viewing of the land from the top of Pisgah. This has been described in detail twice already (see the comment on 3:23-29; see also 32:48-52). One can stand at this spot today and confirm the general accuracy of the description of the view. Gilead lies to the north in Transjordan. Dan and Naphtali are the northernmost areas of the territory better known as Galilee. Ephraim and Manasseh constitute the territory later known as Samaria. Judah lies straight to the west (although one cannot see "as far as the Western Sea" because the mountain range at Jerusalem is about the same height as the Abarim Mountains at Pisgah). The Negeb is the southern area, from Beer-sheba to Kadesh-barnea (which is, strictly speaking, not visible from Pisgah because of the rising vapor of the Dead Sea and the height of the mountains around Hebron). The Plain is defined here as the Jordan Valley from around Jericho to Zoar (the southern shore of the Dead Sea).

The circumstances of Moses' death are not recorded. He is said to have been 120 years old—clear-eyed and vigorous. The figure is probably a round number, signifying three generations of 40 years each. "Natural force," an unusual word in Hebrew, means apparently "life-force." As an adjective, it means "moist" or "fresh" and is used in connection with growing or freshly cut wood (Gen. 30:37; Ezek. 17:24). The writer wants to say that Moses did not die as a result of sickness or old age; he died because God willed it so—because his work was done, his service fulfilled.

The burial place is said to be unknown, but it is located generally as "in the valley in the land of Moab opposite Beth-peor" (vs. 6). This valley is probably one of the ravines below Nebo and Pisgah, leading down into the Plain of the Jordan. It was here that Israel was camped when Moses addressed the nation in the sermons recorded in Deuteronomy (3:29; 4:45-46). It was appropriate that the great leader should be laid to rest where an important phase of his life's work was accomplished.

The leadership now passes to Joshua, a man commissioned by Moses (Num. 27:18-23) and "full of the spirit of wisdom"; that is, of practical sagacity and administrative ability as requisites to the carrying out of the divine will.

The book ends with a glowing estimate of Moses' significance: he was the greatest of the prophets, for—unlike all others—he stood in face-to-face relationship with God and learned his will for the life of Israel; and his mighty deeds as God's deliverer from the bondage of Egypt eclipse the accomplishments of any other servant of God.

However, it was given to another writer centuries later to see, after a yet greater Exodus had occurred (Luke 9:31), that "Moses was faithful in all God's house as a servant . . . but Christ was faithful over God's house as a son" (Heb. 3:5-6).

THE BOOK OF
JOSHUA

INTRODUCTION

The Book of Joshua is both a climax and a new beginning. In it is recorded the fulfillment of the promise made to Abraham concerning the gift of the land of Canaan (Gen. 12, 15) and the beginning of a long life for the people of Israel in the national homeland. The Exodus from Egypt and the Covenant in the wilderness have meaning in Israel's history only because a homeland was won in which a redeemed and covenanted people could work out their destiny under God. The book thus looks both backward and forward.

This double orientation of the book has had an effect on its interpretation. It has long been classed with the first five books of the Bible (the Pentateuch), and the six books together have been termed "the Hexateuch." It has been thought that the same basic sources used in the Pentateuch ("J," "E," "D," and "P") lie embedded in the Book of Joshua. The book's relationship with those writings which follow it in the Canon—Judges to Kings—has also been emphasized. Some interpreters argue convincingly that it is part of a great Deuteronomic history of Israel from the time of Moses to the Babylonian Exile of the sixth century. This history began with the Book of Deuteronomy, and Joshua formed its second member.

Such a view is in line with ancient Hebrew thought concerning the place of the book in the Canon. In the Hebrew Bible, Joshua is classified among the "Former Prophets" (Joshua to Kings). Though these books, strictly speaking, are historical writings and not compilations of utterances of prophets, there is some justification for the classification. Some of the material deals with such early prophets as Samuel, Elijah, and Elisha. But, more important, these writings present Israel's history in its homeland from the viewpoint of the prophet: Israel stands in Covenant relationship with God; obedience to the terms of the Covenant has brought and will bring prosperity and security in the land, but disobedience has resulted and will result in national and personal disaster. This was the theological perspective of the Book of Deuteronomy, and the Books of Joshua to Kings show how Israel's history in the land illustrates the truth of this principle.

Author, Sources, and Date

Most interpreters believe that the Book of Joshua was put together from a variety of sources—some of them of early date—by a compiler who lived not earlier than the late seventh century B.C. and probably in the sixth. This writer may have been the author of the Book of Deuteronomy in its present form. The stylistic and theological characteristics of Deuteronomy and Joshua are strikingly similar. It is altogether likely that Joshua is the second number of a great Deuteronomic history of Israel reaching from Moses to the fall of Jerusalem. It seems that some portions of Joshua were added after the great history was completed (possibly Joshua 13-21 and 24).

What sources were used in compiling the Book of Joshua cannot be accurately indicated. It can be debated whether the old "JE" narrative furnished any of the material of chapters 1-12. The "JE" narrative must have contained an account of the fulfillment of the promise made to Abraham (Gen. 12, 15) in the gift of the land, and hence some interpreters hold that it is preserved in altered form in the narrative of Joshua 1-12. The material contained in Joshua 13-21 seems to have come from tribal border and town lists of cities of refuge and Levitical cities, dating probably from the eleventh to the seventh centuries. Those who deny that "JE" materials underlie the story of the conquest of the land in Joshua find the source of this material in sanctuary and tribal traditions freely reworked by the Deuteronomic author. Whatever the sources used, the author has thoroughly recast them and welded them into a narrative of dramatic power.

Historical Significance

Opinions differ sharply on the historical value of the Book of Joshua. It has long been noted that the massive, sweeping, and almost uniformly successful character of Joshua's campaigns, as described in this book, differs from the painful, piecemeal, tribe-by-tribe efforts at conquest detailed in the first chapter of Judges. It has been customary to accredit the Judges account and discredit that in Joshua as consisting of fanciful hero tales told through the romanticizing haze of the years, and as popular stories which arose in explanation of various customs and landmarks. Similarly, little of value for understanding the settlement of the tribes in the conquered land has been seen in the lists offered in Joshua 13-21, so late and confused have these materials seemed to be.

As a result of archaeological research, however, some interpreters have come to see more grounds for confidence in the historical value of the Joshua materials. Excavation has established conclusively that several important cities of western Palestine (Bethel, Lachish, Debir, Hazor) were destroyed in the latter half of the thirteenth century B.C., the probable period of the Israelite invasion. Heavy layers of ash, topped by primitive Israelite structures quite different from Canaanite workmanship, offer mute evidence of the ferocity of the Israelite attack and the completeness of the resultant devastation. These cities are located in the center, the south, and the north of the land, the locale of Joshua's sweeping attacks. It is admitted that the record in Joshua is schematic and overly laudatory of Joshua, that some cities claimed as destroyed by him could not have been thus taken (Jericho, Ai), and that in reality most of the land had yet to be subjugated territory by territory; but the probability of smashing campaigns in the center, in the south, and in the north cannot be gainsaid. Some sections of Joshua seem cognizant of the gradual subjugation of the land (13:2-6; 15:13-19, 63; 23:7-13). It seems that the evidence of both Joshua and Judges is needed for a full picture of the Conquest.

Theology

The point of view throughout is identical with that in Deuteronomy. If earlier materials used in the Book of Joshua had a different theological orientation, it is no longer discernible.

God is regarded as a holy and jealous God, who tolerates no worship of other gods by his people. He is the Lord of history, who works out the pattern of events in such a way as to fulfill his own purposes. (Note the sovereign "I" in 24:2-13.) He has called Israel into being and guided its destiny at every stage. He has given his people a homeland. This has been possessed not by Israel's bow or sword (24:12) but by the terror or panic sent by the Lord on the land's inhabitants. Although much territory remains to be taken, the whole land is included in God's promise, and it will be possessed if Israel will be loyal and obedient to God.

In view of the gracious purpose and deeds of the Lord, Israel should love and serve him faithfully (23:11; 24:14-15). This means abhorrence of other gods, no intermarriage with foreign peoples (23:12-13), and complete destruction of forbidden material possessions (ch. 7). The only path to national security and prosperity is exclusive loyalty to God with the whole heart and soul (22:5); for an evaluation of the significance of this general point of view for contemporary Christians see the comment on Deuteronomy 7:1-26 and 27:1—28:68.

OUTLINE

The Conquest of Canaan. Joshua 1:1—12:24

The Preparation for the Conquest (1:1—5:15)
The Events of the Conquest (6:1—12:24)

The Division of the Land. Joshua 13:1—21:45

God's Command to Joshua (13:1-7)
Tribal Allotments East of the Jordan (13:8-33)
Tribal Allotments West of the Jordan (14:1—19:51)
Appointment of Cities of Refuge (20:1-9)
Designation of Levitical Cities (21:1-45)

Final Acts and Instructions of Joshua. Joshua 22:1—24:33

The Dismissal of the Transjordan Tribes (22:1-9)
The Altar of Witness at the Jordan (22:10-34)
First Concluding Address of Joshua (23:1-16)
Second Concluding Address and the Covenant Ceremony at
    Shechem (24:1-28)
Joshua's Death and Burial and the Interment of Joseph and
    Eleazar (24:29-33)

COMMENTARY

THE CONQUEST OF CANAAN
Joshua 1:1—12:24

The book begins with a backward look at the passing of Moses, the last event mentioned in Deuteronomy. There a quick reference is made to Joshua as the new leader who possesses Moses' spirit of wisdom (Deut. 34:9). Thus the two books are connected by the Deuteronomic writer. The style and ideas of Joshua 1 are strikingly like those of the Book of Deuteronomy. The charge to Joshua by God is practically a summary of the point of view of that book. Throughout chapters 1-12 the reader is constantly made to know that Israel's successes were wholly due to complete obedience to the Law, as set forth in the Book of Deuteronomy, and to the resultant help of God.

The Preparation for the Conquest (1:1—5:15)

God's Charge to the New Leader (1:1-9)

The Lord's charge to Joshua revolves around three foci. Joshua is told, first, that the time of fulfillment has come. He and all the people should now rise up and take possession of the land. In the Book of Deuteronomy the nation is pictured as standing between promise and fulfillment: it had been delivered from the bondage of Egypt, it had entered into a Covenant with God, but it had not yet possessed the land in which the terms of that Covenant were to be carried out. But now the hour was come; and Joshua hears the command, "Arise, go over this Jordan . . ."

The limits of the land to be possessed are vaguely described: it stretches from the southern wilderness to the Euphrates River, far to the northeast, and westward to the Lebanon Mountains and the Mediterranean Sea. "All the land of the Hittites" (vs. 4) refers not to the entire Hittite empire (which would involve much of the territory now known as Turkey—an area never promised to Israel) but to those parts of that empire which lay between the Euphrates and the Mediterranean, that is, northern Syria. Israel never, as a matter of fact, actually controlled all this territory, but David's kingdom covered most of it.

The charge next assures Joshua that he will be invincible, for God will be with him (vss. 5-6). Joshua's strength will be as the Lord's. God will not "fail" (literally, "let drop") Joshua or abandon him in the difficult enterprise.

Thirdly, the charge affirms emphatically that the promise of God's help is conditional on complete obedience to the Law (vss. 7-8) and on complete confidence in God (vs. 9). If the Law is to be fully obeyed (without the slightest deviation to the right or to the left), it must be fully known by all. Therefore, it must be the subject of constant conversation and meditation (see Deut. 5:29-33; 6:4-9).

The inhabitants of Qumran by the Dead Sea, who gave us the Dead Sea Scrolls, took literally the command given here and other similar statements in the Old Testament (Pss. 1:2; 119:97). The Law was studied around the clock by individual members who succeeded one another in shifts; and the entire community arose at about two o'clock in the morning to recite and expound Scripture and say benedictions. Thus was knowledge of the Law promoted in order that the members might be fully obedient.

Confidence in God is here connected with assurance of his presence. Joshua is to have courage because God will be with him. Paul, in the midst of great trouble at Corinth, was told by the Lord, "Do not be afraid . . . for I am with you . . ." (Acts 18:9-10). "If God is for us, who is against us?" (Rom. 8:31).

The Responsibility of All Israel (1:10-18)

The principle on which Israel is here represented as working is: All for one and one for all. No man can rest and enjoy the fruits of conquest until all have won their inheritance. The passage testifies to the strong spirit of solidarity that characterized the Israelite tribes. But it is clear that this spirit was not always equally strong, as a consideration of Joshua 22:10-34; Judges 12:1-6; and Judges 21:5-14 will show. The later division of the Israelite kingdom into Northern and Southern, after the united kingdom of David and Solomon, was one step among others leading to the eventual dissolution of both kingdoms. Ancient Israel again and again bears testimony to the truth that in unity there is strength.

That the history set forth in this passage is to a certain extent idealized seems clear. It is hardly likely that the wives, children, and cattle of the two and one-half tribes were left beyond the

Jordan completely unprotected. Some fighting forces must have
been left behind to guard them in the lands so recently captured.

The strong support of Joshua by the two and one-half tribes
and their willingness to undertake the assignment given them
(verse 14 suggests that the warriors of these tribes, being without
their wives and children, were to form the spearhead of the invasion) is based upon the assumption that Joshua will always be
God-led and God-empowered. In early Israel the right to leadership was conditioned upon evidences of possession of God's Spirit.
The coming of the Spirit of God on Saul (I Sam. 10:6-13) qualified him to become king; and when that Spirit departed from him
(I Sam. 16:14), David was empowered by the Spirit for leadership (I Sam. 16:13). The tribes thus say to Joshua: We are willing
to follow you, as we did Moses, if we can continue to see that
God is with you as he was with Moses. Much trouble would have
been spared the world if loyalty to leaders had always been thus
conditioned.

Reconnaissance Operations (2:1-24)

Numbers 13 reports spying operations conducted in southern
Canaan from the wilderness to the south. As a result of these
operations, the hope of invasion from the south was given up and,
after long wanderings, an attempt from the east was decided
upon. Again espionage was resorted to.

The story told here is dramatic and full of human interest.
Israel was camped at Shittim, the Abel-shittim (meaning "brook
of the acacias") of the plains of Moab (Num. 33:49) located at
the foot of the mountains across the Jordan Valley from Jericho.
The presence of a large invading force encamped there was obviously known to the Canaanite inhabitants of Jericho, who are
represented as terror-stricken (vss. 9-11). The king of Jericho
(actually a kinglet who ruled over a tiny city-state, of which there
were many in Canaan at this time) and his soldiers were on the
alert for any signs of aggressive activity on the part of the invaders. How the presence of the spies in the house of Rahab the
harlot became known is not reported. But anyone who has lived
in a tight little oriental village knows how hard it is for strangers
to enter undetected and to remain concealed. In choosing a harlot's house they entered the only dwelling where strangers would
be reasonably certain of a welcome.

Rahab's decision to protect the spies by hiding them under

the drying flax on the roof is attributed to her desire for self-preservation. Certain that the invaders would be victorious in the coming attack on Jericho, she saw a way to ensure her safety and that of her relatives. She is represented as confessing the supremacy of Israel's God (vs. 11), a confession which probably owes something to the faith of the Deuteronomic writer (see Deut. 4:39). The panic which will seize Israel's enemies is also a Deuteronomic theme (see Deut. 2:25; 7:23; 11:25).

To seal the agreement that in exchange for the protection of the spies Rahab and her relatives will be spared in the coming invasion, an oath is extracted from the spies in the name of the Lord. Oaths in the name of a deity or deities were common in the ancient world. Amos, for example, condemns those who swear by the god Ashimah of Samaria and the gods of the shrines of Dan and Beer-sheba (Amos 8:14). The oath was accompanied by symbolic acts: the raising of the hand toward heaven (Gen. 14:22, which is literally: "I have raised my hand unto the LORD . . ."; see also Dan. 12:7); the laying hold of some sacred or potent object (Gen. 24:2; 47:29); and sometimes the cutting asunder of sacrificial animals, between the halves of which the contracting parties passed (Gen. 15:10, 17; Jer. 34:18). The oath formula in the Old Testament is commonly, "God do so to me and more also, if . . ." I do or do not thus and so (II Sam. 3:35; see also I Sam. 3:17; 14:44). The swearer thus makes himself liable to the most severe punishments by the Deity if the oath is violated. In the oath sworn by the spies they agree to "deal kindly" (the Hebrew word means "loyally," in conformity to the terms of the agreement) with Rahab and her household, if she keeps her part of the compact.

Sir John Garstang thought some years ago that he had found in his excavations at Jericho part of the city walls (an outer and an inner wall, some twelve feet apart) astride which Rahab's house was built. Recent excavations have shown, however, that these walls come from a period some three hundred years earlier than Joshua's conquest and that the city in his time was small and relatively weak defensively. Very little of Rahab's city has been recovered. Wind, rain, and the diggings of archaeological explorers in the infancy of the science have obliterated most of the remains of the city of Joshua's time.

The story of Rahab was a favorite one in Judaism and Christianity. According to Jewish tradition Rahab was the ancestress of eight prophets and priests, including Jeremiah. It was even asserted that Joshua married her after she became a proselyte! In Hebrews 11:31 she is regarded as a heroine of faith and in James 2:25 of works. The Christian scholar Origen in the third century allegorized the story in a most interesting way. According to him, the spies represent the forerunners of Jesus, particularly John the Baptist; Rahab stands for the publicans and sinners who responded to the Baptist's message; the scarlet thread hung out the window was a type of the saving blood of Christ; the fact that Rahab's relatives were promised safety only if they remained in her house suggests that it is only in the Church that salvation through the blood of Christ is to be found. In view of Rahab's help in a time critical for the future of the people of God, it is small wonder that her act has been thus immortalized.

The Crossing of the Jordan (3:1—5:1)

In this section it becomes evident to the careful reader that the writer has welded his material together from various sources without smooth and complete integration. One finds duplications and inconsistencies here and there. For example, 3:17 and 4:1 represent all Israel as having crossed the bed of the Jordan, but 4:10-11 alludes to this again, as if the people had not yet passed over. It is said in one place that the twelve stones taken from the bed of the Jordan were set up at Gilgal, the place of encampment not far from Jericho (4:3, 8, 20); in another passage we read that they were set up in the middle of the Jordan, at the place where the feet of the priests who bore the Ark had stood (4:9). We have two passages dealing with Joshua's appointment of twelve men to carry stones from the Jordan (3:12; 4:2). The meaning of the stones is twice explained (4:6-7, 21-24). It is obvious that older materials are being combined without careful editing.

The story of the crossing of the Jordan emphasizes the truth set forth in Joshua 1:1-9: the conquest of the land is not Israel's achievement but the deed of God. Obstacles like the swollen Jordan River are to God no obstacles at all. Joshua's command to the people to sanctify themselves (that is, to purify themselves ceremonially) as a preparation for the appearance and manifestation of the holy God in their midst (3:5) and the key role said to have been played by the Ark of the Covenant in the events of the crossing underscore the event as wholly God's doing. Israel can only obey the Lord's directions, as spoken through Joshua, and trust implicitly in him. The memorial stones are set up to let Israel's descendants know what God did at the Jordan in drying up its waters, even as he did at the Red (Reed) Sea (4:23-24).

Some details of the story are of interest. How many people are intended by the phrase "all the people of Israel" (3:1) cannot be said. In 4:12-13 the warriors of the two and one-half tribes are numbered at about 40,000, a figure which agrees quite well with statements in Numbers 26:7, 18, 34 (which list something over 100,000 men in these tribes, not all of whom would be usable in military operations). According to the Book of Numbers (26:2, 51) the total fighting force was slightly over 600,000. This would require us to postulate at least two million people—an incredible number, it seems, for the conditions in such an inhospitable wilderness as that lying between Egypt and Canaan. On the other hand, Exodus 1:15-22 assumes that two midwives could service the needs of Israel in Egypt, and Numbers 10:2 implies that all Israel could be summoned to the Tent of Meeting by the blowing of two trumpets—hardly possible for two million people! Someone has pointed out that two million people, when marching, would constitute a column twenty-two miles long, fifty abreast with one yard between each rank. If the numbers are to be taken literally, they represent computations of a later time, perhaps in some way paralleling the figures of the census made by David (II Sam. 24; I Chron. 21) or possibly the numbers of the tribes of Israel in the period of the Judges. It has also been held that the number of fighting men was derived from the numerical equivalents of the Hebrew letters in the phrase "sons of Israel," which add up to 603. According to Numbers 1:46, one count was 603,550. However the figures are to be explained, it is hardly likely that the refugees from Egypt and the invading tribes numbered more than a few thousand souls.

The role of the Ark of the Covenant in this story is interesting. The origin of the Ark has been much debated. In Deuteronomy 10:1-5 we are told that Moses made the Ark as a container for the two tablets of stone on which the Ten Commandments were written. In Exodus 37:1-9 (see also Exod. 25:10-22) its origin is assigned to Bezalel, who worked at Moses' direction. The Deuteronomic passage seems to represent it as a simple wooden chest, whereas the Exodus passages describe it as an elaborate golden shrine, topped by a golden mercy seat and two gold cherubim and carried by poles overlaid with gold. Some interpreters have held that the Ark was in form a miniature temple and that it was taken over, probably from the Canaanites, after Israel's settlement in the land. It is likely, however, that it originated in the Mosaic period, that it was much simpler than the description of it in the Book of Exodus, and that it was carried into battle in the period of the wilderness wanderings (Num. 10:35-36).

What conception Israel had of the purpose and significance of the Ark is equally difficult to determine. It probably changed considerably through the centuries. In the early days the Ark seems to have been regarded as a portable throne for the invisible presence of God (I Sam. 4:4). Kings of the ancient East were represented as sitting on thrones supported by cherubim. The putting of the tables of stone inscribed with the Law of God into the Ark would enhance the authority of the Law and conform to the practice of depositing covenant documents in sacred places. When the Ark was carried into battle, the warriors would feel that their God was going before them and victory was assured. It must have been a shock to Israel's faith when the Ark failed to bring victory and was even captured by enemies (I Sam. 4:1-11).

In the light of Israel's view of the Ark as the visible throne of the invisible God, it is not strange that Joshua sent it ahead of the people at the crossing of the Jordan. The two thousand cubits' (about three thousand feet) separation of Ark and people was meant to keep the people away from the awful Presence of the Lord. In seeing the Ark going before, they would know that "the living God is among you" (3:10-11).

The cutting off of the waters of the Jordan at flood time (in April, due to the melting snow of the Lebanon Mountains) may have resulted from an earthquake shock which threw down the high mud banks of the river about twenty-five miles north of the Dead Sea. An Arab historian reported such an occurrence in 1267; it happened again in 1909 and yet again in 1927. In the latter year an earthquake caused the west bank to collapse near the location of ancient Adam, and the Jordan was dammed up for more than twenty-one hours. The miracle is not minimized by a suggestion of the means by which it happened.

The setting up of commemorative stones is mentioned numerous times in the Old Testament (Gen. 28:18; 31:45-49; Joshua 7:26; 8:29; 24:26). The appeal to remembrance was a dominant emphasis in Israel's religion. The children of each generation must be taught concerning the deeds of God and the meaning and the requirements of the Covenant into which he had entered with Israel (Exod. 12:26-27; 13:14; Deut. 6:20-25). The children must not be allowed to forget God's mighty deed at the Jordan. They are to live in gratitude and to fear and serve the Lord forever (Joshua 4:24).

Two piles of stones—one in the bed of the Jordan where the feet of the priests had stood (4:9) and one at Gilgal, the place of encampment after the crossing (4:8, 20)—are suggested in the present form of the narrative. But directions were given by Joshua for the setting up of just one pile (3:12; 4:3, 5, 8). It is evident that two traditions persisted concerning the place where they were set up and that the traditions have been joined in this narrative. To have set up the stones in the bed of the Jordan would have been fruitless, once the water had returned to its normal flow. The word "Gilgal" means "circle of stones" and undoubtedly refers to sacred stones of the type said to have been erected here. This place—probably modern Khirbet Mefjir, some one and one-fourth miles east of Canaanite Jericho—was investigated in 1954 by archaeologists and was found to contain artifacts from about 1200-600 B.C. During much of this period, according to biblical evidence, Gilgal served as a military base and religious center. Some historians assume that some of the traditions lying behind the Book of Joshua were preserved at this sanctuary center.

Religious Preparations (5:2-15)

The religious preparations for entrance into the land consist of two acts of fulfillment of the Law by all the people and one of worship on the part of their leader. These acts illustrate the twin emphases enunciated in chapter 1 and throughout the book: if Israel is to succeed in the Conquest, it must fully obey the Law; and if it does, it may be certain of God's presence and leadership.

The act of circumcision recorded here (5:2-7) is explained as required by the non-practice of the rite during the days of the wilderness wandering. The males who had come out of Egypt under Moses had been circumcised, but their sons who had been born since the Exodus had not. Without the obedience of this new generation to the Law in respect to this rite, Israel could expect no help from God in the conquest of the land.

The circumcising is to be done with flint knives (vs. 2). At Joshua's time (the thirteenth century B.C.) tools of bronze had largely replaced stone implements, and soon afterward (from the twelfth century on) bronze was gradually replaced by iron in Palestine. But in religious customs of long standing, ancient materials and methods persist long after general cultural changes.

When Israel adopted the practice of circumcision and exactly what it meant at first have been strongly debated. Circumcision was practiced by the Egyptians and by most of the ancient Semites. Wall reliefs from Egypt of the third millennium B.C. show the operation being performed. The Babylonians, Assyrians, and Philistines did not circumcise. The latter were contemptuously labeled by the Hebrews "the uncircumcised" (Judges 14:3; 15:18; I Sam. 14:6).

Some have argued on the basis of the Septuagint text of Joshua 5:2 (which does not have the words "again the second time") that circumcision was adopted by the Hebrews in the time of Joshua—at the event described in Joshua 5:2-9—and that the claim that it was instituted by Abraham (Gen. 17:9-14; 21:4) is a late and unhistorical view. But in view of the antiquity of the rite among ancient Near Eastern peoples, the traditions that connect it with Moses (Exod. 4:25-26; 12:43-51) and Abraham, the use of flint (rather than bronze or iron) knives, and the actual unfeasibility of strict practice of the rite in the conditions under which Israel lived in the wilderness period, it is better to credit its origin among the Hebrews to a time considerably before Joshua, as this passage affirms.

In Israel circumcision was an act of initiation into the Covenant community (Gen. 17:11), whatever it may have meant to surrounding peoples (perhaps preparation for marriage or sacrifice of powers of fertility to the deity or tribal mark, or some combination of these). Without the mark of membership in the Covenant community, uncircumcised Israelites would have no assurance of God's help.

The explanation of "Gilgal" as the place where the Lord "rolled away the reproach of Egypt from you" (vs. 9) is an alternate and inferior explanation to that provided in 4:19-24. It is likely that Gilgal ("circle of stones"), an early and important

Israelite sanctuary, was a place where circumcision was practiced and that this secondary explanation of the name grew up at a later time.

The second act of religious preparation was the celebration of the Passover, which appropriately followed upon circumcision. According to Exodus 12:43-49 no uncircumcised male could eat the Passover. Now all Israel was fitted for the sacred feast of remembrance. What greater support for the uncertain future could be imagined than the remembrance in dramatic ceremony of the mighty deliverance from Egypt under the guidance of God, whose power was so much greater than that of the petty kings of Canaan?

The eating of unleavened cakes and parched grain from the produce of Canaan marked the end of the supply of manna. The people of Israel are said, according to one tradition (Exod. 16: 35), to have eaten manna for forty years, "till they came to the border of the land of Canaan." In the Book of Joshua the manna is said to have lasted until the encampment at Gilgal, west of the Jordan. (For "manna," see comment on Deuteronomy 8:1-20.)

The promise of God's presence with Joshua and his unfailing help in the Conquest (1:5, 9) is now dramatically symbolized in the appearance of "the commander of the army of the LORD" (5:14). Joshua perhaps may be thought of as inspecting the terrain and the defenses of Jericho and planning his attack. Suddenly he becomes acutely aware of the presence of Deity, by whose help alone the victory could be won. The commander-in-chief of the Lord's armies apparently is conceived of as an angel, but the distinction between the appearance of God himself and that of his angel is not very clearly drawn in the Old Testament (Gen. 18; Judges 6:11-18). The "army of the LORD" here is probably the hosts of angels who fight for the people of God (Gen. 32:1-2; II Kings 6:17), though the term does not necessarily exclude the forces of Israel. The point of view is that God and his heavenly hosts fight with and for the armies of Israel.

Like Moses (Exod. 3:5), Joshua is commanded to remove his shoes when standing on ground made holy (taboo) by the presence of Deity. And again like Moses, Joshua is only the servant of the Lord (1:1-2; Deut. 34:5), whose delight is to do the Lord's bidding. In worship and humble obedience will both leader and people find the overcoming power of the Lord.

The Events of the Conquest (6:1—12:24)

The Capture of Jericho (6:1-27)

The narrative of the fall of Jericho, like the story of the cross-ing of the Jordan, shows unmistakable signs of formation by a combination of originally separate written sources or oral tra-ditions. There are two references to the destruction of the city (vss. 21, 24), two accounts of the rescue of Rahab and her family (vss. 22-23, 25), and two different signals for the shout of the people (at the sound of the trumpet—vss. 5, 20; and at the command of Joshua—vss. 10, 16).

The story is so well known as to need no retelling here. A few points of interest may be commented on, however.

The use of the number seven is striking. There are seven priests, seven rams' horn trumpets, seven days, and seven cir-cuits of the walls. These sevens are mentioned again and again in the story (fourteen times). The number seven was a sacred number among many ancient peoples. We have many examples of its sacral use among the Egyptians and the peoples of Mesopo-tamia. In the Old Testament there are seven days in the week, various seven-day festivals (several occurring in the seventh month), seven-day periods for ordination of priests and for conse-crations of altars, seven sprinklings of sacrificial blood, the seven-branched lampstand, seven-year famines, seven eyes of the Lord, seven baths in the Jordan by Naaman, seven-year periods of tribu-lation, and the like. The New Testament likewise abounds in sevens. It seems that the number seven signifies completeness, perfection, consummation. It is clearly conceived of as a number sacred to God. When things exist or are in sevens they are characterized by perfection.

The prominent position of the Ark of the Covenant in the strategy of capture, as in the crossing of the Jordan, is to be noted. Again it is indicated that it was God's presence in the Conquest that brought victory.

We are told that the walls fell down flat after the sevenfold march and the mighty shout on the seventh day. Sir John Gar-stang, who excavated Jericho in 1929-36, thought he had ex-posed the fallen walls of Jericho (see the comment on 2:1-24) and recovered charred beams, carbonized food, and other objects from the city burned by Joshua. But Kathleen Kenyon in five years of digging at Jericho, beginning in 1952, concluded that practically nothing of the city of Joshua's time was found by Garstang (most of the objects uncovered by him date from much earlier periods than he thought) and that very little remains from the city of his time. It is now believed that no great city stood on the mound when the Israelites came in; there was probably only a fort there. It looks now as if the memory of the great Canaanite city that stood there some three hundred years before Joshua has influenced the narrative of the capture of the fort by Joshua.

Alternatively, it has been suggested that the large city of the sixteenth century B.C. (three hundred years before Joshua), whose considerable remains have been found at Jericho, was captured by a group related to the Israelites from Egypt and that the story in later tradition was transferred to Joshua and his followers. It is evident that we shall have to wait for more light on the problem before anything like a defensible conclusion can be drawn.

It is said that Jericho was to be "devoted to the LORD for destruction" (vs. 17). "Devoted for destruction" translates a Hebrew word meaning something taboo or forbidden to common use. In Arabic, sacred precincts in Jerusalem and Mecca and areas forbidden to any but husbands and eunuchs are designated by this word (in variant forms).

In Hebrew usage the word was especially associated with warfare. In the belief that it would ensure victory, a vow was made devoting all spoils, living and inanimate, to God (Num. 21:2-3). The Deuteronomic law requires the complete devoting of the Canaanites and their possessions (Deut. 7:1-5; 20:16-18), so that Israel will not be led into idolatry. Since Canaanite artifacts were all to be regarded as belonging to God and could not be appropriated by the common Israelite (Deut. 13:17), valuable Canaanite metal objects could be placed in the sanctuary treasury (Joshua 6:19, 24), in the custody of the priests of the Lord (Num. 18:14; Ezek. 44:29).

Exception to the practice of exterminating everything that breathes (Deut. 20:16) was sometimes made as a result of explicit or implied instructions from God (Rahab and her family—Joshua 6:16, 22-25; and the spoils at Ai—Joshua 8:2). Israel does not seem to have been consistent in the application of this principle (Num. 31:7-12, 17-18; Deut. 21:10-14; I Sam. 15:8-33).

The destruction of whole populations seems to us barbaric in the extreme. We know from the Moabite Stone that wholesale destruction was practiced outside Israel also. In the postexilic period the practice died out, but it lived on in the expectation of apocalyptic writers, who looked forward to the complete destruction of Israel's enemies at the Judgment Day.

Failure and Success at Ai (7:1—8:29)

This story is told in great detail, for it illustrates dramatically the main contention of the Deuteronomic point of view: Israel's success in the capture and continued possession of the land and its prosperity and leadership of the nations depend on its absolute obedience to the will of God. The slightest deviation will bring disaster for the whole nation.

The story begins with the account of the sin of Achan and the ensuing defeat at Ai (7:1-5). The name "Achan" is similar to the Hebrew word for "man of trouble" (Achar) and to the name of a plain (called in 7:24 "the Valley of Achor") where Achan and his family were put to death. This similarity leads to a pun on the name "Achan" in 7:25: "Why did you bring trouble on us? The LORD brings trouble on you today." The entire story is meant to show that sinning against the will of God as expressed in the Law brings deep trouble.

Achan's sin was the covetous appropriation of taboo items on which he chanced in Jericho: "a beautiful mantle from Shinar [Babylonia], and two hundred shekels of silver, and a bar of gold weighing fifty shekels" (7:21). The mantle should have been burned and the precious metal turned over to the treasury of the Lord (6:19). The metals were in the form of ingots or bars, not coins. The latter were not in use among the Hebrews until about the sixth or fifth century B.C. Two hundred shekels of silver would amount to about five pounds (a shekel weighing about four tenths of an ounce) and a bar (literally, "tongue") of gold weighing fifty shekels would constitute about one and one-fourth pounds. It was a tempting bit of spoil, and Achan could not resist it.

The first attack on Ai by a small force of Israelites was launched after a report by spies (7:2-5). The initial success at Jericho apparently led to overconfidence. Hence, only a small force was dispatched and no adequate strategy was devised. The topography of the territory between Jericho and Ai is accurately reflected in the narrative (vs. 3). Jericho lies some 800 feet below sea level and Ai about 2,500 feet above. The ten or eleven mile climb by the entire fighting force was regarded as unnecessary by the spies sent out by Joshua. The attack apparently was frontal, for we are told that the invaders were chased from the gate of the city to Shebarim ("the quarries," an unknown place on the way of descent to the Jordan Valley).

The defeat threw Israel into near panic (vs. 5). Joshua was as alert to the significance of psychological advantage as modern generals are. When the Canaanites would hear that Israel was not invincible, they would unite and exterminate the invading force. Not only would Israel's name be cut off from the earth but God's as well (vs. 9).

The intercessory prayer of Joshua and the elders, accompanied by the tearing of garments and the putting of dust on the head— conventional signs of mourning (I Sam. 4:12; II Sam. 1:2)—led to the disclosure that Israel had sinned in the matter of the devoted (taboo) things at Jericho. The sinner, by appropriating taboo articles, had himself become taboo and, in fact, had communicated it to all Israel. Israel had become "a thing for destruction" (vs. 12). It was Joshua's responsibility to find the offender and the misappropriated articles and to exterminate both. The people were to be sanctified (prepared by the proper purifying rituals) so that they could appear before the Lord for the casting of lots as a means of discovering the guilty person.

The casting of lots was carried out in the sanctuary at Gilgal, the tribes being "brought . . . near" one by one (vs. 16). The lots were apparently the Urim and Thummim (see comment on Deut. 33:1-29). The guilty tribe was narrowed down to the guilty clan, the guilty household, and the guilty person. When Achan was identified as the culprit, he was told by Joshua to "give glory to the LORD God of Israel, and render praise to him" (vs. 19). God is to be praised because it is he, not Joshua or any human being, who has brought the secret sinner to light. Thereupon a full confession is demanded, the misappropriated articles are located, and the full penalty—apparently the destruction of Achan, his family, and all of his possessions by burning (see vs. 15)—is exacted. The implication that Achan was stoned seems to have arisen because the place of his burning was marked with a heap of stones (vs. 26).

The cause of the defeat at Ai was now eradicated and God's burning anger was turned away (7:1, 26). Joshua next proceeded to a second attempt on Ai (ch. 8). This time a careful strategy was devised. The force was divided: one contingent formed an ambush by night to the west of the city and the other approached the following day from the southeast to a point north of the city. The size of the ambush is given in verse 3 as 30,000 but in verse 12 as 5,000. Material from two sources is being woven together here, with differences of detail (note the two starts from Gilgal, vss. 3, 10; the two accounts of the ambush, vss. 9, 12; the two burnings of the city, vss. 19, 28). Needless to say, the smaller size of the ambush is to be preferred!

When the battle was joined by the aggressive move of the king of Ai and his forces against Israel's main contingent, Joshua's warriors fled before them to the southeast in feigned defeat. Thereupon Joshua, who co-ordinated the movements of his troops from a position visible to all of them, gave the signal for the descent of the ambush on the city. The plan was successful: the city was taken and burned; the fighting force and all the inhabitants of Ai were annihilated; and the king of Ai was hanged on a tree.

It is a dramatic and bloody story. The topographical details (the hills and valleys around Ai) fit nicely the terrain around et-Tell, the mound with which Ai is to be identified. Standing on the spot, about a mile and a half east of Bethel and about eleven miles north of Jerusalem, one can relive the story in detail. But there is just one difficulty: archaeologists who excavated the ruin in 1933-36 found that the last Canaanite city here was destroyed about 2200 B.C. It was not inhabited again until around 1000 B.C., when an Israelite settlement appeared on the site. In other words, the city was a ruin when Joshua came into the land and had been for about a thousand years! How then could he have captured it? And what are we to make of the story in Joshua 7-8?

Several attempts at explanation have been made. (1) The story in Joshua 7-8 was invented to explain the presence of a ruined city in Israel's midst. Since Joshua was lauded in Israelite tradition as the great destroyer of Canaanite cities, it was assumed erroneously that he had destroyed this one. (2) Either the true location of Ai has not yet been found or somehow the archaeologists missed the evidences at et-Tell of the city destroyed by Joshua. (3) The inhabitants of a neighboring city, probably Bethel, occupied the ruins of the old city to check the advance of Israel against their own town. (4) The story of the fall of Ai is really the story of the capture of Bethel. Archaeologists have established the fact that Bethel was destroyed at the time of Joshua, but no story of this capture is recorded in the Book of Joshua. Since Bethel continued to be occupied but Ai remained a ruin, it is understandable that the story of Bethel's fall could have been transferred to Ai to explain the existence of that ruin. The proximity of the two sites would make such a switch possible.

The most likely hypothesis is the last. The first assumes the unhistoricity of most of the stories of Joshua, quite certainly too skeptical a view. The second supposes that the archaeologists have not adequately done their work. In the vicinity of et-Tell no other location is possible for Ai, and it is not possible that the ruins of so large a city as Ai could have been missed on the mound of et-Tell by the excavators. The third flies in the face of the data of the story itself. It is said that there was a king of Ai who was hanged on a tree, and the story certainly does not assume that the city was only a temporarily occupied ruin. The fourth explains the silence in Joshua concerning the capture of Bethel (an event briefly described in Judges 1:22-26). However, if this view is correct, the story of the fall of Bethel was reshaped somewhat to fit the topography of et-Tell. The land around Bethel does not lend itself, as does that around et-Tell, to the concealment of an ambush. There is a complicated history behind our story—that much is evident. But it is quite certainly not a pure fiction.

The story emphasizes several truths. Any disobedience to the will of God is a matter of great consequence. Hidden sins are no less displeasing to God than open ones. No man sins to himself; what he does has its effects on his family and indeed on the entire social group to which he belongs. True strength comes from obedient living and confident trust in God, not from the contemplation of past successes. If God be not for us and with us, no strongholds of evil will capitulate to us.

The Covenant Ceremony at Shechem (8:30-35)

The ceremony of entering into covenant with God and the publication of the terms of that Covenant are described here in terms similar to the ones in Deuteronomy 27 (see comment) and in Joshua 24.

The Gibeonite Deception (9:1-27)

The opening verses of chapter 9 (vss. 1-2) and the account of the Covenant at Shechem (8:30-35) interrupt the connection between 8:29 and 9:3. These two pieces appear to be editorial insertions into an older narrative or tradition.

The story of the ruse of the Gibeonites, in securing from Joshua and the invading Israelites a covenant ensuring immunity from attack, is a first-class example of ancient cunning. The Bible contains various illustrations of people who maneuvered within the framework of antique laws and customs to secure for themselves special advantages (Jacob and the birthright, Gen. 27; Tamar and Judah, Gen. 38; and the like).

It is clear from verses 11 and 17 that the deputation that arrived at Gilgal with the seeming marks of long travel upon the members was made up of official representatives of a league of four cities of the central hill country. All of these towns were within a radius of about five miles of Gibeon. They obviously acted without consultation with other Canaanite cities, as the sequel in 10:1-5 shows, and determined on a desperate gamble to save themselves from what they regarded as certain destruction at the hands of the invaders. Since Joshua had vowed the obliteration of all the peoples of the land, the possibilities open to the Gibeonites were complete victory over the Israelites (which these four cities regarded as impossible), a stratagem leading to self-preservation as a minority group with guaranteed rights in a conquered country, or complete annihilation.

The sanctity of covenant agreements sworn in the name of the Deity (vss. 18-19) and sealed in a common meal (vs. 14; see Gen. 31:54; Exod. 18:12) is clearly attested from the sequel. Discovery of the ruse—how we are not told—led to a hurried investigation of the places from which the deputation had come (vs. 17) and to much violent controversy and accusation against the Israelite leaders, who had trusted their own judgment instead of inquiring from the Lord (vs. 14), possibly by the Urim and Thummim. But in spite of the pressure to overthrow the terms of the treaty in view of the trickery involved (vss. 18, 26), the sanctity of the agreement was upheld and the inhabitants of the four towns were spared.

Their punishment is said to have been reduction to slavery; they became "hewers of wood and drawers of water for the congregation and for the altar of the LORD" (vs. 27; compare vss. 21, 23). The story is told, in part at least, to explain how it came about that Gibeonites served as menials in the Temple service of later times. King Solomon probably used the Gibeonites as attendants at the sanctuary of Gibeon, at which he is said to have offered great numbers of burnt offerings in the period before the construction of the Temple in Jerusalem (I Kings 3:4). It may be that he brought the Gibeonite slaves to the new Temple, since they were experienced cult functionaries.

Recent extensive archaeological excavations at the site of Gibeon show that the founding of the city occurred at about 3,000 B.C. Eight springs of water made possible the city's growth and extensive history until its abandonment in the first century B.C. That the Gibeonites were experienced "drawers of water" is evident from the city's great pool with its interior circular staircase which led down from the heart of the walled city to the source of water eighty feet below. This pool was constructed probably in the twelfth or eleventh century B.C. A more efficient tenth-century stepped water tunnel 148 feet long, cut through the solid rock on which the city stood to the cistern room at the exterior base of the mound, was found nearby. Both cuts through the rock below the city were made to assure access to water in times of siege. The excavators found that the principal industry of Gibeon was the making of wine, which was placed in specially constructed jugs with stoppers and stored in scores of vats chiseled out of the cool rock. Wine-jar handles, inscribed with the name "Gibeon" in archaic Hebrew characters, were found. These fixed beyond question the identity of the city. It is calculated that in the seventh century B.C. the storage capacity of the vats exceeded 25,000 gallons. Unfortunately, the excavators found no stratified remains of the Canaanite city of Joshua's time, though they did open two tombs containing extensive deposits from this period. Perhaps future excavations will tell more about this important city.

The Southern Campaign (10:1-43)

In entering into a covenant with Joshua, the Gibeonites became the Israelites' vassals ("servants," vs. 6). According to the suzerainty treaties of the time, Joshua was then obliged to protect them against their enemies (see comment on Deut. 4:1-14). The reason for the hostility of the five kings is easy to see. Not only had the Gibeonites become collaborators with the enemy, but

Joshua, if not hindered by the surrounding Canaanite kings, would use the resources of fighting men and provisions of the great city of Gibeon (vs. 2) to accelerate his attack against the whole land. The strategy of the kings was to frustrate the projected alliance of the Gibeonites and the invaders.

Joshua lost not a moment. By a forced overnight march from Gilgal near Jericho, still the base of military operations, he was able to pounce unexpectedly on the besiegers of Gibeon and put them to rout. Joshua's success here, as so often, was due not to superior numbers and equipment but to the ferocious courage of his warriors and to the element of surprise. In rugged country like that between Jericho and Gibeon the hills and deep valleys provide excellent cover for advancing troops.

The routed armies fled to the northwest of Gibeon into the Beth-horon pass. This pass provides the only easy means of travel from the central mountains, where Gibeon lay, to the low, rolling hill country bordering the coastal plain, where Libnah, Eglon, and Lachish—three of the five warring cities—were located. The Israelites in a decimating pursuit, assisted both by a sudden downpour of hailstones and—according to the prose interpretation of a poetic piece from the "Book of Jashar" (vss. 12-13)—by a miraculously lengthened day, achieved a smashing victory.

The hailstones and the standing still of the sun require a moment's comment. The Old Testament frequently claims that natural phenomena played a part in Israel's successes. One thinks of the plagues in Egypt (some of which seem clearly related to aggravated natural conditions native to that territory), of the strong wind at the Red (Reed) Sea, of the probability of earthquake shocks as the cause of the damming up of the Jordan River at the time of the crossing, of the storm at the time of the defeat of Sisera by Deborah and Barak (Judges 5:19-21), and the like. To one who believes in the providential ordering of history, as the Hebrew writers certainly did and as the Christian faith seems to require, the convergence of natural events and the divine purpose will not seem strange. Many may find it difficult to believe that God *sent* hailstones at that moment; but is it not possible that God *used* hailstones and other natural phenomena in the achievement of ultimate moral ends through the free choices of both the Israelites and their enemies? (See comment on Deuteronomy 7:1-26.)

In verses 12-13 a poetic fragment from the "Book of Jashar"

is quoted. This book, from which another poem is excerpted in II Samuel 1:18-27, apparently consisted of a collection of ancient heroic songs, possibly compiled about the time of David or Solomon. The writer of the Book of Joshua seems to have literalized (vs. 13b) the figurative, dramatic language of the poem. One surely should not, for example, take literally the statement in Judges 5:20 that the stars fought against Sisera! In the poem the meaning is perhaps that there was enough time left in the day— it seemed miraculously—for Joshua to complete the destruction of his enemies.

The rest of the chapter records Joshua's follow-up campaign against the strongholds of the southwestern hill-country (Makkedah, Libnah, Lachish, Eglon) and the capture of Hebron and Debir in the mountainous territory south of Jerusalem. The exact location of Makkedah, where the five kings hid in a cave, is not known. Excavations have shown that three of the towns Joshua is said here to have captured (Lachish, Eglon, Debir) were burned at about this time. The destruction of two of them (Debir and Lachish) can be quite precisely dated at about 1250-1200 B.C. —a time into which Joshua fits very well. Gezer, an important stronghold of the low hill-country, was not captured at this time (16:10; I Kings 9:16), though a contingent of troops sent by the king of Gezer to assist Lachish was defeated (vs. 33). Jerusalem was not captured by the Israelites until the time of David (II Sam. 5:6-9).

The summarizing statements in verses 40-43, while somewhat overly sweeping, are not to be entirely discounted on the basis of Judges 1, where a more gradual conquest seems to be described. It is inherently likely that Joshua carried out smashing campaigns into the center of the land (Jericho, Ai-Bethel), into the southwest and south (the six cities mentioned above), and into the north (ch. 11). Later sections of the Book of Joshua (11:13, 22; 13:2-13; 15:63; 23:12-13) show clearly that the writer knew that Joshua had not "utterly destroyed all that breathed" (vs. 40), but that much remained yet to be done after his time. Enthusiasm for Joshua's exploits naturally led to exaggerated statements.

The Northern Campaign (11:1-15)

Israel's successes were now so impressive that it became apparent to all the remaining Canaanite kings that a decisive stand against the Israelites would have to be attempted. The lead in the north was taken by Jabin, king of Hazor, who formed a powerful coalition of northern states. Their military strength rested not alone on huge numbers of available troops but upon strong contingents of horses and chariots (vs. 4). All were encamped near the waters of Merom, a valley carrying water from a perennial spring, some eight miles southwest of Hazor and ten miles northwest of the Sea of Galilee. It was a formidable host, and Joshua was rightly fearful of the outcome (vs. 6).

Again Joshua's strategy was unexpected attack, probably after a long, forced march. The rugged hills and valleys of this area were ideally suited to Joshua's type of guerilla fighting. It is probable that the Canaanites expected to meet the Israelites in a more open area for effective use of their horses and chariots. But Joshua forestalled this and scored a smashing victory. He hamstrung their horses, so that they could not later be corralled and used by other Canaanites, and he burned their chariots (vs. 9).

Joshua then turned back from the pursuit and destroyed the great city of Hazor. How great it was has been revealed in recent excavations. In the time of Joshua the city covered about 200 acres. It consisted of an upper city, which rested on a mound 25 acres in size—the oldest part of the city—and a lower city to the north, surrounded by a great beaten-earth wall. The area occupied by the lower city is so large that it was thought some years ago to have been only an enclosure for horses and chariots. But excavation proved the area to contain the remains of a well-built city. It is calculated that about 40,000 people lived in Hazor when Joshua captured it. The archaeologists found conclusive evidence that Hazor was destroyed about the middle of the thirteenth century, a date which agrees remarkably well with the statements of Joshua 11. Its history covers the period 2700-150 B.C., twenty-one city levels in all. Only part of the great site has been excavated during the four seasons of digging. But the discoveries (for example, of four Canaanite temples and well-preserved cult objects, which reveal that the religion of Hazor centered in the worship of the sun-god in association with a bull) are of sensational importance in understanding what Canaanite civilization was like in the time of the Hebrew invasion.

Summary of Israel's Conquests (11:16—12:24)

The summary of Joshua's achievements here is sweeping and

misleading to the casual reader. The generalizing statements "So Joshua took all that land" (11:16) and "So Joshua took the whole land" (vs. 23) by themselves give the impression that Joshua's victories were both quick and complete. But these impressions must be qualified by the more sober statements, such as: "But none of the cities that stood on mounds did Israel burn, except Hazor only" (vs. 13); "Joshua made war a long time with all those kings" (vs. 18); and "there remains yet very much land to be possessed" (13:1), said to have been spoken near the end of Joshua's life. The facts seem to be that Joshua did launch and carry through a series of smashing attacks on key Canaanite strongholds of the land; he demoralized the Canaanites and gained a foothold for the Israelite tribes in the land, but many areas of the land were too strongly fortified for his military capability. These were gradually overcome (Judges 1), and complete subjugation of the land was achieved only in the time of David two centuries later.

In verse 20 it is said that the Lord hardened the hearts of the Canaanites so that they would resist and be exterminated rather than surrender and be spared. According to the Deuteronomic point of view, all the Canaanites were to be wiped out. The statement that the decision to resist was the result of God's hardening the hearts of the Canaanites in order to achieve their ultimate extermination is similar to that made in Exodus 4:21 and elsewhere concerning Pharaoh. Hebrew thought did not hesitate to ascribe the origin of evil and evil acts to God, who would make them turn out to the advancement of his purposes (see I Kings 22:19-23; Job 2:10; Isa. 45:7; Amos 3:6). Later an evil spirit (Satan, Belial, Mastema, Be-elzebul) was seen as responsible for the instigation of evil, both natural and moral, and it was emphatically affirmed that God would destroy him and his works at the Last Day.

Chapter 12 consists of a general summary of the kings defeated and captured by Moses and Joshua, both to the east and to the west of the Jordan. It is not said that all of their cities were occupied and destroyed. Jerusalem and Gezer lost their kings (10: 22-27, 33), but we know that the cities were not captured until much later (Joshua 16:10; II Sam. 5:6-9; I Kings 9:16). The list of kings here (vss. 9-24) is drawn from the record as presented in Joshua 2-10 and from some unknown source. (Several kings listed here have not been mentioned previously in the book.)

Archaeological work has shown how strongly fortified the cities of Canaan were at this time and how advanced their civilization. Joshua's achievements at the head of poorly equipped and provisioned bands from the desert must be regarded as phenomenal!

THE DIVISION OF THE LAND

Joshua 13:1—21:45

The material in chapters 13-21 is very complicated, from the standpoint both of its literary history and of the complexity of its data. The Deuteronomic writer obviously has used old city and boundary lists in compiling his account of the allotment of lands to the tribes of Israel. It is now believed by many that the lists were of diverse origin and were drawn up at various times and revised between about the eleventh and the seventh centuries B.C. For a variety of reasons it seems possible, for example, to date the list of cities (grouped probably according to administrative districts of Judah) contained in Joshua 15:21-62 in the time of Jehoshaphat (about 873-849 B.C.). The Deuteronomic writer has woven several lists into an account of the territorial allotments made to the tribes by Joshua.

God's Command to Joshua (13:1-7)

Joshua, now an old man, is commanded by God to divide the land west of the Jordan among the nine and one-half tribes. Following this, we are told how Moses had apportioned the territory east of the Jordan among the two and one-half tribes.

The reference to Joshua's age (the Hebrew says that he was "advanced in days") and the reminder that there is much land yet to be taken are not meant as a prod to Joshua to undertake the remaining military tasks before his end comes. They rather suggest that before his death he must bequeath the unconquered portions to their future owners. One is reminded here of the blessing of the tribes by Jacob (Gen. 49) and by Moses (Deut. 33). The allotment is thus represented here as a kind of last will and testament, whose terms, according to oriental conceptions, were perpetually binding. (For two other views of the method and significance of the allotment see the comment on 14:1-5.)

The lands yet unconquered are enumerated roughly from south

to north. They lay chiefly on the coastal plain between the "Shihor" (probably "the Brook of Egypt" of 15:4, 47—a gorge on the Egyptian frontier) and upper Phoenicia. Claim is even laid to the whole Lebanon region, including the great valley between the Lebanon and Anti-Lebanon ranges. Israel never occupied all this north country, although, as we see here and elsewhere, the nation had designs on it. The northernmost point of Israel's expansion in the time of David and Solomon did reach to "the entrance of Hamath" (vs. 5; I Kings 8:65; II Kings 14:25), that is, to the southern border of the kingdom of Hamath at some point in the valley between the two Lebanon ranges; but the Phoenician coastal cities maintained their independence of Israel.

Tribal Allotments East of the Jordan (13:8-33)

For the allotment of territory east of the Jordan to the two and one-half tribes, the student should see Joshua 12:1-6 and Deuteronomy 2:1—3:29 (see also comment). It must suffice here to say that these territories run from the Arnon River (about midway on the east shore of the Dead Sea) to a line running roughly east to northeast of the Sea of Galilee. The eastern borders of these tribal territories are not defined.

Tribal Allotments West of the Jordan (14:1—19:51)

Preliminary Explanation (14:1-5)

The reader of Joshua 13:1-7 would conclude that the division of the land was made by Joshua alone shortly before his death. From 18:2-10 one would conclude also that, as a result of the casting of lots in the presence of the Lord, it was Joshua who declared how land should be assigned. Two other traditions exist concerning the way in which allotments were determined. Some passages suggest that the responsibility lay with "the people of Israel" (14:5; 19:49-50). Still others ascribe a prominent role to Eleazar the priest and to "the heads of the fathers' houses" (14:1; 19:51). It is likely that all three points of view contain truth. Since it was the practice of Israel's leaders to determine the will of God by the use of lots (Urim and Thummim; see comment on Deut. 33:1-29), we would expect Israel's priests and political leaders to share in the ceremony. The act could then be referred to as Israel's doing, or Joshua's, or the priests' and the heads of families'. But behind all three explanations is the conviction that it was God who made the allotment.

That some kind of formal division of the land was made is inherently likely. Otherwise the land-hungry tribes would have consumed each other's strength by infighting and all would have become easy prey for their powerful Canaanite enemies.

Caleb's Inheritance (14:6-15)

The allotment to the tribe of Judah is recorded first (14:6—15:63). It is prefaced by a story concerning the assignment of the Judean city of Hebron to Caleb, one of the courageous spies of the Mosaic period (Num. 13-14; Deut. 1:19-40).

Caleb is called here a Kenizzite, a tribe descended from Kenaz in the land of Edom (Gen. 36:9-11). He is said in Numbers 13:6 and 34:19 to belong to the tribe of Judah. This is to be explained by the fact that the early Hebrews sometimes assimilated outside tribal groups. These accepted Israel's religion and culture and gained full rights in the Israelite community. It is interesting that Caleb, a "foreigner," should occupy a position of honor in Israel's traditions and stand along with Joshua as a great hero of the faith (Num. 13-14; Deut. 1:34-38). Of a piece with this is the tradition that Ruth, a Moabite, became an honored Israelite and an ancestress of King David (Ruth 4:13-17). It is a common-place with biblical scholars that Israel's assimilative powers brought great enrichment to its life—to its faith, its worship, its laws, its institutions, its architecture, its total culture. But what it assimilated it transformed into new and higher creations.

The story of Caleb's reward in long, vigorous life and now in inheritance of land is designed to show how God keeps his promise to those who wholly follow him (vss. 8, 9, 14). Caleb is thus to the Deuteronomic writer a symbol of the kind of obedience God expects from the readers and of the results that will follow on such obedience.

The time notation in verse 10, when joined with that in Deuteronomy 2:14, indicates that the writer regards the period of the conquest up to the moment of Caleb's request as about seven years.

Caleb's courage is shown to rest both on his physical vigor and on his deep trust in the Lord. Although he is now eighty-five, his strength is unabated; but this alone will not suffice. "It may be that the LORD will be with me, and I shall drive them out as the LORD said" (vs. 12). This statement shows the proper posture of faith. We have no right to make demands on God. We can only wage our war, whatever it may be, and trust that he will help us to win the victory.

Judah's Allotment (15:1-63)

The material of this chapter falls into several parts. First are recorded the south, east, north, and west boundaries of the allotment of Judah (vss. 2-12). This is followed by another reference to the awarding of Hebron to Caleb, including a brief reference to the capture of Debir (vss. 13-19). Next a list of Judean towns (comprising eleven, or perhaps originally twelve, administrative districts) is offered (vss. 20-62). Finally, a reference to the invincibility of the Jebusites of Jerusalem is appended (vs. 63).

The territory here delineated as Judah's is large in comparison with other tribal allotments. But much of it is desert or semi-desert. Its southern boundary runs southwest from the south end of the Dead Sea to Kadesh-barnea (about 55 miles) and northwest along "the Brook of Egypt" to the Mediterranean Sea (about 60 miles). The eastern boundary is the full length of the shoreline of the Dead Sea (about 50 miles). The north boundary runs irregularly (some 60 miles) from the north end of the Dead Sea to the Mediterranean just south of Joppa, skirting Jerusalem on the south.

A touch of romance is introduced with the story of the capture of Debir (Kiriath-sepher, known today as Tell Beit Mirsim). According to the story in verses 15-19 (told in almost identical language in Judges 1:11-15), Othniel—Caleb's brother or nephew —won his wife (Caleb's daughter) as a reward for the capture of the city. Caleb subsequently gave Othniel a field and some springs (or perhaps cisterns) of water, probably as a dowry, since Debir belonged to Othniel by right of conquest.

How the capture of Debir as described here is to be related to the conquest of Debir by Joshua (Joshua 10:38-39) is a problem. Excavations conducted at the site of Debir revealed that toward the end of the thirteenth century B.C.—the time of Joshua —the city was violently destroyed. So intense was the burning that in places the ashes were three feet thick. Either we have variant and discrepant accounts of the conquest of the city or a second assault was necessary somewhat later than the one by

Joshua. The latter is not impossible, since Joshua's military efforts were scarcely thorough enough to achieve permanent subjugation of the areas initially captured.

The list of cities (vss. 20-62), grouped according to administrative districts, probably comes from the time of Jehoshaphat in the ninth century B.C. It was David who began administrative districting. This late list, reflecting the situation in Judah of the ninth century, was used by the Deuteronomic writer as a source of information concerning the allotment of land during the earlier period under Joshua.

Jerusalem, a strongly fortified Jebusite city on the border of Judah, was not conquered until the time of David (II Sam. 5: 6-10).

Joseph's (Ephraim's and Manasseh's) Allotment (16:1—17:18)

There are confusing data and overlapping sections in chapter 16. Verse 5 must be read in connection with verse 2. "Bethel to Luz" (vs. 2) can scarcely be correct, for they are variant names of the same place (see 18:13).

It is clear, however, that the southern border of Ephraim is placed on a line running from Jericho to Bethel, to Gezer, and to the Mediterranean Sea. The northern border cut from east to west near Shechem and terminated at the Mediterranean just north of Joppa. The eastern border was the Jordan.

The allotment to Manasseh (17:1-13) consists of territories both east and west of the Jordan. The eastern section comprises areas southeast and east of the Sea of Galilee (Gilead and Bashan) and the western territory between Shechem on the south and the Plain of Esdraelon on the north. Again the east and west boundaries are the Jordan and the Mediterranean.

The allotment of land to the daughters of Zelophehad (vss. 3-6) is made in accordance with a decision attributed to Moses concerning inheritance rights in sonless families (see Num. 27: 1-11).

The request for more room made by the Joseph tribes (vss. 14-18) results in a challenge by Joshua to clear the forested areas of their mountain territory and in a promise that the entrenched Canaanites in the lowlands of the territory belonging to them will be driven out. The Hebrew foot soldiers were understandably afraid of the horses and iron-plated chariots of the Canaanite armies.

Allotment to the Remaining Tribes (18:1—19:51)

The previous allotments are said to have been made at Gilgal (14:6). The scene now shifts to Shiloh, the place of the Tabernacle and the Ark of the Covenant in the period of the Judges.

Joshua reproves the remaining tribes for their lack of zeal in claiming and occupying their future homelands, in contrast to Judah and the Joseph tribes which are represented as settled in theirs (vs. 5). Three men from each of the seven remaining tribes are to survey the land yet available, divide it into seven portions, and return to Joshua for decision concerning assignment. This is to be made by lot "before the LORD" (vs. 6).

Benjamin is assigned a small piece of land between Ephraim and Judah, bounded on the east by the Jordan and extending only halfway to the Mediterranean on the west. Jerusalem lay just within its southern border.

Simeon is assigned to a portion of the large area given to Judah: to the area around Beer-sheba (19:1-9). It seems strange that two tribes should be promised some of the same areas. By the time the lists used here were drawn up, Simeon probably had been absorbed into the tribe of Judah.

Zebulun is assigned to a small area within the territory later known as Galilee, with Issachar to the southeast, Asher to the west (western Galilee and the Phoenician coast), and Naphtali to the east and north.

Dan fares badly. It is given a small piece west of Benjamin and between Ephraim and Judah in the low hill country west of Jerusalem. Verse 47 relates that Dan, unable to capture its territory, subsequently migrated northward to Leshem (at the headwaters of the Jordan), where it dispossessed the inhabitants and settled down (see Judges 1:34; ch. 18).

Appointment of Cities of Refuge (20:1-9)

The function of cities of refuge has already been discussed in connection with the Deuteronomic law providing for them (see comment on Deut. 19:1-21). Here it will suffice to identify them and to explain the reason for their particular location.

They are six in number and are located in the north, center, and south of both sides of the Jordan River. Kedesh lay in northern Galilee, near the foot of Mount Hermon. Shechem was the old tribal center between the mountains of Ebal and Gerizim in central Samaria. Kiriath-arba is Hebron in the hill country of Judah. The exact location of Bezer is unknown, but since it is placed in the territory of Reuben, it lay east of the north half of the Dead Sea. Ramoth is Ramoth-gilead, an important site near the edge of the eastern desert, about twenty-five miles southeast of the Sea of Galilee. Golan in Bashan is somewhat farther north, probably about seventeen miles straight east of the Sea of Galilee.

Accessibility to the people of all the tribes was a prime factor in the location of these cities. But beyond this was the fact that all these towns contained shrines (see Joshua 21). From earliest times sanctuary was allowed at the altar of the Deity. The accused put himself under the protection of the Deity until the charges could be heard by constituted authority and the case fairly tried (Exod. 21:12-14; I Kings 1:50-53; 2:28). The principle of blood-revenge was a deterrent to homicide, but safeguards against its abuse had to be constructed in the interest of justice.

Designation of Levitical Cities (21:1-45)

The Levites were set apart for priestly service, pledged by vow to the Lord. (For the function of the Levites see the comment on Deuteronomy 16:18—18:22.) They were to have no tribal inheritance as such but were to be scatt.red through the tribes to officiate at the local sanctuaries. When the local sanctuaries were destroyed in the time of Josiah and worship was centralized in Jerusalem (see comment on Deut. 12:1—16:17), the Levites were offered a place at the Jerusalem sanctuary and an appropriate share of the sacrifices and first fruits.

The number of Levitical cities is said to have been forty-eight (vs. 41). The list of them here probably dates to the tenth century B.C. The list seems originally to have located four of them in each of the twelve tribes. It is likely that Hebron and Shechem were not in the original list but are secondary additions. Note that nine cities (including Hebron) are listed from Judah and Simeon (vss. 9-16), where one would expect eight. Shechem is included as being in Ephraim (vs. 21), but in actuality it was in Manasseh. In the original list Jokme-am (see I Chron. 6:66-68) seems to have been included, Shechem later taking its place. The list thus has experienced alterations in the process of transmission and editing.

It is unlikely that the Levites were the exclusive possessors and inhabitants of all the towns mentioned. Debir, for example, was captured by Othniel—a non-Levite—and was thus his possession (15:15-19). When Debir is listed here as a Levitical city (vs. 15), it can mean little more than that Levites lived in it along with others. Whatever may have been the exact situation concerning the settlement of the Levites at the beginning of the occupation of Palestine by the Hebrews, it appears that the Levites soon scattered themselves widely throughout the land.

FINAL ACTS AND INSTRUCTIONS OF JOSHUA

Joshua 22:1—24:33

Following a sweeping summary at the end of chapter 21 (vss. 43-45)—obviously somewhat overstated in view of the clear evidence that at Joshua's death much land was yet unconquered and fierce battles with the inhabitants of the land still lay ahead—the text of the book turns from border and city lists to narratives concerning the post-Conquest acts of Joshua.

The Dismissal of the Transjordan Tribes (22:1-9)

According to 13:1, Joshua undertook the division of the land when he was "old and advanced in years." Chapter 22 seems to reflect a much earlier period, immediately after the smashing initial campaigns of Joshua and his troops. It is hardly likely that the Transjordan tribes would have remained west of the Jordan until Joshua was old—especially since their wives and children were in their allotted lands east of the Jordan (1:14).

The situation described here is then this: the warriors of the Reubenites, the Gadites, and the half-tribe of Manasseh have completed their service of assisting their brethren in the conquest of the land west of the Jordan. They are now ready to return and work out their destiny in the lands allotted to them by Moses.

In a parting address to these warriors at Shiloh (vs. 9), where the Tabernacle and the Ark of the Covenant are now located, Joshua first commends them for their fidelity to the service required of them by Moses (vss. 2-3) and then exhorts them to obey all the laws of Moses and to cleave with all their heart and soul to the exclusive worship of the Lord (vs. 5). Following a blessing by Joshua, they start out for their new homes.

The Altar of Witness at the Jordan (22:10-34)

The story of the erecting of the altar at the Jordan by the returning tribes is full of human interest and pathos. It appears that the altar was patterned in love and adoration after the altar of the Lord at Shiloh (vs. 28), though it may have been somewhat larger (vs. 10). Its purpose was entirely misunderstood. It was meant to be a memorial altar, to remind posterity of the unity of the tribes on both sides of the Jordan in the bonds of brotherhood and worship of the common Lord. But its purpose was taken to be exactly the opposite: to set up a rival worship at a new center and thus to divide the tribes and nullify the Covenant they had so recently entered into together. The report aroused the western tribes to a white heat of resentment, to the point where they actually were ready to wage war against the brethren who so loyally had helped them in the western campaigns.

Fortunately, a delegation was sent to find out the true motives: ten chiefs representing the nine and one-half tribes and the priest Phinehas, the latter probably representing the Levites. Phinehas is known in Old Testament narratives as zealous for the Lord and actively hostile to pagan practices. He is said to have thrust a spear through the bodies of an Israelite and a Midianite woman and thus to have stayed a plague sent by the Lord on Israel because of unlawful intercourse (literal and figurative) with the Midianites (Num. 25:6-18). But even this zealot for pure religion was satisfied, after investigation, that the motive in the erection of the altar was good and legitimate (vss. 30-34).

The story is told to drive home several points: the absolute importance of the worship of one God at one sanctuary—the dominant motif of the Books of Deuteronomy and Joshua; the utter folly of idolatry ("Have we not had enough of the sin at Peor [Num. 25] from which even yet we have not cleansed ourselves . . . ?"—vs. 17); and the importance of seeing both sides of the Jordan, not merely the western, as the Lord's land.

The story illustrates the foibles of human nature. How easily people misinterpret the motives of others! How quickly they turn from warm comradeship in a common enterprise to suspicion and bitter hostility! It counsels us to be slow to judge and quick to investigate.

First Concluding Address of Joshua (23:1-16)

The book is now concluded by two addresses of Joshua. The first (ch. 23) is clearly a farewell address (vss. 1-2). In ancient Israel and among the nations of antiquity in general, the parting words of tribal leaders and heads of families were highly regarded. Before death a blessing was pronounced on the immediate children and on descendants yet unborn (often also curses on personal and tribal enemies) and guidance was offered for the future. One thinks, for example, of the last words of Jacob (Gen. 49), Moses (Deut. 32-33), and David (II Sam. 23:1-7; I Kings 2:2-9).

The address in Joshua 23 catches up the main themes of both Deuteronomy and Joshua. It revolves around the familiar three foci: what God has done; what you (Israel) must do; and what God will do.

Joshua first reminds the people of what they have seen with their own eyes—how God has fought for them in the destruction of many peoples (vss. 3-4, 9), how one man has put to flight a thousand because of the Lord's help (vs. 10), and how the Lord has kept all the promises made to his people (vs. 14). This is the burden of the addresses of Moses in Deuteronomy 1-11. The key word there was "remember." The appeal here is likewise an appeal to remembrance.

Joshua then points out bluntly and explicitly what his hearers must do if God is to continue to fight for them until the land is fully won and the nation permanently established in the land. They *must* steadfastly obey all the prescriptions of the Law of Moses (vs. 6). These consist basically in exclusive, wholehearted worship of the Lord and the abhorrence of idolatry in any form (vss. 7-8, 16). As a safeguard against being led astray, there is to be no intermarriage with the heathen inhabitants of the land (vss. 12-13; see Deut. 7:3-4). Obedience is to spring out of love for God (vs. 11).

Finally, the consequences of obedience and disobedience are pointed out. *Behold* what great things the Lord will do for you, if you wholly follow the Lord! He will drive out the remaining nations from the land (vs. 5), and Israel will fully take possession of the promised inheritance (vs. 4). The perils of disobedience are likewise stressed. Intermarriage, leading to idolatry, will result in extinction from the land after untold trouble at the hands of the native peoples. The anger of the Lord will be hot against Israel (vs. 16).

Joshua's message is identical with that of Moses: Israel stands once more between good and evil and between life and death (vss. 15-16; Deut. 28:1-15). The venerable leader urges the people to choose life.

Second Concluding Address and the Covenant Ceremony at Shechem (24:1-28)

The Book of Joshua comes to a dramatic climax in an impassioned address by Joshua to all Israel assembled at the sacred city of Shechem, in a call to decision for or against the God of the fathers, and in the entering into a solemn Covenant with this God by all the people. A brief section at the very end (vss. 29-33) records the death and burial of Joshua and the interment of Joseph and of Eleazar, the son of Aaron. The effectiveness of Joshua's leadership is noted in the statement that "Israel served the LORD all the days of Joshua, and all the days of the elders who outlived Joshua" (vs. 31).

Chapter 24 impresses the careful reader as duplicating (in part at least) both chapter 23 and 8:30-35. Chapter 23 seems to round off the book and would form an excellent conclusion to the whole, as it summarizes admirably the major themes the writer has been emphasizing throughout. The contents of chapter 24 are not dated to the end of Joshua's career, as is the case with chapter 23. The events described in chapter 24 could thus have occurred earlier in Joshua's life. The strong similarity of the narrative concerning the institution of the Covenant here with that to be found in 8:30-35 and in Deuteronomy 27 leads to the possibility that Joshua 24 contains an alternative version of that ceremony. It may have been added here because it was thought to be a more effective conclusion to the book than chapter 23. It affirms that Israel wholeheartedly accepted the Lord God and vowed eternal loyalty to him.

Deuteronomy 27-28 deals with the great Shechem Covenant ceremony (see comment). Only the striking features of the record in Joshua 24 will be indicated here.

That Shechem was an old city is evident both from the Book

of Genesis and from archaeology. Abraham is said to have built
an altar there by a sacred oak (Gen. 12:6-7). An Egyptian official of the nineteenth century B.C. refers to the capture of Shechem by an Egyptian king. Recent archaeological investigation
of the site has revealed that Shechem was long a sacred city
(that is, it contained a shrine). The excavators found a large
temple area which had passed through many rebuildings between
about 1800 and 1100 B.C. Around 1650 B.C. a massive fortress-
temple of unique type was constructed there on the stumps of
earlier temples. Following a destruction of the city in the sixteenth century B.C. by the Egyptians and a period of ruin, yet another temple was built on the spot in the fifteenth century. A
huge sacred pillar of white limestone, carefully smoothed, set up
somewhere between about 1450 and 1200 B.C. not far from the
altar of the temple, was recovered by the archaeologists. In Canaanite religion such stone pillars seem to have symbolized the
presence of the deity, probably the male deity.

The fact that the Old Testament records no Israelite conquest
of Shechem may mean that people were living there who were
known to be relatives of the Hebrews. They may have joined
Israel in Covenant relationship with Israel's God (which may
have been identified with the traditional god of Shechem). However it be explained, Shechem seems from the first days of the
conquest of Canaan to have been regarded as a legitimate place
of worship.

Joshua's address recites the gracious deeds of God in the call
of Abraham, the migration to Canaan, the deliverance from
Egypt, the victory over the Amorites, the deliverance from the
machinations of Balak and Balaam, the capture of Jericho, and
the defeat of many Canaanite nations. On the basis of God's
mighty deeds the people are challenged to be loyal to him and
to put away all false gods. Joshua here preaches for a verdict:
"choose this day whom you will serve" (vs. 15). Like Elijah in
a later time (I Kings 18:21), he seems to be pushing for a clear-
cut decision. Double-mindedness cursed the Israelites through
most of their history. Both Joshua and Elijah knew that part-
time service of God is no service at all.

Joshua's psychology here is noteworthy. He knew the power
of example: You can do as you will, he says, "but as for me and
my house, we will serve the LORD" (vs. 15). This evokes from
the people a burst of enthusiasm for the worship of the God of

Israel. Now Joshua drives their decision deeper. He seems to be saying that no superficial choice will be of any significance. God is a holy and jealous God; he will tolerate no vacillation. Breaking the Covenant after it has once been entered into will be a serious offense which may bring destruction on them. Think twice, he seems to say. The caution had its desired effect, for the people affirm, "Nay; but we will serve the LORD" (vs. 21). This is followed by Joshua's demand that they act immediately in harmony with their decision by casting away their false gods. Joshua knew that decision must be implemented by action if it is to have any permanent results. False gods tucked away for the time being are sure to reappear later on the mantel of the home or on the throne of the heart.

The Covenant ceremony is not described here (see Deut. 27 and Joshua 8:30-35). The part that the stone plays in this passage is of interest (vss. 26-27), especially in view of the archaeological recovery of a sacred stone at Shechem. It is obvious that the stone here is regarded as representing the Deity, as if the Deity were actually present in the stone and a witness to the people's solemn declarations and actions. Jacob is said to have set up a stone at Bethel and poured oil on it as a testimony to God's presence in that place (Gen. 28:18). For Joshua, not only was the stone at Shechem a symbol of the Deity's presence but it was probably also a monument—visible to all for the days ahead—of the Covenant which had been entered into that day. The condemnation of the sacred stone and the sacred tree in Deuteronomy 16:21-22 probably reflects the attitude of a time later than that of Joshua, for both are considered legitimate in Joshua 24:26.

Joshua's Death and Burial and the Interment of Joseph and Eleazar (24:29-33)

The sacredness of Shechem to the Israelites at this period is further evidenced by their burial of the bones of Joseph there. We are told that Jacob had bought land at Shechem; Joseph was thus laid away on family property. The burial of Joseph's bones in the land of Canaan is said to have been in accordance with his dying request (Gen. 50:25).

The death of Joshua is doubly recorded: here (vss. 29-31)

and in Judges 2:8-10. Both passages record the fidelity of the people during the days of their great leader's life and those of the eyewitnesses of the stirring events of the Conquest. Thus indirectly is the power of personal experience and eyewitness testimony disclosed.

The influence of Joshua on Israel's history cannot be fully assessed until one takes into consideration the work of another "Joshua" ("Jesus," whose Hebrew name was "Joshua" or more accurately "Yehoshua"). Both of these Joshua's abundantly demonstrated the truth signified by their name, which means, "the LORD [Yahweh] is salvation."

Other Works by Patrick Jennings You Might Enjoy

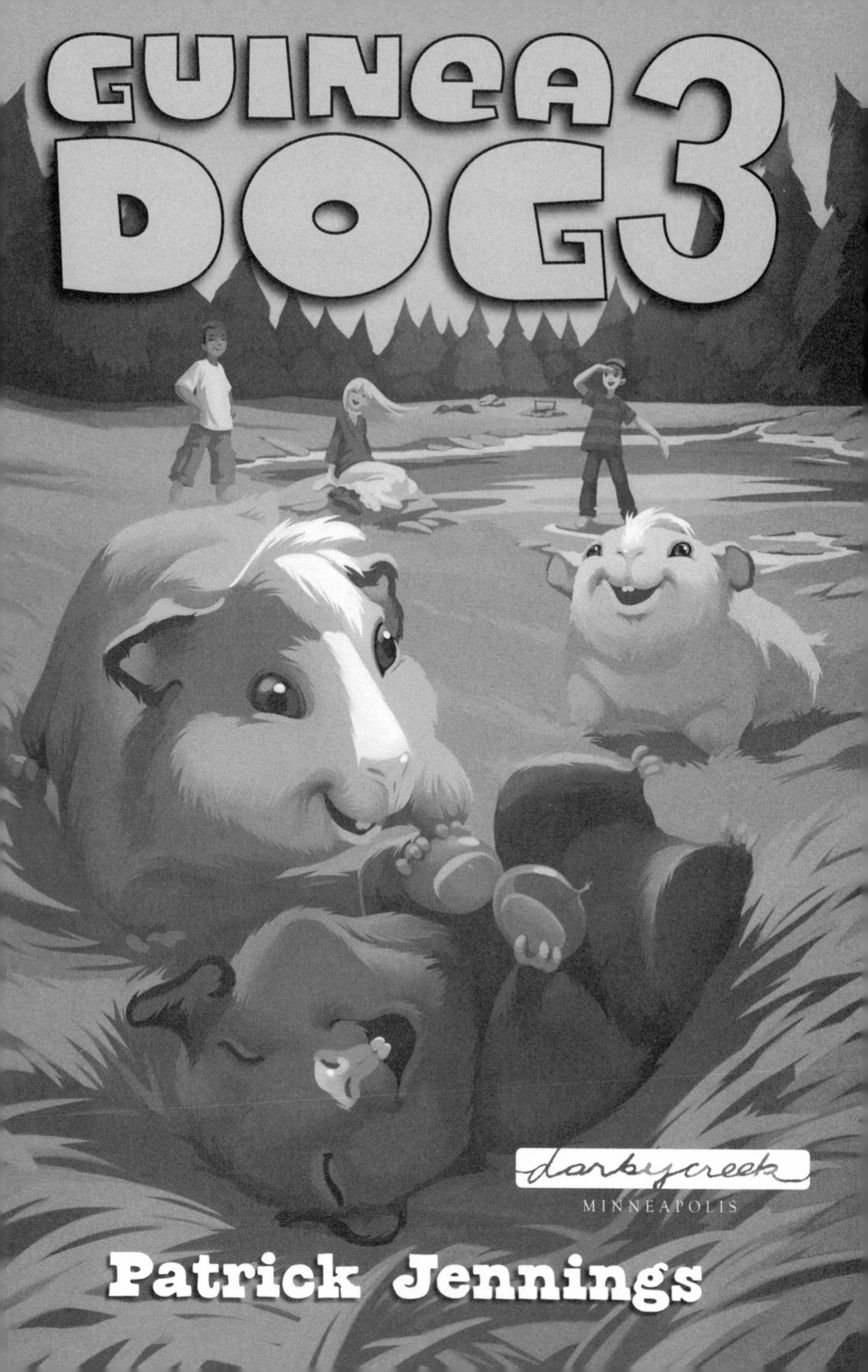

GUINEA DOG 3
darbycreek
MINNEAPOLIS
Patrick Jennings

For Regina Griffin,
Eagle-eyed, Lionhearted
Queen of Editorship

First published by Egmont USA in 2014

Darby Creek
A division of Lerner Publishing Group, Inc.
241 First Avenue North
Minneapolis, MN 55401 USA

For reading levels and more information, look up this title at www.lernerbooks.com.

Library of Congress Cataloging-in-Publication Data

Jennings, Patrick.
      Guinea dog 3 / Patrick Jennings.
         pages cm
      Summary: When Pedro admits that he has a paralyzing fear of water, his friends try to cheer him up with a pet. Only this one won't leave the water! The third installment of the Guinea Dog series.
      ISBN 978-1-60684-554-7 (hardcover)
      ISBN 978-1-5124-0132-5 (eb pdf)
      [1. Guinea pigs—Fiction. 2. Family life—Fiction. 3. Camping—Fiction. 4. Fear—Fiction.] I. Title. II. Title: Guinea dog three.
   PZ7.J4298715Gug 2014
   [Fic]—dc23   2013044867

Manufactured in the United States of America
2-42462-20854-10/5/2016

Contents

1. I need a vacation.

All the fuss at school about my guinea dog, Fido, has worn me down. Everyone kept bugging me to see the guinea pig that acted like a dog, or asking me where to get one, or otherwise being very annoying. It was exhausting.

Fortunately, next week, my family is heading to White Crappie Lake for our annual camping trip. (The lake is filled with white crappies, which is a kind of fish, but, even so, I'm sure they could have come up with a better name.) My best friend, Murphy, and his family are coming, too. They go with us every year. It's a summer vacation tradition that traces back to when we were in kindergarten together. We've been friends that long. Murphy's the greatest guy in the whole world. I'm lucky he's my best friend and I'm his, because everybody loves Murphy—including Dmitri.

My worst friend, Dmitri, has been trying to replace me as Murph's best friend ever since he moved to Rustbury last summer. He's always trying to impress Murph with all the cool devices and clothes and stuff his rich parents buy him. But Murph doesn't care about that kind of stuff. He would have accepted Dmitri as a friend anyway. His motto is "The more the merrier!"

Murph and I always have so much fun at the lake. We swim, dive off the floating pier, jump off the tire swing, go boating, explore the woods, and just, you know, hang out, without any interruptions, from school or from Dmitri.

This will be Fido's first trip to the lake, of course. I mean, I've only had her a little while. Murph loves her, and so does his dog, Buddy, who is probably the greatest dog in the whole world. Murph says Fido's the greatest guinea pig in the whole world. He's the one who came up with the idea of calling her a "guinea dog."

Right now I'm busy packing for the trip, but

it's hard because every time I put something in my duffel bag, Fido dives in and drags it out and wants to play Tug-of-War. Or she hides it under my bed. Or she tries to chew it to pieces. She chews a lot of things to pieces, and not just my stuff, but Mom's and Dad's, too. Mom laughs it off. Dad doesn't. One of the bazillion reasons he won't let me get a dog is that dogs chew things up.

"Put that down," I say to Fido. "I'm not interested in playing Tug-of-War with my underwear."

She holds on and growls. She wants to play.

So do I. I hate packing.

I dig under my bed and find a sock that hasn't been chewed to bits. She drops my underwear and dives under the bed, snatching the sock before I can get to it, then races in circles around the room, the dirty sock in her tiny teeth.

"Hey, you," I say, pretending I'm sore at her. "Bring that here. Fido, here!"

This is an order, and she obeys. She's a good

dog that way. She inches toward me with her butt up in the air, growling in her deep voice, which is about as deep as a mouse's.

"Come on," I say. "Give it here. Give it. Fido? Fido? Give me the sock."

She hunkers down, her ears low.

I lunge forward and grab the other end of the sock. She tightens her grip, digs her claws into the carpet, and starts shaking her head back and forth. We both tug. I have to pretend she might actually jerk the sock out of my hand, which is impossible. If I wanted to, I could lift it up in the air with her dangling from it by her teeth.

A knuckle knocks on my door.

"Rufus?" my mom says, poking her head inside. "Can I come in?"

"Can't you see I'm busy?" I ask.

"I can," she says, with a that's-so-cute smile. "I just thought I'd tell you the exciting news."

"Exciting?" I ask.

Mom's idea of exciting and mine are pretty different.

"I just got off the phone," she sings. Singing

her words is a sign she's about to break some bad news. This is not looking good.

"Oh?" I ask.

Fido keeps growling and tugging.

"Another fa-mi-ly will be joining us on the tri-ip!" Mom sings.

"What family? And just say it, Mom. Don't sing it."

She sucks in her bottom lip and makes her oh-you're-getting-so-smart-and-grown-up face.

"*Who*, Mom?" I demand. "*Who* is coming with us?"

She opens her eyes and mouth wide in fake anticipation, as if she were building suspense. If I had a drum set, I'd give her a drum roll, but Dad says I can get a drum set when I'm grown up and living on my own, not before.

"*Mom*," I say. I wonder if she's read that book I've seen on her bookshelf, *How to Talk So Kids Will Listen, and Listen So Kids Will Talk*. If she did, she didn't learn anything.

She steps inside the room. "I thought it'd be fun," she says, "to have another family join us on our White Crappie trip this year, so I invited . . ." She pauses for effect.

I scream at her with my eyes: *Go on!*

"I invited Dmitri and his family!"

I let go of the sock, and Fido rolls away like a coconut.

2. My mom invited my worst friend again.

I'm both shocked and unsurprised. How is that possible?

Leave it to Mom. After all, this is the woman who invited not only Dmitri, but also his vicious chow, Mars, to my last birthday party. She also invited Lurena, the annoying, rodent-crazy, old-fashioned-clothes-crazy, *crazy*-crazy girl who has been following me around ever since I got Fido.

Mom has been pressuring me to be friends with Lurena ever since they met. Can't Mom see she's a girl? A *weird* girl? Does she not remember that Lurena once asked her parents for a pet *squirrel*? (Which she got, in a way, when Fido gave birth to a guinea pup that acted like a squirrel.)

Yeah, I gave her Fido's baby. It just made sense. The weird thing about it, though, is that it made us sort of related. That doesn't mean we're friends, of course. Mom hasn't succeeded in making that happen, but I'm sure she hasn't given up.

Inviting Lurena and Dmitri to my birthday party was clueless, but inviting Dmitri on our summer trip to the lake goes beyond normal, everyday parental cluelessness. I'm furious.

"Are you *nuts*?" I yell. I know a person shouldn't yell at his mom, and deep down, I feel bad about it, but on the surface, where my mouth is, I'm too furious to stop myself. "You invited *Dmitri*? Are you *nuts*?"

Fido yelps and runs under my bed.

Mom seems genuinely surprised that I'm angry. Which, again, is shocking but unsurprising.

"How could you?" I'm still yelling. I'm also puffing hard through my nose, like a bull in a bullfight, or like Dad when I put recyclables in the regular garbage. "Don't you remember how mean Dmitri was at my birthday party?

Don't you know by now that I can't *stand* him?"

"I just thought . . . ," she starts to say.

"No, you didn't! You didn't *think*. You *couldn't* have!"

"You know, I'm going to come back when you're ready to talk about this respectfully . . ."

"Respect? You want to talk about *respect*? I'll talk about respect! Respect—"

"I'll come back," she interrupts, and edges toward the door. "Try to calm down. You're scaring Fido."

I growl. Not like a guinea dog. Like a lion. I'm a bull and a lion combined. I'm a savage lionotaur on a rampage. Look out, Mom.

She slips out, but before she pulls the door shut, she stops to flash a toothy, hopeful smile, like I'm an angry guard dog and she just stepped over the line into my territory. Then she says, "I kind of invited Lurena's family, too." And closes the door.

"WHAT?" I scream. The lionotaur pounces at the door, snorting, fangs bared. I pull it open with my claws. Mom is fleeing down the hall.

"I won't go!" I scream. "I won't! I'm not

going! I'm staying here! You hear me? *I'm not going!* I'll stay here alone! Just me and Fido!"

I hear whimpering from under the bed, and the fire of my anger fades, doused by guilt. I'm scaring the poop out of my guinea dog.

I kneel down and peek under the bed. She's there, curled up in the farthest corner, shivering.

"Did you hear that?" I whisper. "Mom invited Dmitri and Mars."

She shivers harder. She doesn't like them any more than I do.

"Unbelievable, right? She also invited Lurena."

Fido stops shivering. She wags her tail— well, she wags the spot where a tail would be if she had one. She likes Lurena okay, but, to her, Lurena means Queen Girlisaur, Fido's daughter.

I sit down on the carpet. This is over. Mom wins. Lurena and her rodents, and Dmitri and his giant puffball are coming on the trip. On top of that, I realize I have to apologize to Mom for yelling at her.

I hope one day I have kids. I'll let them have whatever pets they want, and whatever friends they want. I won't push anything they don't want on them, or deny them anything they do want.

Except cats, of course. I won't live with a cat. That's a no-brainer.

Fido scoots out from under the bed and jumps up into my lap. She gets up on her hind legs and looks me straight in the eye.

"Yeah," I say. "Queen Girly is coming on the trip."

She starts licking my face as if it were an ice-cream cone.

3. My dad needs a vacation.

But he doesn't like vacations. Especially camping trips. Does he have a single reason for this? No. He has a million reasons:

- His study is at home. (He works at home.)
- His kitchen is at home. (He does all the cooking.)
- His washing machine and dryer are at home. (He does the laundry.)
- His bed is at home.
- His bathroom is at home.
- He doesn't like driving.
- He definitely doesn't like driving far from home.
- He doesn't like sleeping in a crowded

pop-up camper without a decent kitchen, washing machine, dryer, or study.

- He doesn't like sleeping on a camper mattress.
- He doesn't like sharing a camper with a guinea pig.
- He doesn't like the way guinea pigs smell.
- He's not crazy about the way I smell.
- He says frogs and crickets keep him up all night.
- He hates mosquitoes.
- He despises ticks.
- He doesn't like cooking over an open fire.
- He doesn't like campout food, not even marshmallows.
- He doesn't like campfires.
- He doesn't like campfire smoke.
- He doesn't like that kids and dogs run around all the time, making lots of noise and going to the bathroom outside.
- He doesn't like swimming in lakes because they're filled with fish, snakes, turtles, dogs, and screaming, splashing kids.
- He doesn't like swimming in lakes because

fish, snakes, turtles, dogs, and kids go to the bathroom in lakes.

- He doesn't like camping in the summer because it's hot and humid, and there's no air-conditioning or even electric fans.
- There's also no Wi-Fi.
- There is nowhere to get a decent cappuccino.
- Porta-Potties.

He's been packing the car and the camper all day. He's like that. Everything has to go in just so. If Dad played video games (he doesn't), he'd love Tetris.

He's sweaty and grouchy, and I'd love to stay miles away from him, but Fido thinks that Dad's putting the stuff into the car and the camper, then taking the stuff out of the car and the camper is a game, so she keeps jumping into the car or the camper, then jumping out of the car or the camper with something Dad just packed. I have to hang around to make sure Dad doesn't kill her.

"Will you get this blasted creature out of

my way?" Dad says, without parting his teeth.

"I'm trying," I say.

"Why don't you put a leash on her and take her for a walk?"

"Okay," I say.

I get Fido's leash—it's actually a leash for a ferret—and click it on to her ferret collar.

"Come on, girl. Let's go for a walk."

Fido digs in. She doesn't want to walk. She wants to play with Dad.

I tug on the leash. She tugs back.

"She doesn't want to go," I say to Dad.

He gives me the Stony Stare. "Well, show her who is the boss."

"Right. Come *on*, Fido," I say, jerking the leash a little harder. She chokes.

I turn to Dad. "She—"

"Get her out of here!"

"Check," I say—forgetting that saying this annoys him—and bend down and scoop up Fido.

She whines.

"Sorry, girl, but Dad needs some space. How about a little Frisbee?"

She immediately stops whining and starts panting.

"Let's go out back," I say, and carry her around to the backyard.

The Frisbee is lying in the grass. It has tons of tiny teeth marks in it. I unhook Fido's leash and toss the disc into the air. She runs it down, makes a sweet aerial catch, then drags it back to me.

"Good one," I say, and scratch her on the head. She pants. She wants me to throw it again.

I do, again and again, and she catches it each time and brings it back. She could do this all day, but I get tired of it and sit down on the grass. She runs over to me and hops up and down. She doesn't want me to quit. Where does she get all this energy?

Funny, that's what my mom always says about me.

"We're going to have some vacation," I say to her. "With Dmitri. And Lurena. And Dad."

I roll my eyes.

"At least Murphy will be coming."

Fido starts whining and clawing at my shirt. She looks up at me with her big puppy eyes and cocks her head to the side. It's hard to refuse.

"Okay," I say, standing up.

I toss the Frisbee for the fiftieth time, and she darts after it.

I'm glad she'll be coming, too.

4. I thought caravans had camels.

Not necessarily. Sometimes a caravan is just cars traveling together.

Our caravan (it's Dad's word, of course) is Mom's hybrid pulling our pop-up camper; Murph's dad's Jeep pulling the wooden teardrop camper Murph's dad built himself; Dmitri's parents' RV that's bigger than a school bus, which is pulling one of their SUVs; and Lurena's parents' hybrid, which isn't pulling anything. They have their dome tent packed in the hatch.

"Did you know they used a camel for Chewbacca's voice?" Murph asks.

He's riding with us on the way to the lake, and I'm riding with his family on the way back.

I'm a firm believer in saving the best for last. Murph's dad is very cool. Not only does he own a Jeep and build cool things like campers, but he doesn't ever think about recycling or vocabulary. He's a regular, dog-loving dad. Unlike mine.

Mine said Murph's perfect dog, Buddy, couldn't ride with us in our car.

"Who or what is Chewbacca?" Dad asks, which is a perfect example of how weird he is.

"He's a character in *Star Wars*, Art," Murph politely explains. Murph's nice to everyone, even dog-hating dads who dislike camping and don't know anything about *Star Wars*. "He's a Wookiee, which is this alien species that are really tall and furry but act pretty much like us. He has arms and legs, and sits and even operates a spaceship, but his face looks like a Maltese."

"Does he chew tobacco?" Dad asks.

Murph and I look at each other. Then Murph says with a laugh, "I never thought about that! You're so smart, Art!"

I hadn't thought of it, either. *Chewbacca* has

always just been the character's name, like my name is Rufus. It never meant anything more than that. I'm sort of proud that my dad came up with the connection.

I'm also impressed that Murph compared Chewbacca to a Maltese. It's true. Chewbacca does have a face like a lapdog. Plus he knows that they used a camel for his voice. I wish I had something smart to say.

"Did you know that camels don't actually spit at you?" Murph asks before I can come up with anything. "They vomit at you."

My mom peeks in her rearview mirror at us. She's driving. Dad's riding shotgun. "Really? That's so gross."

Murph may be a smart guy, but that doesn't mean you should trust the things he says. He not only loves fooling you with made-up facts, but he also fools you by saying things that sound crazy so that you accuse him of making it up, when actually they're totally true. Like when he claimed there were frogs that had claws and hair skirts. I didn't believe him. I should have.

"Spitting is shooting saliva from your mouth," Murph says. "But when a camel gets angry, it shoots digested food from one of its four stomachs. It pukes at you."

My mom glances at my dad.

"Oh, he's right," he says, nodding. "Though I don't know if I'd call it 'puking.' It's more like 'regurgitating.'"

For once, it's good to have Dad around. Murph could have kept me going on that one for a long time.

In fact, I should probably doubt the part about Chewbacca's voice being a camel's, but instead of giving Murphy the satisfaction of knowing I'm not sure, I change the subject.

"Mom, you're letting Dmitri's dad pass you again," I say.

The Sulls' giant RV roars past us. It's like a gray whale on wheels. A gray whale towing an SUV. Fido stands up in my lap and scratches at the window.

"It's not a race, Rufus," Mom says.

She's wrong, of course. Everything is a race, or can be if you let it. Dmitri and his dad want it to be. They like being the best.

"Dmitri just texted me," Dad says. "It says, 'NYAAH NYAAH!' All in caps."

"Aren't you glad you invited them, Mom?" I ask.

"The more the merrier!" Murph blurts out, totally missing my sarcasm.

Mom smiles at him in the rearview mirror. "Well put, Murphy!"

I may spit like a camel.

"Another text," Dad says, looking at his phone. "It says, 'Rotten egg!!!' Are three exclamation points ever necessary?"

In the mirror, I see Mom's eyes narrow. She flicks on her turn signal.

"We'll see who's a rotten egg!" she says, and guns the motor.

5. We don't rest in the rest area.

We spend our break trying to keep our pets from eating one another.

Most of the terrorizing is done by the puffball. What a demon dog Mars is. Question: What sort of dog has a black tongue? Answer: an evil one.

First thing Mars does is chase Queen Girlisaur up a tree. Good thing Queen Girly is so fast.

"Dogs are supposed to be kept on leashes," Lurena scolds Dmitri, pointing at a sign that says so.

"Whatever, *girl*," Dmitri says.

"She's right," I say. He's so mean that I even end up defending Lurena. "You should leash your puffball, Dmitri, before it kills someone."

Mars stops barking up the tree and turns on Fido, who is angry and nipping at the beast's heels.

"Uh-oh," Dmitri says with a grin.

I'm not worried. Fido can hold her own with Mars. She's done it before. She barks her little head off and snarls with her teeth bared.

Buddy bounds over and gets in between them. Mars adores Buddy, kind of like Dmitri loves Murphy, but Buddy isn't all that inter-ested. She came over to defend Fido. Eventually, the puffball calms down, gives in, then the three of them run off, playing. Dogs are like that.

"You're lucky Mars didn't eat your precious little guinea dog," Dmitri says.

Dmitri is not a dog. He never calms down, or gives in, or plays nice.

He looks at Lurena. "Or your precious little guinea squirrel."

"If Mars ate Queen Girly, I would eat Mars," Lurena says, and licks her lips.

I believe her. She's kind of scary sometimes.

Murphy comes out of his camper with two tennis balls.

"How about a game of Fetch?" he asks.

Dmitri smirks at me. "You're on, Murph!"

He thinks the two balls are for Buddy and Mars, and he's right. But after flipping one of them to Dmitri, Murph digs into his T-shirt pocket and pulls out a neon-green superball. He hasn't forgotten about Fido.

"Here, Buddy!" he calls. "Here, girl!"

Buddy stops what she's doing and gallops toward us, with Mars and Fido in hot pursuit. Murph hurls a tennis ball over Buddy's head, and, without breaking stride, she leaps up and catches it in her mouth. What a dog!

Dmitri throws his ball, and Mars jumps up, but it bonks him on the head.

Murphy tosses the superball to me.

"Here you go, Fido!" I say, and bounce the ball hard off the pavement. It flies up high in the air, so high I can barely see it.

Fido rushes over, then freezes, her head up, watching the ball like a center fielder waiting for a high fly. She gives a little bark as she waits for it to come down. When it does, she jumps up, timing her leap perfectly, and catches the little green ball in her mouth, her plump body twisting in midair. She doesn't land gracefully, probably because she's so plump and her legs are so short, but she's not hurt. She springs to her feet and carries me the ball as if it's a trophy.

"Great catch, girl!" I say.

"She's amazing!" Murphy adds, and slaps me on the back. "Best guinea pig in the whole world!"

"She is something special," Lurena says. "But I'm not sure she's the best." She picks an acorn out of the pocket of her long, frilly skirt. "Watch this." She looks up into the tree where the guinea squirrel is. "Here you go, Queen Girly!" And she underhands the nut up into the air.

Queen Girly fidgets a moment on her branch, as squirrels do, then darts toward the acorn, leaps, snatches it, and lands on a branch below.

"What an acrobat!" Murph says.

"Wow!" I gasp. I'm smiling. I guess I'm proud. Queen Girly's sort of my granddaughter.

"I want her," Dmitri says. "I'll pay you a hundred bucks for her, Lurena."

"No, you won't," she answers.

Dmitri huffs and stomps his foot. It's pretty funny. He's used to getting what he wants, and hates that neither Lurena nor I will give him our guinea pigs. He even went looking for the store where I got Fido—it was called Petopia—but it had closed up and moved away. So he went to a big chain pet store and bought a guinea pig. It didn't act like a dog. Or a squirrel. It acted like a guinea pig. He was very angry—which kind of goes without saying when it comes to Dmitri.

"Mars, come!" Dmitri yells at his dog.

The puffball whimpers. I don't think he wants to come. I wouldn't.

"Mars, *come*!" Dmitri yells again.

Mars backs away.

"You get over here NOW!" Dmitri shouts, and stomps toward his dog.

Mars drops the ball and runs.

Dmitri runs after him, hollering, "Stop! Heel! Mars, you better stop right now! I mean it! Stop!"

"I don't blame Mars," Lurena says. "I wouldn't stop. I'd keep running and running forever to get away from that creep." She shakes her head. "I can't believe your mom invited him, Rufus."

I look at her. I can't believe my mom invited either of them.

"It promises to be a fun trip," I say.

6. White Crappie Lake isn't as bad as it sounds.

It's actually pretty nice. It's surrounded by tree-covered hills. There's a small beach, and a floating pier, and rope swings for diving, and trails for exploring.

The lake is big enough for boats. We don't have a boat, but Murphy's family has a wooden skiff that Murph's dad made. Dmitri's family owns a speedboat, but, since the lake isn't big enough for speedboats, they didn't bring it. They did bring a couple of kayaks, which they hauled on top of the SUV. Dmitri told me they cost more than two thousand dollars each. Not that I asked. I'm looking forward to paddling around in Murph's rowboat. I doubt I'll get to paddle around in Dmitri's kayaks, and I'm fine with that.

The caravan pulls into the campground, Dmitri's RV first. I guess Dmitri's dad wants first pick of the sites available, and that we're rotten eggs. The sites all look alike to me. The four vehicles park side by side, Dmitri's, then Murphy's, then ours, then Lurena's.

Mom hooks us up to the utilities, then asks me to help her open our camper. Fido dives in and out of the camper while we do this.

"She is *so* cute!" my mom squeals.

Mom is different from Dad.

Dad unloads the folding chairs, the charcoal grill, the coolers, then starts setting up his "outdoor kitchen" on a picnic table.

Next door, Murphy and his dad unload their rowboat. His mom sets up the folding chairs and coolers and stuff. Murph's little sister, A.G., is sitting on one of the chairs wrapped in a blanket, no doubt claiming she has some terrible disease no one has ever heard of. That's why she didn't come out of the Jeep at the rest stop. Poor Murph. I'm so glad I don't have a sister.

And I'm so glad Murph is going to be my temporary next-door neighbor!

Lurena's mom and dad are setting up their dome tent while Lurena, their only child, talks to her pets. She's brought along her chinchilla, China C. Hill, her hamster, Sharmet, and, of course, Queen Girlisaur. The names she gives her pets are anagrams of the kinds of animal they are. For example, she mixed up the letters in *chinchilla* and got *China C. Hill. Queen Girlisaur* is a rearranged *Guinea Squirrel.* I like anagramming, too. It's one of the two things we have in common. The other is owning rodents. But I'm not into rodents the way Lurena is. I don't actually think of Fido as a rodent.

Lurena has decided to keep her rodents locked in cages at the campground because of what happened at the rest stop (Mars running around free), and because she worries about other animals living in the area: dogs, cats, raccoons, even bears. I hope we see bears. China C. and Sharmet seem worked up, but Queen Girly is going bananas. She's running around her cage and shaking the bars with her tiny fists. My guess is she wants to get out and climb some of the big trees all around us. I wonder if Lurena will let her.

Dmitri's dad pops out of their RV long enough to hook up the utilities. The rest of the family stays inside. That includes Dmitri's older brother, Austin. He didn't come out at the rest stop, probably because, one, he's thirteen and wouldn't want to hang out with a bunch of little kids like us, and, two, he was probably playing video games on the RV's giant flat-screen TV. That's what he's doing now. I can hear muffled gunfire and screams.

The Sulls' RV has not only a TV but also, according to Dmitri (I've never been inside it), a bathroom with a shower, a kitchen with a refrigerator and microwave, plus a washing machine and dryer. I don't think what Dmitri's family is doing is camping. It's more like staying in a mobile hotel room.

As I'm looking at the RV, wondering what they're all doing inside, a long, thin aluminum box attached to the vehicle opens and a blue-and-white-striped awning starts automatically coming out of it. The awning is attached to two struts that hold it up as it unspools.

Right then the side door bursts open and bangs against the side of the RV. Dmitri runs out, wearing only a bathing suit that goes below his knees. It's bright red with a pattern of inky black pictures of angry-looking sharks with their jaws open wide.

"Murph!" he yells, looking right through me, "time for a swim!"

"Shut the door!" his mom's voice yells from inside. "The air-conditioning's on!"

7. "Coatimundi!"

That's what Murphy yells before he lets go of the rope swing and plunges into the lake.

We've been yelling this ever since Murph gave me a tail on a stick for the new bike I got for my birthday. He claimed the tail was from a real coatimundi, an animal that looks like a skinny raccoon and lives in South America, Central America, and southwestern North America. (Never trusting Murphy's stories, I looked it up, and it turns out it's a real animal.) The tail isn't a coatimundi's, or a raccoon's, of course; it's fake. Who sells real animal tails?

Anyway, the word *coatimundi* works real well when you go flying over bike ramps and other kinds of jumps. It's kind of like *Cowabunga!* or *Geronimo!*

When Murph comes out of the water, he hugs himself and shivers.

"Is it cold?" I ask, not seriously. I know it's cold. White Crappie Lake is always cold.

"No," he says, his teeth chattering. "It's like bathwater! Come on in!"

What a con man.

Buddy bounds into the water after him.

"See?" he says. "Buddy's not cold!"

"Buddy has a fur coat," I say.

Fido dives in and dog-paddles after Buddy. I knew Fido could swim. She once fell through a sewer grate and didn't drown (obviously).

"Fido's not cold!" Murph laughs.

"She also has a fur coat."

"I'm not afraid of cold water, Murph!" Dmitri says, and catches hold of the rope.

"I didn't say I was afraid," I say. "I just asked if it was cold."

Mars runs around Dmitri, barking and snapping.

"Back off, Mars!" Dmitri yells at him.

Mars keeps circling.

"Stupid dog," Dmitri mutters, then swings

out over the water. "Cowamundi!" he hollers as he lets go.

No one gave him permission to use our private holler, but I don't mind, since he said it wrong.

He splashes into the water near Murphy.

"It's totally not cold!" he says, trying not to shiver. "Only wimps would think it was cold. Right, Murph?"

Mars runs into the water after him. He swims with his head up. It looks completely ridiculous, this fluffy dog head bobbing above the water.

"Your turn, Roof!" Murph yells.

"Yeah, come on!" Dmitri says. "Don't be a wimp!"

I walk over to the rope.

"Or *do* be a wimp," Lurena's voice says from behind me.

I jump. Not into the water. Just an inch into the air. "Where did you come from?"

"What do you care what Dmitri thinks of you?"

"I actually want to go in the water. I

was going to go in, then he butted in . . ."

"So go in, then."

"Would you like to go first?" I ask, holding out the rope to her.

I know she wouldn't. She's wearing lace-up boots and one of her long, frilly skirts. Is this her idea of camping attire?

"No, thank you," she says. "But I'm not a wimp."

"Neither am I."

"Look at him, Murph," Dmitri yells. "Trying to get a *girl* to go before him! Ha!"

"Do your best to land right on top of him," Lurena says behind her hand.

I smile, then pretend I didn't. I don't want Dmitri seeing me smiling at a girl.

I grip the rope to pull myself off the ground with both hands, back up a few steps, then pull myself up in the air. I stand on the big knot at the end of the rope and start swinging forward, first over the bank, then out over the water. It's fun. Really fun.

"Coatimundi!" I yell, correctly.

For a second, I see them all below me—

Murph, Buddy, Fido, Dmitri, Mars—then, before I've found an opening for me to land, I let go of the rope and belly flop onto Fido.

8. I have no idea how to give CPR to a guinea pig.

Surprisingly, neither does Lurena. But Fido's lying on the bank, not breathing, so I give it a try.

I roll her onto her back, and her mouth falls open. Her eyes are just staring. It's scary. She's soaked to the skin, like she was after she fell in the sewer and Murph and I doused her with a hose. She looks like a drowned rat. What if that's what she *is*?

"Give her CPR! Hurry!" Lurena says. She's soaking wet right down to her lace-up boots. She must have jumped in after I landed on Fido.

Queen Girly is chattering in her cage. Worried about her mom, I guess.

I've seen people giving CPR in movies and on TV shows lots of times. They use two hands and push real hard on a person's chest, which would be excessive when you're dealing with a rodent. I don't want to break her ribs. Or crush her flat. Instead, I set my fingertip where I think her heart is, and press. Nothing happens.

"Puff air into her mouth!" Lurena says.

"Yeah, blow into your rat's mouth." Dmitri laughs.

Lurena slaps him across the arm.

"Hey!" he says.

"Do it, Roof," Murph says. "Breathe into her mouth."

I lean down and place my mouth over Fido's snout. Her fur is bristly, even when wet. She feels cold. Shouldn't she be warm? She's a mammal, after all.

I don't want to explode her lungs, so I puff softly. Nothing happens.

"Harder!" Lurena says.

I puff harder. Nothing.

"More heart massage," she says.

I'm starting to feel real panic. It's like I have

a fever and I'm being stabbed with a thousand little needles in the back, neck, and scalp.

I press down on Fido's chest. She doesn't breathe. I press a bit harder. I puff in her mouth again.

"It's not working!" I shout. "What do I do?"

"Call the pet coroner?" Dmitri says. The creep is actually grinning.

Lurena slaps his arm again and tells him to shut up. I like her in situations like this.

I don't like situations like this.

I scoop Fido off the ground and hold her upside down. I shake her.

"Come on, girl—breathe! *Breathe!*"

She has to start breathing. She has to! If she doesn't, she'll—

"Give her a squeeze," a voice from above us says.

We all look up to see a boy lying on a branch on his stomach, his tan arms and legs dangling. His hair is jet-black.

"Who the heck are you?" Dmitri asks, but I don't care. I'm taking the kid's advice. I'll try anything.

I pick Fido up and squeeze her between my hands, like one of Dad's blue stress balls. Spittle comes out of her mouth, then grows into a bubble.

"Do it again!" Murph says.

I squeeze again, and the bubble pops. I feel Fido wiggle slightly and take a shuddery breath. She's alive!

"She moved!" I say.

"Hurray!" Murph cheers. Lurena claps rapidly.

I'm so relieved I might cry. I blink fast to wipe any tears away. Dmitri sees them anyway.

"Aw, Wufus is cwying ovew his widdew wat!"

"Do I need to slap you again?" Lurena asks.

His smirk turns to a sneer. "You better not!"

I cup Fido in my hands as if she's an egg.

"You all right?" I whisper.

She coughs a few times, then wriggles to her feet. Her tongue spills out. She pants.

"I'm so sorry. I didn't see you."

"I never saw a guinea pig swim," the boy in the tree says.

"That's not all she does," Lurena says, and winks at me.

"You saved her life," Murph says, then asks, "What's your name?"

"Pablo."

"Pablo?" Dmitri says with a snicker.

"Yes," Pablo says. "What's your name?"

"None of your business, *Pablo.*"

It's so like Dmitri to be rude at hello. How can he tell from here that Pablo is someone he won't like? Is it just his name? Names aren't our faults. They're our parents'. Besides, what's wrong with the name *Pablo*?

"I'm Murphy," Murph says. "And this is Rufus, and the one you saved is Fido."

"Hi," I say. "Thanks so much. I thought she was a goner."

Fido looks up at the boy and barks.

"I'm Lurena," Lurena says. "So you're camping here?"

"Uh-huh," the boy says. "We've been here a couple days. Me and my family."

"Does your family hang around in trees and spy on people, too?" Dmitri asks.

Is that it? He doesn't like Pablo because he's in a tree and spying? What's wrong with either of those things? I like doing both.

"That's Dmitri," Lurena says, scowling at him. "He follows us around, bugging us and being a jerk. Just ignore him."

"Is that your black chow chow?" Pablo asks him.

"He's not a 'chow chow,'" Dmitri says. "He's a chow, and you better be careful or he'll rip you up."

"Good thing I'm in a tree," Pablo says.

Murphy laughs. "He's right, you know, Dmitri. Technically, Mars is a chow chow."

Dmitri fumes but doesn't object. He's too interested in becoming Murph's best friend to object.

"Come on down, Pablo," Murph says. "Swim with us."

"Yeah," I say over Dmitri's groans. "The more the merrier."

9. Pablo doesn't swim.

He doesn't come out and say it, but it's obvious. Maybe he doesn't know how. Maybe he thinks the water is too cold. Maybe he's scared. But he doesn't get in the water.

"You don't want to jump from the rope swing, Pablo?" Murph asks.

He and I and Dmitri are back in the water with the dogs, including Fido. I'm proud of her for diving right back in after our collision.

"Or maybe swim out to the floating pier?" I suggest. "There's a diving board on it."

"No, thanks," Pablo says with his hands in the back pockets of his shorts. He came down from the tree and is standing on the shore with Lurena. He doesn't seem afraid. He seems relaxed.

"I bet he can't swim," Dmitri says, then laughs. "Can you believe that? A kid his age that can't swim?"

"Remember what I said about him," Lurena says to Pablo. "Would you like to see my pets? I have a guinea pig, too. She's Fido's daughter, in fact, and she acts just like a squirrel. Her name is Queen Girlisaur."

"The guinea squirrel should be mine!" Dmitri yells.

Which is his opinion, no one else's.

"Come on, Pablo," Lurena says. "I'll show you all my rodents. You can meet China C. Hill, my chinchilla. And Sharmet, my hamster . . ."

Her voice fades as she and Pablo walk away toward her family's tent.

"That kid's a dorkchop," Dmitri says. "Right, Murph?"

"Seems nice to me," Murph says. "Come on. Let's swim out to the pier."

He starts swimming, and Dmitri and I splash after him.

"Last one there's a rotten egg!" Dmitri yells.

Again with the rotten egg.

"How could an egg swim?" I ask.

"They can't. That's why they lose!"

"What are you if you're the first one there? A fresh egg?"

"Shut up and swim."

I can't decide if I want to try to beat him to the pier or drop back and take my time. I don't like competing with him. I don't like *being* with him.

I glance back and see the dogs swimming after us. Fido's moving pretty fast for such a little thing.

I decide to wait for them. Dogs don't call anyone rotten eggs.

When Fido catches up to me, she climbs up onto my back. I keep paddling as she settles on the base of my neck for a rest. I do the breaststroke so I won't knock her off.

"Rotten egg!" Dmitri says from the pier, when I finally arrive.

"I think he's a good egg," Murph says with a British accent. "A right good egg, 'e is."

Good old Murph.

I climb up the ladder with Fido on my

shoulder. Murphy and Dmitri lug their heavy, scrambling, soaking wet hounds up onto the pier. Mars looks ridiculous, with his puffy head sitting on top of his drenched body.

We start running off the diving board, doing cannonballs and flips. Murph pretends to walk off the end accidentally, yelping and flailing his arms and legs all the way to the water. I dive in to "save" him.

"I can't—blub!—I can't swim—blub, blub!" he shouts, saying the word *blub* as if he's reading it from a book.

"Like Pablo, right, Murph?" Dmitri says, then bounces high off the board and, instead of diving into the water, belly flops with a loud *THAP!*

When he comes back up, his face is red.

"Didn't hurt at all," he says, grimacing.

"Glad to hear it," I say.

Then the dogs dive in.

I'm having a good time.

10. Dad doesn't like *hot* dogs, either.

He says he doesn't trust them. There's no telling where the meat comes from, he says. They're filled with nasty chemicals and dyes. They're slimy.

Here are some other normal cookout foods Dad doesn't trust:

- Cheeseburgers (mad cow disease)
- Potato chips (deep-fried foods are fatty and contain too much sodium)
- Potato salad (mayonnaise goes bad in the sun)
- Pork and beans (more weird meat)
- Soda (way too much sugar)
- Marshmallows (all sugar)

- S'mores (marshmallows and chocolate, so double sugar)

For dinner, he sets out weighty, whole-wheat buns, slices of tasteless soy cheese, and brown—not yellow—mustard. When I walk up, he opens the grill, scrapes a big mushroom off the grate, and offers the sweaty, blackened thing to me.

Fido jumps up onto the picnic table, sniffing the air. When she smells the mushroom, she turns up her nose.

I've been swimming all afternoon. I'm tired, sunburned, and, most of all, starving. I don't want a fungus.

"Seriously?" I say to Dad. "A mushroom? At a cookout?"

"You want something else?" he asks.

"What else you got?"

"Grilled eggplant and grilled yam wedges. They're better than French fries, believe me."

I don't believe him, and I can't believe this is his idea of a cookout. Eggplant? Come on!

"Hey, Roof!" Murphy calls from over by

the campfire. We have one big community fire for all four families. "Let's roast us some dogs!"

He holds up a package of hot dogs and two sharpened sticks. He knows what my dad considers food. He's bailing me out.

Fido dives off the table and zooms over to him. It may be the fastest I've ever seen her run. I follow after her.

"No offense, Art!" Murph calls to my dad. "I'm sure your dinner is delicious!"

Dad waves his spatula. "None taken."

Nobody can ever be sore at Murphy Molloy.

"Thank you, thank you, thank you!" I say as I take a stick. "The guy made grilled mushrooms and eggplant, if you can believe it."

"Eggplant? Wow. Your dad's one in a million."

"Yeah. I won the lottery when I got him."

Murph elbows me and laughs. "Here, take a dog."

I do. It's pretty slimy, before you roast it, that is. I poke it with my stick, then Murph and I sit with our dogs in the fire. What's better than roasting hot dogs over a campfire? Not much.

Fido scampers around my feet, whining.

"No begging," I say. "I'll give you one in your bowl."

"Aw, here," Murph says, holding out the hot dog package. "Give her one. It's a campout."

He's right. We're cooking outside with dirty sticks over an open flame. We're going to eat dinner outside. This is no time for house rules.

I take out a dog and hand it to Fido. She snatches it in her paws and starts gnawing on it. Guinea pigs don't usually eat meat, but Fido's not your usual guinea pig.

Lurena walks up with a plate. "Mind if I sit down?" she asks.

Yes.

"Not at all," Murph says. "What have you got there?"

"A portobello sandwich and some grilled veggies, courtesy of Art. The man's a wizard with a grill." She nibbles a yam wedge. "Mm, just scrumptious!"

"They do look good," Murph says. "Can I try one?"

Is he serious?

"Absolutely," Lurena says. "They're much better than French fries."

Is she serious?

"Would you like one, Rufus?" she asks.

"You should, Roof," Murph says, chewing one. "They're tasty."

Tasty is not a word he would use if he liked the yam wedge.

"Thanks, no," I say. "Saving room for about a hundred hot dogs."

Dmitri walks up. What's better than a wienie roast with Lurena and Dmitri? A wienie roast without them.

"What's up, Murph?" he asks, then squeezes between us on the log. He's holding a stick with a giant hot dog pierced on it. I've heard of a foot-long dog before, but this one's a foot and a half, and three inches thick. It's like a rolling pin made of meat. I'm jealous.

"Rufus just said he could eat a hundred hot dogs," Murph says.

"Yeah?" Dmitri says. "I could eat two hundred."

"If you do, I'll give you Queen Girly," Lurena says.

"You're on!" Dmitri says.

Murph says, "You know, I read online just yesterday that the world record for eating hot dogs, with buns, is sixty-eight. This kid named Chestnut won."

"His name was *Chestnut*?" I ask.

"It was his last name. Something Chestnut."

Yeah, right.

"I could do that easy," Dmitri says. "Except that the hot dogs my mom buys are so ginormous."

"I'll trade with you," I say.

"Excellent solution!" Murph says. "Trade with Roof. And don't worry, we have plenty more normal-size hot dogs. I think my mom brought a dozen packages. That's like, what? Two hundred dogs?"

Murph's not so hot at math. I had to tutor him so he didn't fail it this year. He didn't fail it.

"Eight in a package," I say, "times twelve. That's ninety-six dogs, Murph."

"Well, that's still plenty."

"Why don't I trade with *you*, Murph?" Dmitri asks.

Obviously, he doesn't want to give his monster dog to me.

"Because I'll be competing right alongside you!" Murph says.

"And I won't be," I say.

Dmitri shakes his head slightly. "Figures. Chicken."

"No, not chicken. I just don't feel like stuffing myself with hot dogs till I puke."

I swap sticks with him. Considering the size of the thing now at the end of my stick, I will be stuffing myself with hot dogs after all.

"Thanks," I say. "Good luck breaking the record."

"I won't need luck," he grunts. "I have skill."

"Well, good skill, then."

11. Dmitri can't keep the sixth one down.

Then the other five start coming back up. He runs off to the woods to take care of that.

The giant hot dog he gave me, by the way, was delicious.

"So he doesn't get Queen Girly after all," Lurena says, smiling.

"He came so close," Murph says.

"He ate five," I say. "The record's sixty-eight. That's close?"

"You didn't let me finish. What I was going to say was 'He came so close to puking all over us.'"

"Thank goodness he didn't," Lurena says.

"What happened to Dummy?" a voice says behind us.

We turn around. Dmitri's brother, Austin, is walking toward us.

"Who's Dummy?" Lurena asks. "Do you mean Dmitri?"

"Yeah, I've always called him Dummy. Like, short for Dmitri?"

Austin is taller and skinnier than Dmitri, but they're definitely brothers. Austin has the same sharp nose and chin, and mean mouth.

"Funny," Lurena says sarcastically.

"Thanks," Austin says. "So why'd Dummy go running off to the woods? He got the runs? Get it? Running because he has the runs?"

"Also funny," Lurena says with an eye roll.

"Are you Dummy's girlfriend?" Austin asks.

"Now, that's *not* funny," Lurena says, and stands up. "Excuse me." She walks away.

"Wow," Austin says. "She's cool. Cool as a campfire. Right?" He snorts.

"Good one," I say. I don't know why. It wasn't. In fact, I'm not even sure I get it.

"Let's go find Pablo," Murph says, saving me.

"Yes, let's," I say.

"Who's Pablo?" Austin asks.

"A new friend of ours," Murph says.

"Well, give me the hot dogs before you go, dude," Austin says, pointing at the package on the log between Murph and me.

"There's only one left, but it's all yours, Awesome Austin," Murph says, and hands the package to him.

Austin laughs. "That's good, man. 'Awesome Austin.' I never thought of that. Nice work, dude." He slaps Murph on the shoulder.

Everyone likes Murph. Sometimes I wonder if that's a good thing.

We go looking for Pablo's camp. The night is warm and clear. Stars peek through the treetops, and fireflies float around us like little stars. The campground smells of smoke, meat, and citronella. People are gathered around fires, talking and laughing, or are inside tents with lanterns, their silhouettes fluttering. Kids are running around with flashlights, whispering and giggling, looking for animals or ghosts. Dad doesn't know what he's talking about: camping is great.

We don't see Pablo anywhere, so Murph calls out his name, cupping his hands around his mouth. Does that really make your voice carry farther? I try it with cupped hands, then without, and realize there's no way for me to tell.

"I'm over here," Pablo answers.

We find him reading with a flashlight on a lounge chair outside a gigantic white RV. It's bigger than Dmitri's. Sections of it slide out like big dresser drawers, which make it even bigger. The lights are all on inside.

"This your rig, Pablo?" Murph asks.

Pablo looks confused, then realizes what Murph means. "Yeah, it's ours."

"Does it have a spa?" Murph asks.

"A spa?"

"Kidding," Murph says with a laugh. "Want to come over to our campfire and roast s'mores with us?"

I'm sure glad Mom invited Murphy's family. Otherwise, we wouldn't have marshmallows, not to mention s'mores.

Pablo looks down at his book, like he's torn

between s'mores and reading. Is that really a choice?

"Uh...sure," he says. "Let me tell my parents I'm going."

He opens the door and steps up into the RV. We hear him inside saying something in another language (I think Spanish), then we hear a woman (probably his mom) answer in the same language. Then he comes back out.

"Okay. Let's go."

"What were you reading?" I ask as we walk.

"*Twenty Thousand Leagues Under the Sea,*" Pablo says.

"Is it good?" Murph asks.

"Really good."

"What's it about?" I ask.

"In the beginning, everybody thinks some monster is attacking all these ships at sea, but they're wrong. You want me to spoil it for you?"

"No," we both say.

"The writing is sort of old-fashioned. Like *Treasure Island*. Did you ever read that one? It's about pirates."

"I've read it," Murph says. "You know, for a

kid who doesn't like water, you read a lot of books about the sea."

Pablo shrugs.

"I brought a rowboat," Murph says. "Do you want to go out in it with us tomorrow? It seats three."

"No, thanks," Pablo says. He kicks a rock. "I like reading about boats and stuff, but I'm not so into being . . . *in* them."

"Do you know how to swim?" I ask.

It gets quiet a moment, then Murph says, "Let's get some s'mores before my sister devours them all. The girl's a marshmallow *fiend*."

Pablo looks back over his shoulder. "So is my sister. Plus, she taps on my aquariums all the time. Which drives me crazy."

Another quiet moment.

"Aquariums?" I finally ask. "Plural?"

Before Pablo can answer, Murph yells, "S'mores!" and takes off running.

We follow him.

12. Solar energy from the moon.

That's what Murphy claims scientists are currently working on.

"They want to put up solar panels all over the moon's surface," he says. "Just cover the whole moon with them."

We're sitting on the beach—Murph, Pablo, Buddy, Fido, and me—looking up at the moon, which is a little less than full. Even so, it's lighting up the lake like a giant flashlight.

"How will they get the energy to Earth?" Pablo asks.

"That's the tricky part," Murph says. "They're thinking very long extension cords."

Pablo and I groan.

"What?" Murph says.

"It's a long way to the moon," I say. "Really long."

"Two hundred thirty-eight thousand nine hundred miles," Pablo says.

Murph and I look at him.

"That's the average distance, of course," Pablo says. "It changes during the course of the moon's orbit. It's closer at the perigee and farther at the apogee."

"How do you know all this?" I ask him.

"I don't know," he says. "I just do."

"It wouldn't work even if the scientists did have extension cords that long, because both the Earth and the moon are spinning," I say. "The cords would get all tangled up."

"I'm just telling you what I heard," Murph says. "Read, actually. In *National Geographic*."

I roll my eyes. "Don't believe him, Pablo. He's always making stuff up. It's his idea of fun."

"I only speak the truth," Murph says as he picks up a stick and hurls it down the beach. Buddy and Fido tear after it.

"I've never seen a guinea pig play Fetch," Pablo says. "Did you train her yourself?"

"No. She came that way. From the pet store."

"Did she cost extra?"

"My mom bought her, and I don't think she had any idea Fido acted like a dog."

"Which store? I wouldn't mind having one myself."

Murph laughs. "You and everyone else at our school!"

"So the store doesn't have any more?" Pablo asks.

"It's kind of a long story," I say. "You see, my dad wouldn't let me have a dog. . . . It's hard to believe, but he doesn't like dogs . . . so my mom bought me a guinea pig. My dad didn't like the guinea pig, either. . . . He doesn't like a lot of things . . . so he said we had to bring it back to the store. But the store wasn't there anymore. It had closed up and moved away."

"That's weird," Pablo says.

"Tell me about it. So then I discover Fido acts like a dog, and pretty soon word gets out, and everyone at school wants one . . ."

"Including me," Murph says.

"But especially Dmitri," I say. "Boy, does he want one!"

Right then Buddy starts growling.

"What is it, girl?" Murph calls out. "What do you see?"

"Isn't she just growling at Fido?" Pablo asks.

"It's a different growl," I say. I like that I can tell Buddy's growls apart. "It's an intruder growl. Must be another animal."

"Probably just a strange dog," Murph says.

We go over to check and hear a peeping sound, like a bird, then a splash. A sleek, dark animal swims away from the bank, its head above the water. Buddy barks, and it dives under the surface. A long, thick tail is the last thing we see.

"An otter," Murph says.

There are always otters at the lake.

Fido growls. She has the stick in her mouth. She beat out Buddy for it!

"Good girl!" I say, petting her head. I pry the stick out of her mouth and throw it. She and Buddy run after it.

"So Fido had a baby that acts like a squirrel?" Pablo asks.

"Yeah. She must have been pregnant when Mom bought her. It was weird, because I wanted a dog and got a guinea pig that acted like one, and Lurena wanted a squirrel and she got a guinea pig that acted like one."

"I like tropical fish," Pablo says. "I wonder what I'd get."

"No point in wondering, unless you can find a Petopia," Murph says.

"What's a Petopia?"

"Petopia is the name of the store where my mom bought Fido," I say. "But it disappeared."

"I think I saw one on the way here," Pablo says.

Murph and I gasp at the same time, then both say, "Where?"

"Jinx!" Murph says, then starts counting.

"Idaho Jinx," I say, and he stops. That's how we work jinxes.

"I'm not exactly sure," Pablo says. "It was in a mini-mall, I think. I saw a sign—"

"Was it far from here?" I ask. "Which way did you come from?"

"We live in Mechanicsburg. West of here."

"We came from Rustbury, which is the other way." I look at Murph.

"So we wouldn't have passed it," he says.

"Right. Are you sure it said Petopia? Not something else? There are lots of pet stores with really punny names . . ."

"Like Pawsitively Pets," Murphy says. "That's a pet store in Wheeling . . ."

"I'm sure," Pablo says. "In fact, I'm *paws*itive."

Murph laughs.

"I'll ask my parents to stop there on our way home," Pablo says. "I'll tell them I want to see what fish they carry."

"But the store will be gone by then!" Murph shouts. "We have to go sooner."

Whoa. I hadn't realized how much he wants a guinea dog. I don't know why he does. He has the best *actual* dog in the whole world.

"Maybe we could go tomorrow," I say. "We'd just have to talk someone's parents into taking us."

"I don't know if my mom or dad would want to go looking for a pet store," Murph says. "Maybe if I told them Pablo saw a Petopia . . ."

"Well, *my* dad won't do it," I say.

"How about your mom?" Murph says. "Wouldn't she be excited to find another Petopia?"

She might be at that. She's pretty pleased with herself for bringing home such a special guinea pig. I'm pretty pleased with her, too.

"I'll ask, but we'd have to sneak away without Dad seeing us."

"If you found the store, what sort of pet would you look for?" Pablo asks. "Another guinea pig?"

"I'd sure like one," Murph says.

"So would Lurena," I say.

"And Dmitri," Murph and I say together.

"Jinx," Murph says. "One, two, three . . ."

"Idaho Jinx," I say. "Listen, Pablo, we can't let Dmitri know you saw a Petopia, okay?"

"Why?" Pablo asks.

Why don't I want Dmitri to get his own guinea dog? Good question. Is it because his parents give him everything he wants? Because he's spoiled rotten and a big show-off? Because he bought a guinea pig and when it didn't act like a dog, he didn't want it anymore? Because he's mean and—

"Hey, Murph!" Dmitri calls from behind us. "What are you doing? I've been looking for you everywhere! Didn't you hear me calling? Why are you hanging out with these two losers?"

"That's why," I say to Pablo.

13. Adults, rodent cages, and a girl in a long skirt.

That's what Murph, Dmitri, and I find around the campfire when we return. None of them is my idea of fun.

What I want to do is have a word with my mom. I want to tell her about Petopia, but I don't want my dad, Lurena, or Dmitri to hear. Unfortunately, all the parents, plus Lurena, are sitting around the campfire. My mom loves parties, which is probably one of the reasons that she invited the other two families. I'm sure to her a campout is just an excuse for a big barbecue. I know she wanted to get to know Lurena's and Dmitri's parents better. Murph's she's known for years. Why wasn't she content with that?

When we walk up, she's in the middle of telling a story.

"So I put the can in the paint shaker..." Mom works in the paint department at a hardware store. "... Did I mention it was pink? That this man wanted pink paint? Did I say that?"

"You did, Raquel," Dad says without emotion. "You mentioned it thrice."

Dmitri's dad, Scott, is leaning back in his chair, smiling, one leg crossed horizontally over the other. He's shaking his foot like it's a dog's happy tail. I don't know what keeps his flip-flop from flying off. His wife, Carol, is not smiling. Her face is wearing a frown and an awful lot of makeup for a camping trip. She pretends to be listening to Mom's story, but mostly she keeps stealing looks at her phone. She's not wearing a watch. I think she's checking the time.

"Okay, *Art*," Mom goes on. "For the *fourth* time, it was pink...*so* pink...like a sunburned flamingo."

Scott laughs.

Carol doesn't.

"I can't imagine what they were planning to paint with it! Maybe a . . . a . . ."

"A baby's room?" Billie asks. Billie is Murph's mom. She's sitting next to my mom.

Murph's dad, Sam, is poking at the fire with a stick. I get the feeling he's the one who keeps it burning. He's good at useful things like that.

Lurena's parents are there, too. Her dad, Jimmy, has this habit of running his fingers through his very curly brown hair, which causes it to stand on end and make him look like a clown. Someone should tell him. His wife, Elaine, has straight blond hair that goes down to her waist, like Lurena's, only whiter. She doesn't wear old-timey clothes, though. She's wearing normal clothes, including a white T-shirt with words on it. Her hair hides most of the letters, so I can't read what it says.

Both of them are pretty normal, unlike their daughter. I wonder where she gets the weirdness from. Then again, my parents are both weird, and I turned out normal. Where did

I get my normalness from? Maybe weirdness and normalness aren't passed down, like eye color is.

Lurena is sitting on the ground between her parents' chairs, peering in through the bars at her pets and talking to them in a high voice. I can't make out what she's saying over my mom's loud story, which is a relief.

"But this isn't baby-room, pastel pink," Mom says. "This is *hot* pink. Anyway, I put the paint can in the shaker and I . . ." She laughs into her palm. "I was *positive* I'd hammered the lid on good and tight. I mean, I shake hundreds of cans of paint a day. I *never* forget."

"No!" Scott says.

"I can see where this is going!" Billie says.

"So—*splat!*" Mom says, spreading her fingers really fast.

Everyone but Dad and Carol laughs. Dad's heard it before. Carol is doing something on her phone.

"Luckily, the Plexiglas door was shut, but it was instantly painted hot pink, and then paint oozed out from around the edges. It looked like Pepto-Bismol. It took a full hour to clean it all up."

Jimmy asks, "So you mixed them up another can of pink paint?"

Mom says yes by lifting her eyebrows. "We have two shakers."

Everybody nods.

Her story is over. I'm hoping someone else will tell the next one, so I can steal her away.

"That's a sweet canoe you got there, Sammy," Jimmy says to Murph's dad, whose name is Sam, not Sammy.

"It's a skiff," Sam says. "But thanks."

Dmitri's mom sighs aloud, then stands up. "I'm ready to turn in. Good night, all." She walks away.

"Can I have more s'mores, Mom?" Dmitri calls after her.

"Whatever," she says, without turning around.

Dmitri starts putting one together.

"How about me, Mom?" Murph asks Billie. "Can I have s'more s'mores?" He beams at her.

"How many have you had?" she asks.

"One?"

More like six.

"Okay, but only one more," his mom says.

Everyone lets Murph slide. Especially his mom.

I look at my mom. She looks at my dad. I look at my dad. I don't have to ask. It's n'more s'mores for me.

"I need to marinate some vegetables for breakfast," Dad says, and leaves the circle.

Here's my chance.

I jump into his seat and whisper in Mom's ear, "I need to tell you something."

"Okay," she says. "What is it?"

I look around the circle. Nothing like whispering to get everyone's attention.

Murph holds up a stick he has stuck about eight marshmallows on.

"One more s'more!" he says with a laugh.

This distracts everyone long enough for me to tell my mom what Pablo saw.

14. The only way to get one off you is to chop off its head.

That's how the story always goes. The beast sleeps at the bottom of the lake or pond, waiting, then you come by and—*chomp!*—it bites down on your ankle and refuses to let go, no matter what you do. You can drag it out of the water and beat it with a stick, and it won't let go. You can't pry its jaws open with a crowbar. The only thing you can do is cut off its head.

It's an old story, one I've heard all my life: the story of the giant alligator snapping turtle in the lake (or pond). And I'm hearing it again, this time from Dmitri.

"You're smart to stay out of the water,"

Dmitri says to Pablo. "You don't want one of those things to get you."

We've all come down to the beach to launch the boats. Dmitri's dad and brother are in the two kayaks, paddling away. Murph and his dad are carrying the skiff into the water. Buddy's swimming around them. Fido's chasing Buddy. Dmitri, Pablo, Lurena, and I are sitting together on the bank.

"It happened to a friend of mine back in Irondale," Dmitri says.

Dmitri moved to Rustbury this year, from Irondale, which, according to him, was better than Rustbury in every way possible. I guess having confirmed alligator-snapping-turtle attacks is another example.

"I think turtle attacks are just urban myths," Pablo says. "Did you actually see the turtle's head after they chopped it off?"

"No," Dmitri says, rolling his eyes. "The doctors didn't *keep* it. They destroyed it. That's what they do. Don't you know anything?"

"I know some things," Pablo says. "I

know when someone is making stuff up, and when he's being insulting."

Lurena and I laugh.

Dmitri's face turns red.

A bunch of ducks squawks suddenly and starts flapping out onto the lake. It's Fido. She can't leave ducks alone.

"Fido, come!" I say.

"You really should keep her on a leash," Lurena says. "They have signs up about it."

"They say to keep your *dog* on a leash," I say. "Fido's not a dog."

"She's frightening the wildlife."

Fido pads up to me, her tongue hanging out.

"Should I keep her in a cage?" I ask as I bend down to pet her.

The ducks settle down and float peacefully on the water. Then Mars woofs and plunges in. The ducks squawk again and flap and splash.

"That one should definitely be on a leash," Lurena says.

"He's on vacation, too," Dmitri says. "I'm not going to put him on a leash." He stands up. "Hey, Murph! You ready for me?"

I don't know why he thinks Murph is going to let him go instead of me. Murph and I are best friends, and have been since kindergarten. Dmitri can wait for one of the kayaks.

But then I think about Pablo, staying here on the shore with Lurena and the cages. Plus, I want to tell him what my mom said.

"Roof's going first!" Murph calls back.

Good old Murph.

"It's okay," I say. "I'll wait."

Dmitri smacks my arm with the back of his hand. "Thanks," he says, then adds, "sucker!"

He runs into the water toward the skiff, Mars on his heels.

"You didn't have to stay with me," Pablo says.

"I know." I glance at Lurena. I don't want her to know about Petopia. "So what do you like to do here, since you don't go into the water?"

"I look for shells and stuff," he says, "to put in my aquariums."

"How many aquariums do you have?" Lurena asks.

"Three," he says.

"Big ones?" I ask.

"Two are just twenty-gallon tanks. One is a thirty-gallon hexagonal."

"Do you have any sharks?"

"A couple."

"Cool. Let's go look for some shells and stuff," I say, hoping Lurena won't want to join us.

"I know a good spot," she says.

Of course she does.

15. Lurena the Pest.

That's what I'd call a book about her.

She shows up places uninvited. She invites herself. And she won't leave, no matter what I say. Here are some examples of what I've said in the past:

- "I was just heading out."
- "Murphy's coming over."
- "I have a ton of homework to do."
- "My dad says I have to mow the lawn."
- "I have a terrible headache."
- "I have laryngitis." (I wrote this down.)
- "I have mad cow disease."
- "Fido is a carrier of rodent flu."
- "A guy's coming over with his pet grizzly bear that eats girls."

- "Our house is being demolished today, so . . ."
- "I think I'm allergic to you."
- "I'm going to throw up."
- "I think you need to leave now."
- "Leave, Lurena. Now!"
- "Just *go* already!"
- "I'm calling the police if you don't leave."
- "Get lost!"
- "OUT!"

She doesn't take hints very well.

She leads Pablo and me to the spot she talked about. It's a small, rocky beach. We start poking around for shells.

"What do you like about fish?" Lurena asks Pablo.

"I don't know," he says.

"Do you like that they're so sparkly and colorful and pretty?"

Like that's what a boy would like about anything.

"Sure," he says.

He's just being agreeable.

"Do you like their big eyes and their big kissy mouths?"

That's too much!

"Seriously?" I say. "'Kissy mouths'? Pablo is a boy, Lurena."

"What does that mean? Boys can't appreciate a kissy mouth?"

"I just like watching them," Pablo says. "They make me feel calm."

"Yes," Lurena says. "They are calming. And serene. And tranquilizing. *So* tranquilizing."

"What are you, a thesaurus?" I ask.

"Why do you like rodents?" Pablo asks her.

"Oh, for so many reasons, Pablo. Thanks for asking. They're soft and furry, of course. And adorable. And cute. And cuddly. And—"

"Thesaurus," I say under my breath.

"And they're loyal. *So* loyal. My rodents *love* me."

I guess someone has to.

"And they talk to me. They tell me they love me."

"They *tell* you?" I ask.

"Of course they do!"

"What are they saying now?" Pablo asks.

She leans over her hamster's cage.

"They say they love me oodles and oodles."

"I'm going to throw up," I say.

"Doesn't Fido talk to you?" Lurena asks.

"Nope. My guinea pig doesn't speak to me. Isn't that strange?"

"Maybe she doesn't love you." She winks.

I stay calm. Serene. Tranquil.

"I think I hear your mom calling you," I say.

"I think I hear Queen Girly calling her mom," Pablo says.

True, the guinea squirrel is whining in her cage, and Fido is running around it, also whining.

"Can't you let her out for a while?" Pablo asks Lurena.

"She might run up a tree. There might be raccoons in the tree," Lurena says, still poking through the rocks. "Here's a good one, Pablo." She holds out a shell to him.

Fido grips the bars of Queen Girly's cage and shakes them.

"Maybe you could let Fido *in*," Pablo suggests.

Lurena thinks about this, then says, "Okay. But help me. I don't want Queen Girly escaping."

We huddle around the cage in case the guinea squirrel tries to make a break for it, while Lurena unlatches the cage door and opens it a crack. Queen Girly does try to get out, just as Fido scrambles to get in. With some effort, Lurena is able to push Fido in, then relock the door.

"What's Queen Girly saying now?" Pablo asks.

Lurena cups her ear. "She says, 'Thanks, Lurena. I love you so much!'"

Oh, brother.

16. 2 guys + 2 dogs + 1 skiff = fun x 5 trillion.

Especially when the guys are Murphy and me and the dogs are Buddy and Fido.

Lurena stays with Pablo.

"I couldn't get rid of her," I say to Murph as I row. "She just sticks to me like glue. Like barnacles, more like. Lurena's a barnacle."

Murph laughs. "I'll get her to come out in the skiff with me. She can even bring her cages. The more the—"

"It isn't merrier to me to have Lurena around. It isn't even merry. But I'm sure you'll have a merry voyage with her and her rodents."

He laughs again. I don't know what he finds funny, but his laughing makes me laugh, too. He has that effect on people. It's hard to stay grouchy around him, even when you want to.

He lies back, his arms bent at the elbows, his hands in the water.

"Ahhhhh!" he says. "This is the life, ain't it, Tom?"

"It ain't bad, Huck," I answer. I read the book *Tom Sawyer* this year after Murph recommended it. He's like Pablo: he likes old books. The characters in the book spoke funny, but I got used to it.

"We should just drift away forever," he says. "Drift all the way downriver to Jamaica and lay in the sun all day, eating coconuts."

"Sounds like heaven, Huck," I say. "But this here's a lake, not a river."

"Well, it ain't bad here, neither."

"No, it ain't."

"Paddle us 'round the lake a couple times, will you, Tom? That'd be ever so kind of you."

"It'd be my pleasure, Huckleberry."

"Let me know if you spot any alligators or snappy turtles, and I'll help you wrassle 'em."

"Will do. Say, Huck, ain't those ducks over there poisonous?"

Murph once tried to persuade me that a flock of poisonous ducks had landed in our town. I didn't believe him, but I did go to our local lake with him, just to check. There were ducks on it, but they weren't poisonous.

Murph sits up, shades his eyes. "Where, Tom?"

I point to a flock of ducks floating off, starboard side.

Fido, who'd been curled up in the hull with Buddy, napping, perks up. She rushes up onto my lap, sets her paws on the gunwale, barks, then dives into the lake and starts swimming in the direction of the ducks. The ducks quack and scatter.

"That's a fine bird dog you got there, Tom."

"Thanks, Huck."

Buddy, seeing Fido jump overboard, gets to her feet and growls.

"Easy there, girl," Huck . . . I mean Murphy . . . says. "Don't rock the boat now . . ."

But Buddy does rock the boat. She rises up on her hind legs, sets her forepaws on the gunwale, and woofs a big *woof*. What a dog!

Then her hind legs start scrambling around the hull, trying to find a foothold, and the boat starts rocking. Before Murph can tell her to sit, her paws slip off the gunwale, she falls hard onto her chest, the boat tips, Murph and I fall over sideways, and we capsize. The boat lands upside down over us. Buddy sniffs and paws at the outside, whimpering. We reach up and grab hold of the bench seats.

"Thought I might go for a swim, Tom," Murph says, grinning.

"Thought I'd join you, Huck," I say.

Fido pops up out of the water between us, soaked to the skin. She looks at Murph, then twists around and looks at me.

"Your bird dog is here to rescue us, Tom," Murph says.

"Yup, she sure is, Huck."

17. Tom Sawyer dries off in the gigantic RV.

He changes into some of Pablo's clothes in the master bedroom, then Pablo's mom puts Tom's clothes in the dryer.

"This place is amazing," I say.

Pablo's RV is like Dmitri's: it has the washer and dryer, a bathroom, a fridge, a microwave, and a big flat-screen TV. It's like a mobile hotel room. I guess Pablo's family has a lot of money, too. But Pablo acts a lot differently from Dmitri. A *lot* differently.

We're sitting at the kitchen table, which is in the part of the RV that slides out. His mom puts a bowl of tortilla chips and a plastic container of salsa on the table. Fido sits on the floor, begging.

"Quiet!" I say to her.

She stops whining.

"Thank you, Mrs. . . ."

"Covarrubias," she says.

It's pretty, but I can't say it. I smile instead.

"You can call her Yolanda," Pablo says.

"*Sí*," she says, with a big smile. "Yolanda."

Pablo pronounced it, *Yo-lan-da*, but she said, *Jo-lan-da*.

"Thank you, Yolanda," I say, with a *y* sound, since I don't speak Spanish.

She nods, then speaks to Pablo in Spanish. He nods and answers in Spanish. Then she goes outside.

"It's cool you speak Spanish," I say.

"Thanks," he says. "My parents were born in Mexico. I was born in Mechanicsburg. My sister, too. My parents don't speak very much English. Most of their friends and co-workers speak Spanish. My sister and I speak it to them, too. So they don't learn English."

"So it's cool you speak English, too," I say. I feel like the things I'm saying are sort of stupid. None of my friends speaks another language, so this is new to me.

"Yeah," Pablo says.

We quietly eat a few chips. That is, we don't talk; you can't eat tortilla chips quietly. The salsa turns out to be very hot. Pablo gobbles it up anyway. My lips are on fire.

Fido whines again.

"Can I give her one?" I ask Pablo.

He says, "Sure," so I drop a chip—without salsa—on the floor. Fido crunches it.

"We'd better get going," I say, "while Murph and Lurena are still in the skiff."

After we got the boat upright, I came here with Pablo. Murph insisted he didn't need to dry off, but I claimed I did. I really just wanted to talk to Pablo without Lurena around. Then Murph persuaded Lurena to ride in the boat with him. He can persuade almost anyone of almost anything.

"Let me see if I can go," Pablo says. "Wait here."

He goes out to where his mom and dad are sitting and speaks to his mom. She answers, then he returns.

"She says it's fine," Pablo says.

"What about your dad?"

"He didn't say anything, so it must be fine with him."

"It won't be fine with *my* dad. Somehow we'll have to get away without him knowing."

"Maybe Murphy can get him in the skiff, too."

"I doubt it. He's not really a skiff kind of dad."

"Neither is mine," Pablo says, peeking out the window. "He doesn't like water."

His dad is sitting in a lounge chair with a laptop. He's wearing a button-down, short-sleeve shirt; plaid shorts; and leather sandals. His hair is black, like Pablo's, and his skin is brown, too. But he reminds me more of my dad. A laptop on a camping trip. Please.

"Does your dad work in computers?" I ask.

"He's a programmer," Pablo says.

"My dad edits an online golf magazine," I say.

"We should introduce them."

"But your dad doesn't speak English, and mine doesn't speak Spanish."

"True. They could just stare at their laptops and not say anything. Like usual."

"Oh, my dad talks," I say. "He talks plenty."

Pablo laughs. As if it's funny.

"How about your mom? Does she like water?"

"Nope."

"Your sister?"

He shakes his head.

His whole family doesn't like water. I want to ask why, but it feels like it's none of my business. So I don't.

"Ready to go?" Pablo asks, standing up.

I stand up, too. "What about my clothes?"

"They won't be dry for a while. You can wear mine, if that's okay with you."

"It's okay with me if it's okay with you."

"It's okay."

"Okay," I say. "Let's go find Petopia."

18. Mosquitoitis.

That's A.G.'s latest disease. She's lying on a lounge chair by the Molloys' camper with a pained expression on her face.

In the lounge chair beside her is a girl I haven't seen before, but my guess is she's Pablo's sister. She looks like him: black hair, brown skin. She's wearing a bikini, though. And she's younger. Maybe A.G.'s age.

"Mosquitoitis," I say. "Is it serious?"

"I don't know. No Internet," A.G. says.

"Then how do you know you have it?"

"Oh, I know. I know." She coughs.

"I have it, too," the other girl says, and also coughs.

"This is my sister, Bianca," Pablo says. "She's a conformist."

"What's that?" A.G. asks.

"Someone who'll do anything to fit in."

"I think she's really sick," A.G. says.

"I am," Bianca says, and coughs again. She's getting better at it.

"I hope you two get better and have some fun," I say, then gesture to Pablo that we should keep moving.

"Don't lie around all day, Bianca," he says.

"Good-bye, Rufus," A.G. says. "Good-bye, Bianca's brother. Maybe I'll see you again! Then again, maybe not . . ."

"Good-bye, brother!" Bianca says in a sickly voice. "Bye, cute little dog!"

"It's a guinea pig, actually," I hear A.G. say as we walk away.

"I'm sure glad I don't have a little sister," I say as we walk up to my family's campsite.

"It's not so bad," Pablo says. "She copies everything I do, so we have a lot in common. It's irritating sometimes, I guess."

He guesses? That would drive me crazy.

"Pssst, Rufus!" my mom hisses. She's bent

down behind the hybrid, peeking over the hood. "Over here!"

Pablo and I run around the car and crouch down. Fido follows.

"Where's Dad?" I whisper.

"He went for a stroll."

A stroll is what my dad calls a walk.

"I unhitched the camper," Mom whispers. "Climb in. And stay down."

I open the door, and Pablo and I crawl into the backseat. Fido hops in after us. My mom gets in behind the wheel and slumps down.

"How are you going to drive like that?" I ask. "And why are we hiding if Dad isn't even around?"

"He could come back any second," she whispers.

"You can't drive like that, Mom. You'll hit a tree. Sit up."

She inches up a bit higher and pulls her seat belt across her lap. "Buckle up," she whispers.

We do. She puts the car in gear, and we ease forward.

"Oh, this is ridiculous," I say, and sit up. "It's

okay, Pablo. Sit up, Mom, and let's get out of here before—*There he is! Get down!*"

We all duck.

"Where is he?" Mom asks.

"On the trail. It's okay. His back is to us. We can go."

Mom peeks over the dashboard.

"He's heading to the bathrooms," she says. "When he's inside, we'll go."

Dad walks up to the small building and enters the door with the MEN sign above it.

"Let's go!" Mom says, and hits the gas. The tires kick up some gravel.

"Are you guys afraid of your dad or something?" Pablo asks.

Mom and I answer at the same time. She says, "No"; I say, "Yes."

19. We couldn't find the mini-mall pet paradise.

Mom says the name *Petopia* is a pun.

"They put the word *pet* with the word *utopia*," she says. "*Utopia* is a kind of paradise."

So Petopia means "pet paradise." It also means it's another one of those pet stores with a punny name.

Anyway, we can't find it.

"Sorry," Pablo says. "I was sure I saw the name on a sign."

"It's not your fault," I say, though I've been thinking for some time that he never actually saw a sign for the store at all. There aren't very many mini-malls near White Crappie Lake. We've driven pretty far and found only two little strip malls, but neither of them had a Petopia, or even a pet store.

"Maybe we came in on a different highway," he says.

I glance at Mom in the rearview mirror.

"There's only one highway that goes by the lake," she says.

Fido starts whining.

"Mom, Fido needs to go out," I say.

"Okay," she says, turning on her signal. "I should get gas anyway. Then we'll need to head back. Sorry, guys."

We nod. We're sorry, too.

She pulls off at the next exit.

Fido whines louder and hops up and down on the seat.

"I'm going to take you out as soon as Mom stops the car," I say.

I've always thought it was weird the way people speak in full sentences to their pets. Now I have one, and I do it. I know Fido can't understand English, but I do it anyway. Weird.

Mom pulls up to a bright red pump in a bright red truck stop. The huge parking lot is filled with massive eighteen-wheelers. Next to them, our hybrid seems like a toy.

Across the parking lot is a bright red convenience store the size of a supermarket. This place definitely has a bright red theme going on.

I unbuckle myself, snap Fido's leash to her collar, then open the door. She tries to bolt.

"Fido, freeze!" I say, and wrap the leash around my hand a few times. I want her close to me. She's hard to see. I don't want her getting crushed by a semi.

I climb out first and say, "Fido, heel!" She hops down onto the pavement. I check in all directions for cars, then start crossing the parking lot, scanning for a patch of grass for her to do her business in.

Pablo walks with us. "She's very obedient."

"Sometimes. But like I said, I didn't train her. Petopia—"

Right as I say the word, I see it. In neon. Bright red neon. The red neon word is written in cursive and mounted inside the store's front window.

"Look!" I say to Pablo.

He chuckles. "I knew I saw it!"

"This isn't a mini-mall, though."

"It's the size of one."

We walk up and stare at the glowing red sign. Fido barks.

"I remember we stopped here to use the bathrooms," Pablo says. "Bianca had to go."

"Whoever heard of a pet store at a truck stop?" I ask.

I look back at Mom. She's standing by the car, pumping the gas, but she's looking at us. And smiling ear to ear. She sees the sign, too.

"Go on in!" she calls. "I'll catch up!"

Fido tugs us toward the doors. Maybe she wasn't whining because she had to go out. Maybe she knew we were close. Maybe she heard other guinea pigs.

Or guinea dogs.

20. Truckers must get lonely on the wide-open road.

Driving those big rigs day after day, night after night. All alone.

The store is like a mall for truck drivers. Not only does it have shower rooms and laundry facilities, it has a game room, a food court, a gift shop, an electronics store . . . and one tiny pet shop. Fido led us right to it. There's another red neon sign hanging in its window.

I almost can't believe I'm reading it correctly. Dad searched after Petopia disappeared, and said there wasn't a pet store with that name anywhere in our whole state. And here one is, in our state, just a few miles from where we're camping, in fact. I feel an eerie chill at the back of my neck.

"I don't see any fish," Pablo says disappointedly. "But I doubt it would be a good idea for a trucker to keep an aquarium in his rig."

"I guess a snake would work better," I say, pointing at a fat boa constrictor that's hugging a branch in a terrarium.

Fido tries frantically to crawl up my pant leg, but I'm wearing shorts, so instead she crawls up my skin. Which really hurts.

"Ow!" I howl, and pry her off my leg. Just as I suspected: blood. Not enough to call 911, but still . . .

"She doesn't like snakes?" Pablo asks.

"Apparently not." I scowl at Fido, who has scurried up my shirt and now sits trembling on my shoulder. This is not exactly dog behavior.

A bird squawks. It's a blue and orange parrot resting on a perch in a cage in the corner.

"That might be a good pet for a trucker," I say. "Someone to talk to who might actually talk back."

We walk over. It has a white face with zebra stripes around its eyes.

"You think it talks?" Pablo asks.

The bird squawks again. Its tongue is gray.

"Doesn't seem to," I say.

It squawks again. This time it sounds like "No more!"

"You fellas teasing that macaw?" a deep voice asks.

It's a man wearing a bright red shirt and a name tag that says the name of the gas station and, under it, in capital letters, the word VERNE. I guess it's his name. He has gray whiskers along his jaw that turn into a beard at his chin and so many tattoos I can't make out what any of them are. His eyes are beady enough to be a little scary.

"Aw, I'm just kidding you," he says, then smiles. His eyes soften. "That's Captain Nemo. He's over thirty years old. And plenty smart. Aren't you, Nemo?"

"NEE-mo!" the bird says in its squawky voice.

So not "No more"—"Nemo."

"Like in *Twenty Thousand Leagues Under the Sea*," Pablo says.

"That's right!" Verne says. "You're plenty smart, too, boy. Have you read that book?"

"I'm reading it now, actually. Almost finished."

"That was my old man's favorite book. He named me after the author." He taps his name tag. Even his fingers have tattoos. "Verne. After . . ."

". . . Jules Verne," Pablo says. He smiles.

Verne smiles.

I'm not sure what I'm supposed to do.

"I'm afraid he's not for sale," Verne finally says. "On account of he's mine, I mean. I don't like leaving Nemo at home all day."

"NEE-mo!" the bird says.

"Maybe you want a friend for your little pal there," Verne says, sticking a finger out to Fido. Fido licks it. "He's a friendly little fella."

"She's female," Pablo says.

"Well, I'm not sure you'll want a male, then," Verne says with a laugh. "You'd have guinea pigs all over the place if you did that."

Hmm. That could solve some problems for me. . . .

"I think we do have a guinea pig around here somewhere," Verne says. "Over here . . . yeah, here it is!"

He leads us to a terrarium. There are fake plants and rocks and a little fake cave inside it, all beside a little pool of water. You'd think the terrarium would be for turtles, but inside there's a guinea pig, soaking in the water.

Verne laughs. "He's always in the water like that. Really likes being wet. Funny little fella. Does yours like being wet?"

"Actually, she does," I say.

"Rufus!" my mom says, rushing up to us. "My goodness, what a big place! Whew! I'm out of breath. Hello, there"—she peeks at Verne's name tag—"Verne." She eyes his tattoos.

"These must be your boys," Verne says. "They sure are polite."

"Well, this one's mine," Mom says, setting her hand on my head. I can't wait to grow taller. "This is his friend." She sets her hand on Pablo's shoulder.

"I see," says Verne. "Best buddies, then."

Pablo and I shrug. How embarrassing.

"So this is it," Mom says, looking around. "Petopia. It's smaller than the other one. Strange that it's in a truck stop. . . ."

"NEE-mo!" Captain Nemo squawks.

"That's my macaw," Verne says. "He's not for sale. The boys were looking at that guinea pig right there. The soggy one."

She leans in and looks at it. She smiles.

Here we go again.

21. Why does Mom think a guinea pig is the answer to everything?

We drive back to the campground with two of them, Fido and the soggy one from the terrarium. Pablo holds the new one in his lap on a beach towel Mom found in the trunk. It's a chocolate brown guinea pig with tan fur under its very whiskery chin and on its belly. Its paws are nearly black. It's been making this tiny growly, huffing sound since we left the truck stop, though every once in a while it peeps like a finch.

Fido spends the trip in my lap as well, growling at the new animal.

"I'm going to name it Snapper, after the

snapping alligator turtle Dmitri lied about," Pablo says. "Snapper kind of acted like a turtle, you know, lying in that water."

"Isn't a snapper a fish?" I ask.

"That makes it even better!"

He's acting as though the guinea pig is his when I was under the impression we'd gotten it for Murphy. I mean, what if it's a guinea dog? If it is, it's Murphy's. Period. Sure, then he'd own both a guinea dog and the world's most perfect dog, which hardly seems fair, but Murph deserves it.

"Do you know how to tell a guinea pig's sex?" Pablo asks me.

"No. But Lurena does."

"Right. The rodent expert."

Lurena will probably want the new guinea pig, too, but I don't consider her a candidate. She got Fido's pup. Plus, she already has a chinchilla and a hamster. She's got plenty of rodents. She doesn't get this one.

"So you want to hide Snapper from Dmitri, right?" Pablo asks.

Ack! This is getting as complicated as it was

when Queen Girly was born. I don't want the responsibility again of having to decide who gets the new guinea creature. Technically, since it was my mom who purchased the animal, it belongs to our family, but that doesn't make it my responsibility, does it? Why shouldn't Mom have to choose who gets it?

"It's probably a good idea," I say to Pablo. "Dmitri's going to be all over it, and when he wants something, he doesn't give up till he gets it."

"He didn't get Queen Girly. How did you get him to give up? What did you do?"

Remembering what I did makes me feel better. Less nervous.

"I said no," I say.

Pablo smiles. "So do that again."

I smile back. "You know what? I will."

Dad walks over to the car the second we drive up to the campsite. He pokes his head through the passenger-side window of the car.

"So where did you go?" he asks.

Fido barks. Dad looks into the backseat. His face falls. His shoulders, too.

"You bought another guinea pig," he says to Mom. "How on earth . . . where on earth . . . *why* on earth?"

"We found a Petopia outlet," Mom says in a chipper voice. "In a truck stop. Isn't that incredible!"

Dad looks stunned, confused, frustrated, and angry. Too stunned, confused, frustrated, and angry to find any words to yell, which, for Dad, is pretty darned stunned, confused, frustrated, and angry.

So Mom gets out of the car and walks around to his side. She takes his arm. "Have you started marinating vegetables for dinner yet?"

"N–no," he says. "I haven't had . . . Now listen, Raquel . . ."

"You'd better get started, then," she says, and starts leading him away.

"Your mom's good," Pablo says.

My mom's a lot of things. Embarrassing. Inconsiderate. Pushy. Way too chipper.

Clueless. But, yeah, Pablo's right: she's not bad. I'm particularly happy that she didn't say the guinea pig was Pablo's.

I nod. "Let's get out of here while we can."

"Where to?"

"I want to avoid Dad, Dmitri, and Lurena."

"Should we go to my RV?" Pablo asks.

If we do, it will seem as if it's his guinea pig even more than it already does.

"No, let's find Murph."

22. "Cowamundi!"

This is Dmitri saying *Coatimundi!* wrong again as he jumps off the rope swing. Murph is in the water.

"What do we do?" Pablo asks, cradling the squirming, growling guinea pig that we've wrapped inside the beach towel. The poor thing doesn't seem to like being wrapped in a beach towel, but then what guinea pig would?

"We have to get rid of Dmitri," I say.

"How?"

"You stay here behind this tree, out of sight. I'll call you when he's gone."

"What are you going to do?" Pablo asks.

"I don't know. Maybe a brilliant idea will come to me as I'm walking over there. You just keep the guinea pig hidden. Don't let it get away. I'll take Fido with me so she won't give you away."

Fido has growled and snarled and barked at the new guinea pig since we bought it. That's how she usually treats rodents: China C., Sharmet . . . Not Queen Girly, of course.

"Okay, but hurry," Pablo says. "He's sick of being wrapped up in this towel."

"I know," I say. I know I need to hurry. Pressure isn't going to help me think of a way to get rid of Dmitri.

Here are the ideas I come up with on the way over:

- I could tell him his dad has a new, expensive gadget for him.
- I could tell him I saw a wild guinea dog running through some bushes very, very far from here.
- I could tie him up with the rope swing.
- I could wait till it's his turn to jump, then, when he's underwater, grab Murph and tell him I have a surprise for him.

I decide the last one is best, though tying Dmitri up with the rope is tempting.

Unfortunately, he always lets Murph go on the swing first, then follows right after him, then climbs out of the water with him. The guy is like Murphy's shadow.

"Roof!" Murph yells from the water when he sees me.

Dmitri grumbles under his breath.

Fido runs up to Buddy and Mars, and they start tearing around in circles, Fido nipping at the bigger dogs' heels.

"Where you been?" Murph asks, swimming toward the shore. "I was looking everywhere for you. You were gone an eon."

"I was with Pablo."

"Oh, with Pablo," Dmitri says. "Guess *Doofus* has a new best buddy."

The rope idea gets more attractive all the time.

"Come on, Roof," Murph says. "Dive in with us."

"Uh . . ." I start to glance over to where Pablo is hiding but stop myself. I don't want Murph or especially Dmitri to catch me. "Okay."

I pull off my T-shirt (technically, it's Pablo's shirt) and walk over to the rope. It's nice and strong. With a few good knots and Pablo's T-shirt for a gag, Dmitri would be out of commission for quite some time. . . .

Dmitri steps out of the water, stomps over to me, and snatches the rope out of my hand.

"Murph first!" he yells in my face, so loud I taste his lunch. Yuck.

"That's not necessary," Murph says. "Roof can go ahead of me."

Dmitri snorts like a bull. "No, you go, Murph. Then me. *Then* Rufus."

"I wouldn't think of it," Murph says, going into his proper-English-gentleman routine again. "After you, Rufus, my good man."

I get an idea.

"After *you*, Dmitri, my . . ." I can't say "my good man" to Dmitri. It's not possible. I consider saying the opposite, but instead finish my sentence by adding, "my, isn't it a beautiful day?" I try doing it with a British accent but come nowhere close.

Dmitri glares at me, then turns to Murph, who gives him a gentlemanly bow.

"Oh, all right!" Dmitri grunts, then runs backward with the rope in his hands. "Watch this, Murph—a backflip with a half turn!"

He leaps up, wraps his legs around the rope, then swings out over the water, where he releases the rope and does a feeble half back-flip, without a turn. The second he hits the water, I grab Murphy and start dragging him away.

"Hey, now!" he says. "What's all this, then?"

"I have to show you something. Come on. I don't want Dmitri to see."

"What is it, pray tell?" he asks, putting up a mild fight. "What the dickens has gotten into you, man?"

"Knock it off, Sherlock, and come on. Look, Dmitri sees us."

Dmitri is slogging through the water to the shore, bellowing, "Hey! What's up? Where you guys going?"

I answer, "Your dad got a new . . . uh . . ." That's no good. I'm stuck. I can never come up with stories on the spot.

Murphy, on the other hand . . .

"Jeepers! Your father's kayak has over-turned!" he says, pointing out at the lake. "See it? Oh, drat! It's sunk! I do hope he's all right!"

This would be a lot easier to sell without *Jeepers!* and *drat!*

Dmitri squints out to where Murph is pointing. "I don't see him."

"What's all the excitement about?" Lurena asks, walking up behind us with her cages.

Pablo is standing beside her. The beach towel is slung around his neck. I give him a fierce *where-is-it?* look. He points with his eyes at one of Lurena's cages. Sure enough, the new guinea pig is in one with Queen Girly, huffing and growling. China C. and Sharmet are sharing the other.

Fido runs over and starts growling and barking angrily at the new rodent through the bars. She doesn't like it being in there with her daughter.

"Quiet, Fido!" I say. "Sit!"

She sits and stops barking, but she con-tinues to growl.

Fido has noticed there's a spare rodent in her daughter's cage, but neither Murphy nor Dmitri has.

"Wait! *There's* my dad!" Dmitri says, pointing to camp.

His dad is by the fire, chatting with my dad, who is marinating his vegetables.

"My bad," says Murph. "Must have been someone else tumbling out of a kayak." He claps his hands together. "Looks like dinnertime. Let's eat!"

"Yes, I hear we're having vegetable shish kebabs tonight," I say. Oh, joy.

The trick during dinner will be keeping Dad from mentioning the new rodent.

23. Most fireflies fly higher than guinea dogs.

Fido ran around the campground, snapping at them, then gagging on the few she caught and coughing them back out.

While this went on, we ate dinner. Once again, Murph saved me from my dad's insane idea of camp cuisine, this time with good old-fashioned cheeseburgers. I was able somehow to keep Dmitri away from Dad's big mouth, mostly because Dad was too busy talking about his precious shish kebabs to notice us.

I've been trying to concoct some scheme to get Dmitri out of the way so I can tell Murphy about the guinea pig. The quicker I give it to Murphy, the better. Dad can't be angry that we bought one for Murph. Dmitri will get angry at me for giving it to Murph, but he can't make much of a fuss about it. That would look like he doesn't want Murph to get the guinea pig, and he wouldn't want that.

Will Pablo be upset? Maybe, but he's got his fish, right? And he lives far away, right? So I don't have to worry about him being mad for long, right?

This will all work out beautifully, if only I can ditch Dmitri.

"So you've never been swimming?" he asks Pablo with a strong hint of mockery.

"My parents say I tried it when I was little, but I hated it."

"And his parents don't swim," I add, trying to bail him out. Maybe that's why he doesn't swim. If they never learned, they couldn't teach him. Of course, they could have gotten him lessons. . . .

"Why didn't you take swimming lessons?" Dmitri asks.

It sort of scares me when we think alike.

"They say I would always throw a really big fit—a total meltdown, yelling and screaming—

every time they put me in the water. So they stopped trying."

"Then why the heck do they take you to a *lake* for your vacation?" Dmitri asks.

Pablo shrugs. "We actually live by a lake. Lake Black Gut. So there's nothing weird about it to us. We like being near water. Not everybody who goes to a lake swims in it."

"Lake Black Gut?" I say. "Do all the lakes around here have gross names?"

"How about a game of Ghost in the Graveyard?" Lurena suggests, and gives my arm a quick tap.

Is this her idea for getting rid of Dmitri? It's worth a try.

"I'm in," I say.

"Isn't that kind of a baby game?" Dmitri says.

"I'm in," Murph says. "I like ghosts *and* babies."

Good old Murph.

"I guess I'm in," Pablo says. "Though I'm not sure what it is."

"It's simple," Lurena says. "One person is the

ghost and goes and hides. The rest of us count, 'One o'clock, two o'clock, three o'clock,' all the way to 'twelve o'clock,' then we yell, 'Starlight, star bright, I hope I see a *ghost* tonight!' Then we all go looking for the ghost. The ghost jumps out when someone comes close and tags them, which makes them the ghost, then you start over!"

Dmitri groans.

"The campfire can be base," Lurena goes on. "Who's brave enough to be the ghost first?"

Normally, Murph would jump at the chance, but this time he doesn't, which leads me to believe he knows what's up. Lurena was smart to make it sound brave to be the ghost.

"I'll do it," Dmitri says, then, looking at Pablo, he adds in a sinister tone, "And when I jump out at you, you'll be too scared to run."

"I'm scared already," Pablo says in a flat tone. "Want to feel my goose bumps?"

"I don't *think* so!" Dmitri says, sticking out his tongue.

He runs off into the woods.

"One o'clock . . . two o'clock . . . ," Lurena

starts to count, very slowly, then she whispers to me, "Show him!"

"Yeah," Murph whispers. "What's the surprise?"

Lurena gets the cage with Queen Girly and the new guinea pig in it while continuing to count out, "... four o'clock ... five o'clock ..." She hands the cage to me; I take it; she waves at us to leave. "... six o'clock ... seven o'clock ..."

Murph, Pablo, and I speed-walk away. Fido follows, barking at me.

"Don't worry," I whisper to her. "He won't hurt her."

"Who won't hurt who?" Murphy asks.

When we are deep in the trees, I start to open the cage. Fido starts barking louder.

"Quiet, Fido!" I order.

She stops.

"Pablo, why don't you take her to my mom and ask her to pigsit during the game? Otherwise Fido will give us away with all her barking. When Lurena finishes counting, you two should start looking for Dmitri. Take your time finding him, though."

"Okay," he says, and scoops up Fido. She starts wriggling and snarling.

"Fido, *quiet*!" I say.

She stops snarling but starts to whimper. Pablo carries her away.

That worked out well. I'm alone with Murph at last.

"So?" he says. "What's in the cage?"

I hold it up. It's dark, but the almost-half moon shines enough light for him to see what's inside.

"Hey, there are two of them!"

I quickly tell him about Petopia and buying the guinea pig.

"Does it act like a dog?" he asks eagerly.

"So far, it acts like a guinea pig. Except that it was sitting in a pool of water at the store. And it made a strange growling sound on the way home."

"Fido growls," Murph says.

"This was different. More like huffing. It hasn't obeyed any orders or begged or panted or done anything doglike yet."

"Yet," Murph says hopefully.

He reaches in and takes the guinea pig out. It starts making its weird huffing.

"Lurena says it's a boy." I say. "Pablo calls him Snapper, because he was lying in the pool of water, like a turtle. You know, the snapping-alligator-turtle thing."

Murph laughs. "It's a good name."

The guinea pig stops growling and starts squeaking and peeping.

Murph laughs again. "Listen to that! Maybe it's a guinea bird! Maybe it can fly!"

"Maybe," I say. Is it crazy that this doesn't sound crazy to me?

"Why aren't you guys looking for me?" Dmitri asks, appearing out of nowhere, mad as a monster.

The guinea pig squawks, then leaps from Murph's arms. He hits the ground, and scrambles away into the dark.

24. Who knew Fido was a bloodhound?

Not me, that's for sure.

While we all scratched our heads, trying to figure out how to find the new guinea pig, Fido put her nose to the ground and started sniffing.

"She's got the scent!" Murph says. "Follow her!"

Lurena fetches some flashlights from camp, and we're off.

"What was that anyway?" Dmitri asks. "One of Lurena's rats?"

"Nope," Lurena says. "Not one of mine."

"You were holding it, Murph." Dmitri asks, "Where did you get it from?"

No one answers. Then it hits me: we

don't have to say *where* we got it, just who it belongs to.

"It's mine," I say. "It's my new guinea pig."

"But you have Fido. What do you need another guinea pig for? It doesn't . . ." His eyes grow wide. "Does it act like a dog?"

"Not that I've noticed."

"It makes sounds like a bird," Murph says.

"A bird?" Dmitri says. "Does it . . . *fly*?"

"No, but it chirps," Murph says, and does a bird impression.

"Can we just all focus and find the rodent?" Lurena says. "There are lots of animals out here that might eat a guinea pig. Raccoons, for instance. And coyotes."

"Are there coyotes out here?" Dmitri asks.

I think he might be scared.

"Are you scared, Dmitri?" Lurena asks, smiling at him.

Oh, no. Now I'm thinking like her, too.

"No!" he says. "I just don't know why we're out here looking for a stupid guinea pig with coyotes around. Obviously, we'll never find it. I'm heading back." He starts doing that.

Lurena laughs. "Coyotes won't bother us. At least, not if we all stay together. They might attack a kid out in the woods by himself, though."

Dmitri stops walking. "Why didn't you tell me about that before, when I went off to hide for your dumb game?"

Fido keeps searching, sniffing the ground, stopping sometimes, like she's lost the scent, then barking and moving on again.

"Do you think she can find him?" Pablo asks.

"Of course she can!" Murph replies in a big, confident voice. "She's Fido the guinea dog!"

"Guinea bloodhound," I say.

"Exactly!" Murph says, and slaps me on the back.

"This is stupid," Dmitri says.

"You still here?" I ask.

"I'm going back," he says.

"See you, coyote chow," Lurena says.

I wish she'd stop that coyote stuff and let him leave.

"Ha-ha," Dmitri says, without laughing. "Coming with, Murph?"

Murph and Lurena crack up in unison.

"Fine. I'll go by myself. You're not going to find a guinea pig out here in the dark, I'll tell you that. You'll come back with nothing." And he walks off, the beam of his flashlight wobbling. He's scared, all right.

"Are there really coyotes out here?" Pablo asks.

"I hope so," Lurena says.

Fido leads us out of the trees to the lake. She sniffs the ground right up to the bank, then skids to a stop. She sniffs a moment at the air, which is dotted with fireflies—she doesn't eat any, not while she's working—then she barks out at the lake.

We all walk up to the bank and look down into the dark water.

"Think Snapper dove in?" Pablo asks. His voice trembles, like he's worried. I think he's gotten attached. Darn it.

"Guinea pigs don't generally dive into water," Lurena says.

"Except Fido," Murph says.

"And Snapper," Pablo says. "He was in water when we first saw him."

"At Petopia," Lurena says. "If that's where you got him, there's no telling what he'll do."

"What if he can't swim?" Pablo asks.

"Maybe he's a guinea turtle and can swim beautifully," Murph says.

"But he doesn't have a shell. What if something gets him? What if Dmitri's right and there really is an alligator snapping turtle?"

"There isn't," I say, though I was wondering the same thing myself.

"Can't you guys dive in after him, see if you can find him?" Pablo asks.

"It's too dark," Lurena says. "It'd be impossible. Even Fido didn't dive in. We'll have to wait till morning."

We all stand quietly awhile, staring at the quiet lake. The rope swing is far to our left. We've covered some ground. The moonlight flickering on the water's surface reminds me of the fireflies hovering around our heads.

If I weren't so worried, I'd probably be enjoying this.

I crouch down and pet Fido. "Good girl," I say. "Good girl."

She pants. She likes strokes.

I remember when Fido ran away. I was tired of all the attention I was getting for having a guinea dog and tried to train the dog out of her. Then she disappeared. She was gone all night. I was so scared something would happen to her outside in the dark.

"You think he's okay out there?" I ask Fido.

She yaps, and her little voice echoes across the lake.

"I'll take that for a yes."

25. Guinea turtle?

Guinea bird?

Or just a chirping amphibian guinea pig?

Whatever Snapper is, we're looking for him, in Murph's skiff. Murph, Lurena, and me. It's pretty crowded, but one of us convinced the other two she was "essential to the expedition," being an "authority on rodent behavior." Murph invited her aboard with his usual the-more-the-merrier nonsense.

Pablo stayed ashore.

Fido, our guinea bloodhound, is with us, too, of course. She's perched on the bow. Maybe she's a guinea bird dog that hunts guinea birds.

I'm probably pushing this "guinea" thing too far.

What does *guinea* mean anyway? And

why are guinea pigs called *guinea pigs* when they're obviously rodents? Why not *guinea rats*?

There's a person in this boat who can answer these questions, but I'm not going to ask her. I don't want to waste precious time listening to her rattle off guinea facts.

Not that anyone needs to ask her to rattle off guinea facts.

"Guinea pigs do like water," she says. "Most rodents can swim."

"Yeah, just look at all of them," I say, spreading my arms. "White Crappie Lake is practically a rodent swimming pool."

"I didn't say they *love* to swim. I said that they *can* swim, if they need to. But there are aquatic rodents, you know. Beavers, for example. Definitely rodent. Look at their teeth."

"Where?" Murph says, twisting his head side to side exaggeratedly.

Lurena laughs. "You know what I mean, Murphy Molloy, you big goof."

Fido suddenly scoots to the port side of the boat; she whimpers and wags her bottom.

"I think she smells something," I say, and point off to the left. "That way."

"Right oar, oarsman," Murph says in an Irish or maybe Scottish accent. He rolls the *r* in *right* and *oarsman*. "Rrrow, rrrow, rrrow yerrr boat!"

"Okay," I say. "We're rowing already."

"Gently down the strrrrrream! Merrrrrrrrily, merrrrr—"

"Enough!" I say, though I'm laughing. "We're going in a circle." I try to roll the *r* in *circle*, but can't. I bet Pablo can.

"Oarrrrsman, left oarrr! Rrrow, rrrow! . . ."

"That fixed it," I interrupt. "We're good."

Fido leads us toward some cattails.

"Oarrrs up!" Murph calls.

"I'm right here, you know," I say. "You don't have to yell."

"Sorrrry," he says.

The skiff cruises into the reeds. They graze against the sides of the boat, slowing it down.

Fido barks and barks.

"I think we're close," Lurena says.

"Cowamundi!" yells Dmitri. He's in his kayak. He must have been hiding in the reeds.

He's paddling toward us from starboard. Not fast, since it's hard to paddle through cattails, but fast enough that we can't get out of the way.

"Are you crazy?" Lurena screams.

He laughs like the villain he is as his kayak crashes into the skiff. We all fall to the left.

"Midsea collision!" Murph yells. "Pull the alarrrm! Man the lifeboats!"

I scowl at him. Doesn't he ever just get mad? Is everything fun and games to this guy?

"Where's Fido?" Lurena gasps.

I spin around, looking for her. She isn't on board.

"Dog overrrboard! Dog overrrboard!" Murph hollers.

Fido can swim, of course, so I'm not too worried. But can she swim in these reeds? And I'd be lying if I said I wasn't worried about that mythical alligator snapping turtle, or some other carnivorous creature—one of Lurena's aquatic rodents, maybe—prowling the cattails.

"There she is!" Murph says.

I follow where he's pointing. She's swimming away from, instead of toward, the boat.

"Fido!" I call. "Come *here*, girl! This way! *Come!*"

She glances back but keeps swimming away. She wants us to follow her.

"Oarsmen," I say, "full speed ahead!"

26. Empty speed ahead.

Is that the opposite of *full speed ahead*? Oars are too long to work in cattails. Rowing is impossible. So Murph and I lean over the side and paddle with our hands.

"You guys all right?" a voice calls from the shore. It's Pablo. He must have run all the way around.

"We're fine!" Lurena calls back.

She would say that. She's not up to her elbows in scummy muck. The water's a lot muddier in the reeds.

"Dmitri rammed us with his kayak," I say to Pablo. Where'd Dmitri go anyway? I don't see him anywhere.

I do see Pablo, through the cattails. He's pacing.

"Did you find Snapper?" he asks.

"Not yet," Lurena answers. "But Fido's on his trail."

Much to our surprise, Pablo answers, "I'm coming in!"

Coming in?

I see him step toward the bank.

"Not a good idea," I say. "The bottom here is thick mud. It's slippery and deep."

He stops. "Well, I can't just stand here!"

"If we can get to you, will you get into the boat?" I ask.

He doesn't answer.

"Pablo?"

"I guess so," he says.

Murph looks at me and smiles. I know what he's thinking: he's proud of Pablo. Happy for him. I am, too.

"Let's go get him," I say to Murph.

"I don't think we have room, Roof."

"I'll jump out when we pick him up," Lurena says. "Pablo getting into a boat is worth losing your rodent expert."

"Right," I say. I'm surprised she volunteered,

considering the fancy clothes she's wearing.

"Fido's swimming along the shore," I say to Pablo. "Be ready in case we get close enough for you to climb in. If Fido changes direction, though, we're going to follow her."

"Okay," he says. He sounds shaky. I'm sure he's nervous about going out in the boat.

We keep trailing Fido as she leads us through the cattails. Murph and I start grabbing the reeds and pulling the boat through them. It works better than rowing.

We're moving parallel to the bank, so we can't get close enough to pick up Pablo. He walks along the shore, following us, just in case we find a way to get to him. He's going to a lot of trouble for the new guinea pig. He really has gotten attached.

The cattails start to thin out a little, making it easier for us to get through. Fido's still ahead, paddling like crazy. She never seems to tire. We drift into a small clearing.

"There he is!" Murph says. "There's Snapper!"

I guess that's the name. No sense fighting it.

Snapper is floating on his back about twenty or so feet ahead of us. He has something in his paws. It's flapping around . . .

"I think he has a . . . ," Lurena says, then lowers her voice. "A *fish!*"

"What does he have?" Pablo asks.

I guess that's why Lurena whispered. Snapper has caught a fish, and Pablo loves fish. I wonder if the fish is a white crappie. Or maybe a snapper . . . ?

"You know what he reminds me of?" Lurena whispers. "Swimming on his back with a fish on its chest?"

Before she can tell me, Snapper disappears under the water. He didn't twist and dive in. It was as if he was surprised to be going under, as if he didn't mean to do it. In fact, he made a little squawk before he slipped beneath the surface. It was almost as if something had pulled him under.

27. Heroic, sure, but not smart.

That's what Pablo diving into the pond to save his guinea pig is. It's also surprising, considering how he feels about water. Any one of us could have done it, and we're all fine with water. But Pablo dives in anyway. It's a clumsy dive, but it's his first one ever, so . . . Throw in the possibility that there's something under the water that snatches guinea pigs—a snapping turtle?—and you've got one heroic, foolish, surprising, clumsy, death-defying dive. I love it. If I were a judge, I'd hold up a scorecard with a big ten on it.

Of course, Murph and I do have to jump in to save him. I mean, the kid doesn't know how to swim.

The bottom of the pond is so deep with oozy mud that I can't stand up. I sink in up to my ankles. It's kind of creepy, like I'm being dragged under by a cold alien slime.

"Tread water," Murph says. "The bottom's too muddy."

I lean forward into the water and swim. My feet pull free from the slime and I start paddling. Murph and I swim over to Pablo. I grab hold of one flailing arm; Murph gets the other. Together, we keep Pablo's head up out of the water. Fido swims in a circle around us, barking.

"Snapper!" Pablo screams when he's not coughing up lake water. "Snapper!"

"We'll find him, Pablo!" Lurena yells from the skiff. "Let them save *you* first!"

His struggling makes it twice as difficult to get him into the boat. A couple of times, he almost tips it over. When we finally push him in, Murph taps my shoulder.

"Let's stay in the water. We can pull the boat out of the reeds."

"How?" I ask.

He grabs hold of the mooring line.

"Like tugboats."

He swims ahead, gripping the rope. I take the other line and do as he does. The boat glides behind us. Fido paddles ahead of us.

"Any sign of Snapper, Lurena?" Murph yells out.

"No. Do you think the snapping turtle got him?"

"There's no snapping turtle," Pablo says.

"I know you don't want to hear it, Pablo," Lurena says, "but something took your little friend. It was terribly brave of you to dive in to save him, though, especially with your being afraid of the water and all."

"I never said I was afraid of it," he says. "I said I didn't like it. I've been in it plenty of times. I wish you all would hear me on this."

When we clear the reeds, I see behind us, floating in the cattails—*hidden* in the cattails—Dmitri's kayak. He's not in it.

I tap Murph's shoulder. "Look," I whisper, pointing at the kayak.

He nods. "Let's get in."

"Check," I say.

My dad doesn't like it when I say that. Murph doesn't mind.

We climb aboard the skiff. It's crowded inside. And heavy. It sinks deeper into the water.

"I think we're carrying one too many," Murph says. "How about one of us rides in Dmitri's kayak?"

"Huh?" Pablo and Lurena say.

I point, and they look at where the kayak is drifting, unmanned. It's not sitting still, though. It keeps rocking. As we get closer, I can see why. A hand is holding on to it. Dmitri's hand. He's in the water on the other side of it. He probably couldn't get back in after he swam over, swiped Snapper, then swam back, the whole time underwater. I wonder where Snapper is now. Is he in the kayak? Did he get away?

Fido starts barking.

"Someone over there, girl?" Murph asks.

"Is it Snapper?" Pablo asks, and stands up.

The boat rocks dangerously.

"Sit down, please, sailor, or we'll all end up in the drink," Murph says.

Pablo sits.

Dmitri's kayak suddenly rolls over on its side.

Fido barks louder and looks down at the water. A small, black-colored animal surfaces near the tipped kayak, then immediately submerges again, all in one motion, like a whale, only smaller.

A few feet ahead, it does it again. Is it an otter?

"It's Snapper!" Lurena yells.

Fido dives in after him.

Then Pablo does.

We're back where we started.

28. Dog-paddling isn't just for dogs.

Pablo figures it out pretty quickly. Or did he already know how? He is swallowing a fair amount of water, especially when he calls out, "Here, boy! Here, Snapper!"

What is he, crazy? Does he think Snapper's a guinea dog? It seems more like he's the proud owner of a guinea *otter*. I guess it's a good thing Pablo lives on a lake.

Lurena tries rowing the boat around us, to head Snapper off, I suppose, but instead she almost takes *my* head off with one of her oars.

"Hey!" I splutter. "Oarswoman! Oars down! Oars down!"

"Sorry," she yells back. "Just trying to help!"

"Just don't!"

With Pablo keeping himself afloat and Lurena not swiping at us with wooden blades, Murph and I are free to swim ahead and try to corral Snapper. All we have to do is follow Fido. She never gives up. Like any good dog, she is steadfast.

We chase Snapper to the bank. He scrambles up onto it, stops for a second to shake off some water, then starts running in that funny, loping—yep, otterish—way of his. Fido follows him up the bank, likewise shakes off water, then shoots after him. Being faster, she overtakes him easily and tackles him. They snarl and growl and roll around together in the grass. I think they're playing. I hope they are.

I swim over to the bank and climb up onto it. Murph stays in the water to help Pablo. Since I don't have a fur coat, I don't shake off the water. I run over to the battling rodents. I'm hesitant at first to stick my hands in between the snarling, tangling fighters, then I remember they're guinea pigs, and I reach in and pick them up by their soggy scruffs.

"Okay, that was fun," I say. "Good girl, Fido."

She pants proudly.

Behind me I hear a loud thump. It's the sound of wood hitting fiberglass. Lurena has rammed the skiff into Dmitri's kayak.

"Are you crazy?" Dmitri yells. I can't see him. He's still hiding behind the kayak, which is now upside down on the water. "You'll break it! My dad will kill me!"

"I didn't mean to do it, you big dope," Lurena says. "I'm trying to rescue you. Give me your hand."

"I'm not holding your hand!" he says.

"Fine," she says. "Rescue yourself."

She starts to row away.

"Okay, okay," Dmitri says. "Lower a paddle, and I'll grab it."

"It's an oar, not a paddle," she says, and lowers one.

Murph and Pablo catch up to me.

"Snapper!" Pablo sighs. "Come here, boy!"

I hand him the guinea pig. It's crystal clear that Snapper belongs to Pablo. Murphy's smile shows me he knows it, too.

Lurena starts towing Dmitri and his kayak to shore.

I get an idea.

"Tell Dmitri I had to . . . ," I start to say to Murph, then get stuck coming up with an excuse. Why is this so hard for me? "Tell him I . . . I . . . I had to go to the bathroom? Yeah. That's fine. Then tell him to be careful because there have been snapping turtle sightings here." I wink.

"Gotcha," he says.

"For the last time, there are no snapping turtles here," I hear Pablo say as I run off, toward the cattails. I'm sure Murph will clue him in.

I step into the water, into the mud, and slowly my feet sink in. It's not as oozy close to the bank. I work my way over to the reeds, crouch down in them as low as I can, and wait.

As Lurena and Dmitri near the shore, Murph says, "You should be careful. There have been snapping turtle sightings around here."

Pablo nods. "Yeah," he says.

"Oh, really?" Dmitri says with a little laugh. He climbs out of the boat and steps into the water. "I guess I'd better watch out."

I swim toward him, underwater, and seize his ankle with a viselike grip.

He screams and starts jumping around. He accidentally kicks me in the head, trying to get away. I let go and surface. My ears are ringing, but it was totally worth it.

Murph and Pablo are cracking up. Fido is barking at Dmitri.

"Don't be grabbing me, dude!" he says.

"Don't be stealing other people's pets, *dude.*"

"Don't tell me what to do!"

"You knocked Fido into the water!" I'm getting angry.

"She can swim all right. No harm done."

"What about Murph's boat? You rammed it!"

He looks up at Murph. "Sorry about that, Murph. It was an accident."

"Tell it to the police," Lurena says.

Dmitri glares at her. "So whose guinea pig is that? It's a cool swimmer."

"It's Pablo's," I say. "I bought him at Petopia, and I gave him to Pablo."

"Petopia?" Dmitri asks. "What are you talking about? There's no Petopia around here." He's practically foaming at the mouth.

"It was in a truck stop," Pablo says.

"But I bet it isn't there now," I add.

"Liar," he says. "You didn't get that guinea pig at Petopia. You're lying because you don't want me to have one. But if you bought it at a truck stop, I'll find it."

"They only had one guinea dog, and we bought it," Pablo says.

"You shut up, weirdo," Dmitri says, pointing at Pablo.

We all stand there a minute, his meanness filling the air.

Then he hoists himself up onto the bank, climbs into his kayak, and paddles away.

"You know," Murph says, "sometimes the *less* the merrier."

Whoa. Did I really hear that from Murphy Molloy? Forget the guinea pig acting like an otter. This is the true miracle.

29. The guinea dog chased the guinea squirrel up a tree.

The strangest thing about this is that the squirrel is the dog's daughter.

As she scampers along a high branch that reaches out over the lake, Lurena shouts, "Queen Girlisaurus! Get back here!"

Fido runs under the branch to the water's edge, then looks up and barks at her daughter. She's being scolded by two moms.

Lurena flicks an angry look at me. "Do you see? Do you see why I keep her in her cage?"

"No," I say. "I see that she's glad you finally let her out. You can't keep a squirrel in a cage. You have to let her run and climb."

Lurena sets her fists on her hips. She

frowns. Then her mouth twists so that it's like she's half frowning and half smiling.

"I guess you're right," she says. "But you just better hope a raccoon doesn't get her."

"Or a snapping turtle," Murph says.

"Right!" Pablo laughs.

Snapper runs below Queen Girly, on the ground. He heads for the water's edge, then dives in and starts swimming, otter-style, under the branch. He stops when he's under Girly, then rolls onto his back and floats.

I guess I should find all this really bizarre. But I don't. I'm getting used to guinea pigs not acting like guinea pigs. I'm pretty sure I know now why they don't act like the animals they are. They came from Petopia—or, in Queen Girly's case, from an animal that came from Petopia.

I don't find it strange anymore that the store turned up in the truck stop, or that it had just the pet Pablo needed, just when he needed it. It's not strange that it was there for my mom the night she bought Fido, the perfect guinea pig for a kid who wanted a dog but couldn't get one, or that Fido gave birth to the exact animal Lurena wanted but her parents wouldn't let her have. Guinea pigs that can catch a Frisbee, or climb a tree, or swim underwater? Strange, sure, but it makes sense that they act that way. Petopia is in the business of sensible strangeness.

My guess is the store appears when and where it's needed, then, once it delivers the strange but perfect pet to the lucky new pet owner, it vanishes. Maybe it goes to some other place, some other town, or state, or country, where some other kid needs some other peculiarly perfect pet. Maybe this happens over and over, all around the world.

This time, it showed up for Pablo in a truck stop near White Crappie Lake. Maybe, at this moment, it's reappearing in some faraway place: in a shopping mall in Chicago, or in an airport in Japan, or next to a souvenir shop near the Great Pyramids of Egypt. For all I know, some kid is walking into a Petopia in Africa right this minute and buying a guinea pig that acts like a gorilla, or a kid in Australia is buying a guinea pig that acts like a kangaroo. Who knows, maybe it isn't just guinea pigs. I mean, the truck-stop Petopia had other animals: the boa constrictor, for example, and Captain Nemo. I wonder what he acts like when you get him home. . . .

"Oh!" Lurena shrieks. "Look!"

Queen Girly has gone out to the end of the branch, onto tinier branches of the branch, one of which has cracked under her tiny weight. She's hanging on by a paw; her other three grasp frantically at the air.

Fido goes bonkers. She dives into the water, which frightens Snapper, who chirps and dives under. Buddy then goes bounding down and runs into the lake. (Mars doesn't, because he's with Dmitri and his dad in their SUV, out looking for Petopia. My bet is they won't find it.)

So the strange gets stranger. The guinea squirrel hanging from the limb; the guinea dog and the perfect dog swimming in circles below, barking, one in a deep voice, one in a tiny one; and the guinea otter, surfacing in the nearby reeds, on its back, with a fish in its paws.

"Snapper eats fish," Murphy says, looking at Pablo. "That okay with you?"

Pablo shrugs. "I eat fish."

"Ah," Murph says. "Then all is well."

30. Man eats dog.

A hot dog, that is, and the man, incredibly, is Dad.

"Admit you like it," Mom says.

The adults all laugh.

Dad hesitates, looks down at the remainder of the hot dog in his hand—it's smeared with ketchup, mustard, and pickle relish—then he laughs, too, and stuffs the whole thing into his mouth.

Miracles happen at White Crappie Lake.

A moment later, though, Dad gags on the enormous bite he took, covers his mouth with his hand, and keeps the dog inside—something Dmitri had not been able to do. Of course, Dmitri had eaten five. This is Dad's first.

The guy has really loosened up some on this

trip. All the parents, in fact, are acting pretty chummy. Campfires have that effect on people. Even Austin hangs around the fire at night instead of hibernating with his video games.

The only problem is that being around laughing, joking adults is way less fun than it sounds. When they're happy and relaxed, they're more likely to loudly relate some embarrassing moment from your childhood, or to start singing some song you used to sing, then beg you to join in.

"Let's get out of here," I whisper to Murph.

He looks at me like I'm crazy. "Why? It's merry here!"

I bet he'd love hearing his mom telling an embarrassing episode from his childhood. He'd even get up and reenact it for everyone. He'd happily sing any song he's ever known, including "Baby Beluga" or "Little Bunny Foo Foo." He'd happily belt it out.

Let him. I don't like singing. I'm leaving.

"Ghost in the Graveyard?" he asks. "Is that it?"

"Yes, that's it precisely," I say, though I wasn't

thinking of the game. I was only thinking of getting away. "Let's go play Ghost in the Graveyard. Just shut your mouth and come on . . ."

"Wait, we need people to play!" He jumps up on a stump. "Ladies and gentlemen? I beg your pardon! Quiet, please!"

Oh, help.

"Tonight we have some festivities planned. A rousing match of Ghost in the Graveyard! But we will need participants. Who will play?"

He makes a broad gesture with his arms, as if he's gathering everyone up. The more the merrier. The more the scarier, more like. I don't want to play tag with Lurena's parents. It's bad enough playing with her. Will I have to tag Lurena's dad? Or *mine*?

Several of the adults say, "I will!" and raise their hands, laughing like idiots. Then they nudge the ones who didn't volunteer, and say, "Oh, come on, wet blanket!" or "Don't be a killjoy!" Where do adults learn to talk?

Lurena and Pablo are sitting at the picnic table, peeking into Lurena's cages. Snapper is in one with Queen Girly (who survived her climbing misadventure by dropping into the water and being rescued by her mother—Fido, that is). If Pablo didn't put Snapper in the cage, he'd jump in the lake, and, though Pablo now goes in the water, he doesn't exactly like to. Not to mention it's dark out, and dinnertime. It's reasonable Pablo would want to keep the guinea otter on dry land.

Before you know it, everyone's playing the game, including Pablo's parents, Austin, even A.G. and Bianca. Their mosquitoitis must be better. Only Dmitri's mom absolutely refuses to play. She has a headache, she says, and retreats to the Sulls' RV.

Maybe I should have a headache.

Murphy, of course, is the first ghost. Everyone runs off to hide, giggling and whispering and tripping off into the dark.

I see Pablo climbing a tree and remember that he was in a tree the first time I saw him, when he gave me the advice that saved Fido from choking to death. I'm sure glad I met him. He says he'll tell his parents he wants to coordinate our summer trips so we're at White Crappie at the same time from now on. And he gave me his e-mail address so we can talk all year round.

I hide, too, but I don't giggle or whisper or trip. I swipe a hot dog and a bun, and sneak under the picnic table to eat it. Fido finds me. She jumps up in my lap and starts licking my chin. It could be love, but it's probably the wienie.

"Down!" I command in a whisper.

She gets down and whimpers.

"Quiet!" I whisper-command.

She stops whimpering.

"Good girl." I pat her head. She pants. I break a piece off my hot dog and feed it to her.

Murphy ducks his head under the table. "I s-e-e-e-e you!" he says in a ghostly voice.

"I'm kind of comfortable under here," I say. "Why don't you go find someone else to tag, then come back?"

"Check," he says in his regular, nonghostly voice, and runs away.

I take another bite of my hot dog and feed

another bite to my guinea dog. We watch the fire flicker as we chew.

"It was a fun trip," I say to her. "I didn't think it would be."

She looks me straight in the eye as I talk. I know she doesn't understand English, but I swear she understands me.

Murph returns, out of breath, and climbs in under the table with us. He swiped a hot dog, too. He even took the time to squirt some ketchup on it. I'm jealous. Mine's already gone. And it didn't have ketchup.

"Here, take half," he says, and breaks his dog in two.

"Thanks," I say, and take my half. We both take a bite.

"I'm sorry you didn't get Snapper," I say.

He shrugs, like, *Hey, no biggie.*

And that's all we need to say about it.

"Did you know that the first hot dog wasn't made of pork or beef?" he says through his hot dog.

"No," I say through mine.

"You'll never guess what it was made of."

"You're probably right."

"You're not going to guess?"

"You're not going to tell me?"

He laughs. "Cat! They were actually called *hot cats*."

Fido growls.

I give her another piece of meat.

"No wonder she likes it," I say.

Murph laughs again, harder. I love making him laugh.

"So I ride home with you, right?" I ask.

"Yep," he says.

"You checked with your parents?"

"I don't need to. They will love having you."

"You sure?"

"*Paws*itive."

"Can I tell you something about Petopia?"

"*Paws*itively."

"Okay, it was cute once . . ."

"Sorry." He fake-hangs his head in shame.

"So I can tell you?"

"Shoot."

"I think . . . well . . . the animals they sell . . . I think . . ." I stop. It sounds too crazy.

H*e* lif*ts h*is head. "I agree," he says.

"About what? I mean . . . you do?"

"Pawsiti—Oops. Sorry." He hangs his head again.

"I bet we'll find another Petopia," I say. "We'll get you a guinea something yet."

"Don't worry about it," he says, looking up. "I got Buddy. I got you. I got Fido. What else do I need?"

Good old Murph.

"Another hot dog?" I ask.

"Two, coming right up."

"With ketchup, please," I say. "And yellow mustard. Not brown."

"Is there any other way?"

He bangs me with his shoulder. I bang him back: 2 guys + 2 dogs + ketchup = fun × 100 trillion.

"I found you!" Lurena yells, sticking her head under the table.

I feel too good to let her spoil the fun. Maybe we can add one crazy girl to this equation.

"We're kind of comfortable under here," I say. "Go find someone else to tag, then get three hot dogs with ketchup and come back."

"I'm vegetarian," she says.

"So get a tofu dog from my dad."

"Check," she says. She's picking up my lingo.

Fido barks, then paws at my knee.

"Oh, and get a dog for the guinea dog," I say.

"Be right back with your order," Lurena says. "You need anything else with that? Fries? S'mores?"

"No," I say. "We have everything we need."

Patrick Jennings

is the author of many popular novels including *Guinea Dog, Guinea Dog 2, Hissy Fitz, Lucky Cap, My Homework Ate My Homeword,* and *Odd, Weird & Little.* He won the 2013 Kansas William Allen White Children's Book Award and the 2011 Washington State Scandiuzzi Children's Book Award for *Guinea Dog,* which was also a 2013 Honor Book for the Massachusetts Children's Book Award. In addition it was nominated for the 2010-2011 New Hampshire Great Stone Face Book Award, the 2011-2012 Colorado Children's Book Award, the 2012-2013 Florida Sunshine State Young Reader's Award, the 2014 Washington State Sasquatch Award, the 2014 Hawaii Nēnē Award, the 2014-2015 Indiana Young Hoosier Book Award, and the 2014-2015 Minnesota Maud Hart Lovelace Book Award. He lives in a small seaport town in Washington State.

You can visit him online at www.patrickjennings.com.